GOD HAS PURPOSE FOR YOU

ALLOWING THE SPIRIT TO LEAD YOU TO DIVINE DESTINY

KERWIN D. TUCKER

iUniverse, Inc.
Bloomington

God Has Purpose for You
Allowing the Spirit to Lead You to Divine Destiny

iUniverse books may be ordered through booksellers or by contacting:

iUniverse
1663 Liberty Drive
Bloomington, IN 47403
www.iuniverse.com
1-800-Authors (1-800-288-4677)

ISBN: 978-1-4502-8920-7 (pbk)
ISBN: 978-1-4502-8919-1 (cloth)
ISBN: 978-1-4502-9132-3 (ebk)

Printed in the United States of America

iUniverse rev. date: 1/27/11

DEDICATION

I dedicate this book to the life and legacy of Bria "Poo" Gregory. Words can't even express how much I miss you and love you. Through your death you spoke to more people than you ever could have in your life. It's clear now that God truly had a "purpose for you." May you find eternal rest in the arms of the Father.

December 31, 1991—November 28, 2010

CONTENTS

"God Has Purpose for YOU"
Allowing the Spirit to Lead
You to Divine Destiny

INTRODUCTION

What is my purpose? Why am I here on this earth? When God created me, what did He have in mind? These and more questions are on the minds of everyone as they attempt to pinpoint their purpose in life. Often times this question goes unanswered even unto one's demise. The fear of never obtaining anything substantial in life, the despondency of ultimately feeling like a failure, and the inevitability of not being able to do anything about it, lingers on the minds of countless people each day, and worst yet, it's becoming a worsening epidemic in the church. Romans 8:14 states, "… those who are led by the Spirit of God are sons of God."

One of the greatest advantages of being a child of God is having the benefit of being led by God. What a privilege? What an honor? To know that in the midst of so much chaos and so much improbability, God is there to lead his children just like a father would lead his child. How much better life would be if we made decisions based on the leading and guidance of the Spirit of God, rather than by the frequent changes in our desires and emotions?

At one point in my life, and I'm sure everyone who is reading this book, emotions and feelings were the fuel that drove you. When we are led by feelings and emotions, mistakes become inevitable. This was the story of my life. At one point I was void of drive, void of direction, and ultimately void of purpose. I was living life based on what felt right to me, rather than what God wanted me to do and constantly found myself trying to pull myself out of situations that I had put myself in. I had grown up in the church all of my life; however I had never developed a true relationship with God.

In fact, I spent most of my teenage years up to early adulthood acting in direct opposition to the teaching that had been instilled in me. I drank alcohol, I smoked marijuana, I was routinely put out of school for behavior problems, and I was rebellious against any level of authority, including my parents. I was headed down a road which would surely lead to destruction if I didn't turn my life around. I knew, however, that I couldn't turn my life around by my own will or strength. The only person who could turn my life around was Jesus Christ.

One day I did accept Jesus Christ into my life and he changed my entire life around. Although I had given my life to God, I had yet to truly walk in complete obedience to his will. I was content with being the keyboard player for the choir but God had so much more for me to do. From my youth I sensed that God was calling me into the ministry, but what did I know I was just a kid? I thought that this was the product of me being a "preacher's kid," and I was convinced that as I got older this feeling would go away. Boy was I wrong.

As I begin to truly gain an understanding of Christ by reading his word and praying, the more the call to preach the gospel weighed on me. Afraid to accept the call I continued to work in the church, operating in my position as the keyboard player for the choir, however I had yet to truly be obedient to God and fulfill my true purpose which was to preach the gospel of Jesus Christ.

Are you operating in a position right now that is contrary to what God had shown you that you were going to operate in all because you fear stepping out? Are you content with just staying in that position and never truly seeking and embracing God's purpose for your life? Worst yet, are you looking to something or someone else to define your purpose because you don't feel as though you are capable of fulfilling the purpose that God has for you, you really don't know for sure what that purpose is, or you really don't want to fulfill that purpose because it requires you to do more than what you are comfortable with doing?

Whether we like to admit it or not, we have all found ourselves in one of the above situations before. So much so, that many of us have become satisfied in life with just existing, and never looking to make a difference in our families, our community, and our world. It's my belief that a lack of defined purpose is the catalyst for the lackadaisical society that we now find ourselves living in. A society that no longer wants to wait on God to define their purpose, rather they attempt to identify their purpose by other means. Psychic hotlines, the lottery monopoly, and even false prophets are all lynching on the hopes and dreams of countless people. This uncertainty has left the doors of manipulation wide open for the world and for the church alike.

In a world of uncertainty, there is only one thing that is assured; God is still in control. No matter what your current position is in life, God has the power to take you from where you are, to where He has purposed you to be. How do I know? I know because he did it for me. For the last five years I have served as the youth pastor at Gospel Tabernacle Outreach Center located in Gretna VA. Along with that, I have had the opportunity to proclaim the gospel at many different churches and unto many people in the streets who had never even been to church. God truly did have a purpose for my life, but it was up to me to develop a deeper relationship with God in order to discover what purposes God had for my life, and then to begin working towards them.

I truly believe that God has so graciously chosen me to write this Biblical guide to assist people in discovering their God given purposes in life. I would like to forewarn you that God's purposes for your life are not always what you had envisioned or planned. One thing is for sure however, God has a plan for each and every one of us. Paul states in Ephesians 2:10 (NIV), "For we are God's workmanship, created in Christ Jesus to do good works, which God prepared in advance for us to do." Think about that. Each one of us was designed by God to fulfill specific tasks and to accomplish specific purposes in life. Come along with me as we journey through the word of God, in order to discover exactly what those purposes are.

CHAPTER 1

The Prerequisites for living a Spirit Led Life

Accept Christ into Your Life

It's important to note that it's not until you accept Christ into your life that you prepare the way for the Spirit to begin to lead. 1 Corinthians 2:14 states, "The man without the Spirit does not accept the things that come from the Spirit of God, for they are foolishness to him, and he cannot understand them, because they are spiritually discerned (NIV)." The natural man is the man devoid of the Holy Spirit. Because he does not have the Holy Spirit he relies totally and completely on the wisdom of the world for guidance, seeing as though he doesn't have access to divine revelation which is only provided through the Spirit. Therefore this man will not be able to receive the secret things of the Spirit of God, neither can he know all of the wonderful truths that God wants to reveal to him because they are spiritually discerned from him.

This person will never be able to truly discover their God given purpose in life. Not only does the person void of the Spirit lack the capacity to know the things that God has freely given them, but this person will also forever walk in bondage. This is because it's not until a person allows the Spirit to lead them that they begin to walk in the freedom that Christ promises. Galatians 5:1 states "Stand fast therefore in the liberty wherewith Christ hath made us free, and be not entangled again with the yoke of bondage

(KJV)." You might be trying to figure out what bondage Paul is referring to. Paul was referring to the bondage that the Christians at Galatia were experiencing still trying to live under the Law. They had already been freed from the burden of trying to live without breaking any of the Law of Moses when they accepted Christ into their life. However, because they were so deeply routed in their Judaism traditions, they found themselves constantly feeling pressured to adhere to the Law, rather than walking in the freedom of the Spirit.

The Law of Moses

The Law of Moses was instituted to provide a divine standard to which the sinner could evaluate themselves and their actions compared to what was morally right. The ultimate goal of the Law was to help people recognize that they were sinners and were in need of a savior. While the Law served as a type and shadow for what was to come, in and of itself it fell short in a lot of areas. For instance, observing the Law couldn't provide justification for groups or individuals. The Law wasn't able to give life. By observing the Law one could not receive the Holy Spirit. The Law also couldn't solve the problem of the sin nature. While there were levels of punishment for breaking the Law, the Law didn't provide victory over sin. Without victory over sin one would remain in bondage to the custom of trying to observe the Law, which would ultimately end in failure. Paul understood that Christians who continued to live by the Law would never be able to walk in the freedom that Christ had given them through His Spirit.

Paul states in Galatians 5:18, "But if ye be led of the Spirit, ye are not under the law (KJV)." Are you tired of trying to live right by your own strength only to fail over and over again? If you are then the only way to overcome this is to accept Christ into your life and to receive the Spirit of God who gives you the power needed to sustain in such a sinful world. Therefore, the prerequisite for living a Spirit led life is to have a Spirit filled life. The only way to have a Spirit filled life is to first experience *salvation.*

What is Salvation?

While this book is mostly geared towards pre-existing Christians, I don't want to go any further until I take out time to offer salvation to those who have yet to accept Christ as their savior. The reason being is apart from Christ you will never be able to fully understand your purpose in life. Not only will you not be able to understand God's purposes for your life, but apart from Christ you're separated from God and risk eternal damnation in hell. Hell is a scary topic to talk about, but it's a very important reality that everyone needs to be made aware of.

> For if God did not spare angels when they sinned, but sent them to hell, putting them in chains of darkness to be held for judgment; if he did not spare the ancient world when he brought the flood on its ungodly people, but protected Noah, a preacher of righteousness, and seven others; if he condemned the cities of Sodom and Gomorrah by burning them to ashes, and made them an example of what is going to happen to the ungodly; and if he rescued Lot, a righteous man, who was distressed by the depraved conduct of the lawless (for that righteous man, living among them day after day, was tormented in his righteous soul by the lawless deeds he saw and heard)—if this is so, then the Lord knows how to rescue the godly from trials and to hold the unrighteous for punishment on the day of judgment (2 Peter 2:4-9 NIV).

God doesn't want anyone to be eternally separated from him because of sin. To prove this, he sent his only begotten son to die on the cross in order to "save" all those who would accept him as savior. Therefore, salvation is an act whereby God delivers one from eternal punishment (Hell) by erasing his sins from the legal record and imputing the perfection of Jesus Christ[1]. Contrary to popular belief, salvation isn't something that's unattainable. It's not something that is only reserved for those who have never made a mistake or for those who don't have issues. The Bible says that all have sinned and fallen short of the glory of God. However, if you would confess your sins then Christ is faithful and just to forgive you of

---

1   Elmer L. Towns, *Theology for Today* (Ohio: Cengage, 2008, 2002), 900.

all sins, and cleanse you of all unrighteousness. Why? Because God loves you! John 3:16 declares, "For God so loved the world, that he gave his only begotten Son, that whosoever believeth in him should not perish, but have everlasting life (KJV)."

No matter what you have done, what you are doing, or what you were thinking about doing, God still loves you and He died for you. Many of you feel as though it's no way Christ could possibly love you because you feel as though you have made too many mistakes. You say things like, "It's no way God can use me, and I didn't grow up in the church." "It's no way Christ could have died for me I'm not a good person." We place too much attention on what we have or haven't done, however if salvation were based on human merit then none of us would be saved. The scriptures let us know that when Christ died, He died for everyone who would accept Him as their savior as we are all sinners in need of a savior. That means whether you are a drug addict, drug dealer, alcoholic, prostitute, liar, murderer, or even an adulterer Christ died for you and has a purpose for your life. You may say well I didn't fall into any of those categories. Maybe you say I'm a good person without Christ. Maybe you volunteer your services at your local soup kitchen or nursing home. Maybe you give to the poor and help support local widows in the community financially. Maybe you always buy toys for the kids on the angel tree at Christmas time and you always, always give money to the Salvation Army to help them in their endeavors. As gracious as all this may be and as good as it may make you feel about yourself, if you have yet to make Christ Lord of your life then you are still classified as a sinner since we were all born into sin due to the transgression of our ancestors Adam and Eve.

Repent and Believe

My friend it would be virtually impossible to make an exhaustive list of all the possible sins. The point is, if you are living in this world, you are a sinner in need of a savior. The good part about this is that Christ died for you in order to cover your sins. Christ said come to me all you who are burden and heavy laden and I will give you rest. If you are tired of doing things your own way, and have a sincere mind and heart to give your heart to Christ, then He is waiting there to welcome you into His family and to identify you as a "child of God." The apostle Paul declares, "If you declare with your mouth, 'Jesus is Lord,' and believe in your heart that God raised him from the dead, you will be saved. For it is with your heart that you believe and are justified, and it is with your mouth that you profess your faith and are saved (Romans 10:9-10 NIV)."

Essentially the only thing you have to do is believe that Christ died for you and accept him into your life. Christ has already did all of the hard work when He died on Calvary. He paid the debt for the sin of the world by offering his life as a ransom. The blood that he shed on Calvary over 2000 years ago was sufficient enough to cover all of our sins for all time. Wow who wouldn't serve a God like that? Just repent of your sins, turn away from your old lifestyle and turn towards the Lord. Salvation isn't based on human merit, it's based on faith. Keep in mind that repentance is a way of thinking. You have to be willing to completely realign your thinking to be in accordance with the word of God. When you realign your thinking, your lifestyle will follow. The Bible says that he who is in Christ is a new creature (2 Cor. 5:17). The reason why you are a new creature is because you have been crucified with Christ and therefore you have died to the old man. Once you truly accepted Christ from the heart then he filled you with His Spirit and gave you victory over sin.

When at one time you were a slave to sin and even a slave to the Law, now the Law has been written in your hearts and transcribed in your mind by the Spirit of God. You are now walking in the liberty of the Spirit. Not a liberty that gives you a license to sin, but a liberty that frees you from the oppression of sin. You no longer have to allow sin to rule your life. Contrarily, you can now exercise control over sin in your life. As you begin to read the Bible, which is the written word of God, the Spirit will give you a new mind, a new heart, and a new purpose for living.

Slowly but surely you will begin to let go of the old habits that you thought were going to have power over you forever. When your faith is genuine then it will produce genuine change in your life and the works that you do will reflect this. This is what James meant when he stated, "Thus also faith by itself, if it does not have works, is dead (James 2:17)." Many believe that the Apostle James's view of salvation accompanied with works is in stark contrast with the Apostle Paul's view of salvation solely by faith. On the contrary the two men seem to compliment each other quite well.

The apostle Paul let's us know that "faith" is the vehicle that drives us into right standing with God. Notice, however, the type of faith that Paul references. Paul tells us to "follow in the footsteps of the faith that our father Abraham had before he was circumcised (Rom. 4:12 NIV)." I don't want to venture too far off subject, however I would like to give a brief historical account of the patriarch Abraham to help us better understand the faith of Abraham.

The Faith of Abraham

The Biblical narrative of the patriarch Abraham, then called Abram, begins in the book of Genesis chapter 12. God had instructed Abram to leave his country and his family, and he promised to make Abram a great nation. Just how great? He promised Abram that he would make his descendants as numerous as the stars in the sky. He also promised to make Abram's name great and assured Abram that through him all of the families of the earth would be blessed. Abram believed God and left his land and family just as God had commanded him to do and thus God's covenant with Abram was established.

Years passed and Abram and his wife Sarah still didn't have a child of their own in order to foster any descendants. Yet even in his old age, Abram continued to believe that it would happen and his faith was accredited to him for righteousness. God changed his name from *Abram* to *Abraham*, "father of nations." To make a long story short God kept his promise to Abraham and today the world recognizes Abraham as the father of the Israelites, the Ishmaelites, Edomites, and the Midianites. He's most notably known as being the patriarch of the Israelites who were acknowledged by God as being his chosen people.

However, this special honor was only bestowed upon them because of Abraham's faith in God. To signify the covenant that God had made with Abraham, God instituted circumcision as an outward sign of the covenant that he had made with him. All male Israelites were to be circumcised on the eight day of their life to indicate that they were born into a covenant relationship with God. Circumcision was extremely significant to the Israelites, however in a more broader view God was using this outward sign as the ground work for the inward circumcision of the heart that would be given to all those who would believe in his son Jesus Christ. This circumcision of the heart would be the believer's stamp of approval that they possessed an eternal covenant with God.

In the New Testament many of the Jews still believed that because they had been given the circumcision of the flesh from their forefather Abraham, that this gave them a special advantage over non-Jews as it related to salvation even after the death and resurrection of Jesus Christ. However, Paul is able to demonstrate how Abraham was made righteous before circumcision was even instituted. This would make Abraham not only the father of the Jews who were circumcised, but also for the Gentiles who believed in Jesus Christ as their savior without having the outward sign of circumcision. Paul makes it clear that it's not by any works that we are made righteous, but by faith in Jesus Christ. That's why he tells us to "walk in the steps of the faith in which Abraham had." The word *"walk"* signifies an action. Abraham didn't just say he believed God, but he acted on his belief by stepping out in faith in response to the word of God.

True faith requires an action. If I truly believe then my actions will reflect my belief. This ties in well with what James said when he stated that faith without works is dead. He then goes on to say, "But someone will say, 'You have faith, and I have works.' Show me your faith without your works, and I will show you my faith by my works (James 2:18 NIV)." James was letting us know that it's not possible to separate faith and works. You can't say that you have faith in Christ but your actions say something completely different. Therefore, if one has truly believed from the heart, then his actions will begin to exhibit authentic Christ like qualities.

Do You Believe?

Christ would love to shine through your life. He would love to come into your heart and clean out everything that's not like him in order to give you a new start. It's up to you, however, to respond to his love in faith by believing in your heart that Christ died so that you may live. Maybe you are reading this book and you are a sinner. Maybe you are a sinner and didn't even realize that you were a sinner. Maybe a friend gave you this book and you didn't think you were going to get anything out of it, but now you realize that without Christ you can never fully identify your purpose in life. Perhaps you initially thought that there were many ways to get to Heaven. However, now you see that there is only one way to get to Heaven and that's through faith in Jesus Christ. Maybe you thought that your good deeds were enough to get you into Heaven. You may have even thought that because your parents were saved that you had a guaranteed key into the kingdom, but now you understand that the only way to be saved is to develop a personal relationship through faith in Jesus Christ. Are you ready to accept him into your life?

Don't Wait Any Longer

If you are ready to submit your will to God's will and to accept Him into your life, then don't wait any longer. Some of you are saying well I still curse. I still have a drinking problem. I still practice premarital sex. Let me get rid of those habits and then I will come to Christ. Don't wait to get rid of these habits before you come to Christ. Without Christ in your life you will not be able to break the chains of addiction that are holding you. Come to Christ just as you are, with your issues, with your addictions, and with a willing heart to change. Let Christ help you break these destructive patterns of living. You don't have to go at it alone. If you are ready to accept Christ into your life then before you continue reading, take a moment right now and ask Christ to come into your heart. Grab hold of him with all of your heart, with all of your soul, and with your entire mind. Yes I mean right now.

Now doesn't that feel so much better? Congratulations, now you have become a part of the family of God. Now your true destiny can begin as you surrender your will, to the will of God. Surrendering your will to God's will is not an easy thing to do. On the contrary, it will be a tedious gradual process which must be taken with care. Yes, I said process. Don't expect for everything to change overnight. Although the work of salvation has already been accomplished through the death and resurrection of Jesus, there is a process of salvation which must be completed in us by our faith and obedience to God's word.

The Process of Salvation

Justification

Before I conclude this section on salvation I want to explain a few terms that will be pivotal to your Christian walk. The first term is justification. Justification is the initial step of salvation. Ephesians 2:8 (NIV) states, "For it is by grace you have been saved, though faith..." When you accept Christ into your life then you accept his divine grace, or unmerited favor that he died in order for you to receive. Christ's grace paved the way for the justification of our sins. Justification is God's act of declaring or making a sinner righteous before God in spite of every sin they have committed. When you truly accepted Christ by believing in him from the heart then you were justified for all the sins you had committed in the past and the sins that you would commit in the future and you were given access to an inheritance in the kingdom that you didn't deserve. In spite of everything that you were guilty of, when you accepted Christ into your life you were declared not-guilty. The Christian walk doesn't stop there. After you accept Christ into your life then begins the process of sanctification.

Sanctification

Sanctification means that we as believers are still being saved. This is where you take out time to be intimate with God, in order to deepen your relationship with Him and become more and more like Him. In order to do this you have to spend time reading his word, fasting and praying, and even learning how to serve others in order to better identify with the character of Christ. Philippians 2:12 (NIV) states "continue to work out your salvation with fear and trembling..." The key word there is "work." If you are not willing to work then it's no way you can experience Christ on a deeper level.

There are a lot of Christians who have been in the same spiritual state for years because they are too lazy to work on their relationship with God.

The more of God you receive, the more of yourself you lose. This is what Christ meant when he said, "For whoever wants to save their life will lose it, but whoever loses their life for me will find it (Matthew 16:25 NIV)." We call this process "dyeing to self." Many feel that this happens at the initial state of salvation so it's nothing else that they have to do after that. As a result they don't work on bettering themselves. I believe this belief is the reason our modern day churches have taken on such an apathetic and self-righteous attitude.

Many feel that they have reached the plateau of holiness and there is nothing more that they need to do. Paul refuted this attitude when he said, "Brothers and sisters, I do not consider myself yet to have taken hold of it. But one thing I do: Forgetting what is behind and straining toward what is ahead (Phil. 3:13 NIV)." If Paul who is considered by most as being the greatest Apostle of all the apostles didn't think that he had reached this perfect level of Christ-likeness, what room does that leave for us? Paul understood that he hadn't reached that level yet, but one thing he would do was continue to press forward toward that mark. As long as he was continuing to press forward, dying daily to his flesh, then he would be becoming more and more like Christ everyday.

Sanctification will require us to "work" on ourselves everyday for the rest of our life. We should never think that we are so good that we can't be better. Don't begin the race and then quit running when you're halfway to the finish line. You have to keep pressing forward for the ultimate goal which is glorification.

Glorification

Glorification is the believer's final state of salvation. It refers to a Christian receiving a perfect resurrection body in heaven. We will finally take off this body of mortality and put on our glorified body of immortality. No more sickness. No more pain. No more temptation. The best part about it is that their will be no more sin. Romans 8:30 (NIV) states, "And those he predestined, he also called; those he called, he also justified; those he justified, he also glorified." When you accepted Christ into your life, then at that moment you were considered glorified. It's just a matter of time before you change bodies. Don't think though that because you said a prayer and the preacher laid his hands on you that you were considered glorified. If true repentance never happened and your life didn't change, then you need to check your life to make sure that you are truly saved.

Remember salvation is not brought about by works, but if you are truly saved the works will follow. As I stated earlier, James said show me your faith without your works, and I will show you my faith by my works (James 2:18). James was letting you know that it's no way you can say that you have faith (salvation) and not show works (fruit of the Spirit). The Apostle Paul writing to Timothy states, "Watch your life and doctrine closely. Persevere in them, because if you do, you will save both yourself and your hearers (1 Timothy 4:6 NIV)." We have to constantly examine our life and doctrine to make sure that our lives and beliefs are lining up with the Word of God. Jesus said if you abide in my word then you are my disciples indeed (John 8:31).

You know that you are truly a disciple and thus justified and glorified when you see your life progressively aligning (sanctification) with the word of God. Don't fool yourself. If you know that your life is going in a completely different direction than the standard set by the word of God then it's time to make sure your salvation is authentic. You have to know beyond a shadow of any doubt that you are a disciple of God. Do you believe that Jesus Christ died for your sins? Jesus speaking of this belief states the following:

> The Spirit gives life; the flesh counts for nothing. The words I have spoken to you—they are full of the Spirit and life. Yet there are some of you who do not believe. For Jesus had known from the beginning which of them did not believe and who would betray him. He on to say, "This is why I told you that no one can come to me unless the Father has enabled them." From this time many of his disciples turned back and no longer followed him. "You do not want to leave too, do you?" Jesus asked the Twelve. Simon Peter answered him, "Lord, to whom shall we go? You have the words of eternal life."(John 6:63-68 NIV)

You have to be certain of your faith. Even when you might not feel saved, you have to know that you are. Even when you feel like turning backs towards your old lifestyle, you have to continue to press forward towards "perfect" Christ likeness. This doesn't mean that you want have slip ups. This doesn't mean that you may not have a fall. David said that even if a righteous man falls seven times, he will rise again (Proverbs 24:16 NIV). As a believer you have the assurance to know that even when you fall God has put His Spirit on the inside of you which gives you the power to rise again.

Don't think because you made a mistake God doesn't love you. He still loves you. Don't allow guilt to keep you from confessing your sins to God and asking him for help. When you are a believer your setbacks will never keep you down for long. Now if you say you have confessed Christ but are back to your old lifestyle without any remorse, yet you still feel justified, then you have a false sense of security. Jesus said that no one who puts his hand to the plow and looks back is fit for service in the kingdom (Luke 9:62). Paul echoes this when he says, forgetting those things in the past and pressing forward towards the mark of a higher calling. Pressing forward, however, shouldn't cause you to be ignorant of previous temptations that you struggled with in your flesh. If you previously had a drinking problem, don't expect to go to the bar and not be tempted to drink. If you had a gambling problem then I wouldn't recommend going to the casinos at this time to witness. As a new convert, or as a seasoned saint, placing yourself in the fire is never a good idea. Putting something which was once an area of weakness directly in your view is pretty much the same as committing spiritual suicide. Keep in mind that although the Spirit is willing your flesh is weak. When you do this you are setting yourself up for moral failure and eventually you will get burned. That's not what salvation is about at all.

Surrendering All To Christ

Salvation is not living with the absence of temptation, rather the closer you get to Him, the more He will warn you of certain things to stay away from. You will be tempted to follow your old pattern of living, but for every temptation Christ will provide an avenue of escape for you (1 Cor. 10:13). You also have to know that even though you are saved, if you are not careful, sin could still easily get the best of you. With that being said, salvation should not be viewed as living with the absence of sin either. Rather it's living a yielded life to the Spirit of God, so if you do sin, and you will, you have an advocate with the Father who is faithful and just to forgive you of all sins and cleanse you of all unrighteousness.

On the road to destiny you will make mistakes. When you make a mistake, don't give up, don't throw in the towel. That's what Satan wants you to do. You have to know that He who begun a good work in you, will carry it on to completion until the day of Christ Jesus. Simply put, no matter where you are at right now, God is not through with you yet. The fact that God is still working on you is even more of a reason to make sure that you are willing to surrender your entire being to Christ. If not, you will constantly have to deal with the consequences of trying to handle the temptations of life on your own which always ends with disappointing results.

As I stated earlier, giving your life totally to God is not an easy process. However, it is a necessary process in order to discover your purpose in life. Many of us who have been saved for years still struggle with surrendering our will completely to God. It is for this reason that many of us are still struggling identifying our purpose in life. However, in order to finally walk into your destiny and in order to allow the Spirit to lead you into all truth, you have to be willing to give up control of your life and trust the Spirit to take command. Once you relinquish control don't try to take it back. The reason you don't want to take back control is because the Holy Spirit already knows the path for your life. He knows whether or not at your current location you need to take a left or if you need to take a right. Psalms 37:23 (KJV) states, "The steps of a good man are ordered by the LORD....." He is the global navigation system for your life. He is able to guide you through the peaks and valleys of life until you make it to your intended destination. However, you have to trust God and know that He wouldn't lead you wrong.

This is difficult to do because many times it will appear as though God is leading you the wrong way. Truthfully speaking, looking at life from a human perspective, it sometimes seems easier to take a different route rather than the one that God is leading you on. All the same, you have to know that God has a reason for leading you in an opposite direction than what seems easiest to you. This takes sacrifice and it will be a bit of an adjustment, but it will be well worth it in the end.

Embracing the Spirit's Guidance

If salvation places you in the spiritual boat, then the Holy Spirit begins the rowing process. When he comes into your life you have to be willing to go where he says go, do what he says do, and say what he says say. Your own personal desires and previous itinerary in life no longer matters. If you want to discover your true purpose then you have to be willing to follow the Spirit's lead.

Same Team, Same Goal

When I was about 12 years old I played little league football for the first time. I was very fast. However I was particularly small for my age. Despite my size the coach still welcomed me in with open arms to be a part of the team. He provided me with my uniform, assigned me a number, and assigned me a position on the team. Contrary to my longing to play wide receiver, the coach decided to make me a tail back (Coach knows best). The coach had been teaching a play to the team called a 22 dive all that week. The formation of this play was the key to its effectiveness. To run this play we had to place seven players on the offensive line: split end, left tackle, left guard, center, right guard, right tackle and tight end. You would then position a full back a yard behind and to either side of the quarterback and a tail back directly behind the full back. The object of this play is for your blockers, which consist of your offensive line and your full back, to create an open channel in either the right or left side of the line just big enough for the tailback to squeeze through and pick up some yards. Since I was the tailback I had the responsibility of following my full back and hopefully he could open up a hole for me. The ultimate goal was to make it to the "end zone." What would make this play work is, number 1, my blockers had to be big enough to block for me, and number 2, I had to trust my blockers to do their job and be willing to follow them.

During practice I ran the play fine with no hesitation. It was much easier to run the play in practice because I was running it against my own players. Although they would still hit me pretty hard, they wouldn't attempt to hurt me because we were on the same team. I was very confident in my offensive line as they were all massive guys and I know they had the same goal as me, to make it to the "end zone." As long as these guys were blocking for me, I didn't have a fear in the world that anyone would be able to harm me. When we got to the game on that Saturday afternoon and I saw the size of the opposing team's defensive players, fear gripped my heart. I forgot all about how big the people leading me were and frankly at the time they looked obsolete compared to the opposition. How many times have you found yourself in this place in your spiritual life?

Game Time

When you accepted Christ into your life he became the "coach." He assigned you with the appropriate uniform which He calls the "whole armor of God." He assigned you a number when he wrote your name in the Lamb's book of Life. He also assigned you a position on His team, though it might not have been the position you wanted. Further, He gave you the play that he wanted you to run through the ultimate playbook, the word of God. At the practice facility, the church, it was easy to run the play because you were surrounded by your own players. However, when you stepped out of the practice facility onto the game field, the world, all of a sudden you began to lose heart because of how big the opposing team, Satan and his army, appeared to be.

At some point in all of our lives we all have to step out of the practice facility onto the game field in our lives. Usually everything is fine when we are in the practice facility experiencing comfort in our lives. However, when it's "game time," and the pressures of life began to weigh on us, we forgot how big our God really was and instead of following him we became stagnant. For instance, many of us can talk with local members in our church concerning the goodness of God, but if God moves us to go out into the streets to tell someone about the Gospel who may have never stepped foot in a church, we immediately freeze up and make every excuse in the book why we can't do it. That's because most of us are afraid of the opposition.

Let's look at this from a different angle. What do you do when everything was going good on your job, then without notice your job experiences a huge layoff? We find it easy to be happy when we are living in a nice home, driving a nice car, and eating steak for dinner. However, what do you do when you can no longer afford the mortgage, the car has been repossessed, and Ramon noodles are all you can afford for dinner? Can you still trust God when your world has been turned upside down? Once more let's look at it from a different angle. What if you go to the doctor and when you were once the picture of health, all of a sudden you are informed that you have an incurable disease? The doctor said that it's nothing that they can do and that you should just plan for the worst. Do you throw in the towel and just wait to die? Do you say your life is over because this opponent that you are facing is too big for you? Do you go to the sideline and wait until the game is over? Or do you stay in the game and continue to battle until the end?

Defense: Anticipate, Devastate, Dominate

No matter how good your life appears to be right now, sooner or later life will throw an obstacle your way that will test the validity of your faith. In fact, God has a way of using obstacles in our life as a means of realigning our focus back towards Him. The reason being is because sometimes it's not until our backs are against the wall that we even find ourselves reaching out to God. When everything is going good prayer becomes scarce. When the road of life seems clear, we don't read our Bibles like we should. Why?

Probably because moments of happiness tend to make one forget about the seasons of struggles that they had previously had to endure. God sometimes uses problems to make sure that we continue to defend against the enemy's constant "offensive" onslaught. People go on vacations to get away from their problems. While it's good to take time off in the physical to relax and unwind, it's not always a good idea to take a spiritual vacation.

The reason being is because while you're taking it easy and being comfortable, the devil is working harder than ever before building an even bigger "opponent" to fight against you. Therefore we have to anticipate the enemies attack, devastate his attempts to "score" on us, and dominate him in this "spiritual game" called life. The weapons of the believer's warfare are not carnal, but mighty through God (2 Cor. 10:4). Our weapons have the power to pull down strong holds and demolish every attack of the enemy. What happens however when the enemy catches you without your weapons?

Although my physical man may be on vacation, my spiritual man has to be ever vigilant because we know that Satan is on the prowl. This is why God instructed us to watch as well as pray so that we don't fall into temptation (Matt. 26:41). As tempting as it may be not to pray, I know that I have to in order to sustain against the enemies attacks. If Satan catches you in relax mode then you will not be able to handle his attack. Most likely you want even see him coming and he will catch you with your guard down. The Bible says that if we recognize the devil then he will flee. However, if the enemy can get us distracted, then we want even recognize when he has stepped into our camp.

17

CHAPTER 2

Maintain Your Position

In the 16ᵗʰ chapter of the book of 1 Samuel we are introduced to a shepherd boy by the name of David who was destined to become the King of Israel. David's opposition to the thrown was the current King at that time named Saul. Saul had been rejected from being King; however he was determined to keep David from inheriting the thrown. After several near death experiences by his adversary King Saul, David decides to flee from his people and to take up residence in a foreign country, with men who had once been the enemy of his people and his land.

In 1 Samuel 29, King David and his men were attempting to go with the Philistines, who David was now allied with, to fight in a battle against the Israelites who were David's natives. All of the men's children, and their wives stayed back in the city of Ziklag alone and unprotected. David was confident enough to believe that the women and children would be alright, even though they were in foreign territory. This fed right into the enemy's plan because without the men in the camp, the covering was removed.

No doubt David didn't believe that he was doing anything wrong. He thought that he was offering help to someone who had helped him in the past. What David didn't realize though was that he was allowing a distraction to lure him out of position. If the enemy can lure us out of position then we leave ourselves and the things that are connected to us unguarded and vulnerable for attack. That's why it's important that we always maintain our position.

Don't Give Satan Access

Sometimes the devil will lure us away with something or someone who appears to be good, however, it was just a setup to give him access into our lives. How many times has the devil knocked on your door, and found your home unprotected? There are a lot of men right now who have left their families to pursue what they feel is success. Often times it's more of a mental abandonment than a physical one. Nevertheless, now their wife and their children are left to fend for themselves. Their wives are also forced to assume a position that they were not created to operate in.

What David didn't realize was that the battle he was attempting to fight was just a diversion to lure him away from where he needed to be. This battle didn't even belong to David. Some of you have been attempting to fight someone else's battle for so long that you have lowered your guard in your own life. Now the enemy has been given the opportunity to deliver a blow in your life that could be catastrophic. Even though David was denied the opportunity to fight in the battle, the damage had already been done.

When David returned to Ziklag in 1 Samuel 30, his enemies the Amalekites had come in and taken all of the women and children captive and burned the city. David had lost everything all because he hadn't maintained his position. Whatever you do in life you have to make sure you maintain your position. Don't let life's issues affect your Christian standing. The Bible says that David was greatly distressed and it was at this time that David encouraged himself in the Lord. It's usually when we have been stripped of everything that we realize that we need the Lord. While David was able to pursue his enemies and recover all that he had lost and some more, he wouldn't have had to go through this if he would have just stayed in the right position.

The beauty of this story is that even when we do step out of position for a moment and allow the devil to attack our belongings, God can use our loss as an opportunity to show just how powerful he is. If you have allowed the enemy to take some things from you don't get discouraged. Don't get so distressed that you quit moving forward. God has the power to turn that entire situation around for your good. Unfortunately, when many of us face a situation that seems too big for us to handle we will just stop moving forward. This is what has happened to a lot of Christians today. They have experienced a blow in their life and now they feel as though they are stuck.

Stuck in Limbo

Have you ever come to a place in your life that you felt as though you were stuck? Some feel that they are stuck on the job they are on. Others feel as though that they are stuck in a relationship. Many who have been trying to lose weight for years feel as though they are stuck with the body that they are in. While others feel as though they are stuck in debt and there is no foreseen way out. To go along with that, there are also many who feel stuck in their spiritual lives.

They feel as though that they are stuck at the dead church they attend. They feel as though they are stuck with the same level of anointing. Many preachers who have been preaching for years feel as though their ministry will never get off the ground. When someone is stuck that means that they are rendered completely immobile and all forward advancement has ceased. It's bad enough to be stuck in a place of inadequacy and immobility, but it's even worse when you begin to sink deeper and deeper into what you are stuck in.

People who are in debt usually sink deeper into debt. People who are overweight tend to become more and more overweight. This is because the very thing that causes you to be stuck is now the thing that you feel you need to survive. Your issue has now become your source of strength. It has become your source of happiness. It becomes an addiction that you feel you just can't live without. You feel as though you need it in order to keep going and without it you can't advance. As is the case with any addiction, the longer you wait to deal with your problem, the harder it will be to overcome it.

I remember watching these old treasure hunting movies. In these movies you would usually have a scene where a person would be running through the jungle and as they got deeper and deeper many times they would step into something called quick sand. Once the person stepped into the quick sand they would begin to sink at a very rapid rate. As they begin to sink many times they would grab the first person's hand they could find to help pull them out. Frequently the person's hand that they grabbed wasn't strong enough to pull them out, and most of the time both of the people would sink.

The reason why many of us continue to sink deeper and deeper into certain issues is because we keep connecting ourselves to the wrong things or people to attempt to bring us out. If I'm struggling financially then I can't expect to connect to someone who doesn't know how to manage their money to attempt to pull me out. If I'm struggling with losing weight then I can't connect with someone who can't stay out of the buffet line. If I have a drinking problem then I can't continue to go to the bar with my alcoholic friend. If my spouse and I are having marital problems then we don't need to connect with a couple that's on the verge of divorce. If I'm attempting to grow spiritually then I can't connect with someone who waivers in their relationship with Christ. I think you get my point.

In whatever you do, you have to make sure that you connect with people who have been in your position and overcame it. You also have to make sure you make connections with people who are either striving for, or are already doing what you intend to do. Mike Murdock, the senior pastor of The Wisdom Center, explains this best when he states, "your goals for your life should choose your mentors." Most people, however, do the exact opposite of this. They choose people who either have no direction, or who are going in a completely different direction than they are.

Break the Cycle

The book of Matthew 15:14 (NIV) states, "...And if the blind lead the blind, both shall fall into the ditch." How many of you have found yourself frequently falling into a ditch in your life because of the instruction you have chosen to follow? Most of us have found ourselves in some sort of ditch a time or two in our life because of other people who steered us in the wrong direction. It's very important to keep in mind that the instruction you follow will determine the future you create.

Psalms 1:1 (KJV) says, "Blessed is the man that walketh not in the counsel of the ungodly..." Simply put, you can't take advice from everybody, including your own. There are a ton of Christians right now who are still stuck in the same place that they were 10 years ago because they have been taking advice from the wrong people. So instead of walking forward into their destiny, they are stuck in a place of despair and hopelessness. Galatians 5:7 (NIV) states, "You were running a good race. Who cut in on you to keep you from obeying the truth?"

Whose instruction are you following? Who is hindering you from obeying the precepts that have been affirmed in the word of God? Are you allowing the Spirit of God to direct your steps, or are you being led more by what you believe to be true? Are you allowing negative people to influence your actions, or are you bringing every decision under subjection to the will of God? So who or what is really hindering you from obeying the truth of God's word?

The answer is quite obvious, you are. How many times have you attempted to blame other people for your misfortunes? Some blame others for the fact that they don't have a better job. Others place the blame on everybody but themselves because their credit is dreadful. A lot of people attempt to say they are where they are because their parents never did any better. Still others blame their lack of advancement on their race, gender, or even their disabilities. We say that if we had of grew up in different circumstances then our life would be so much better.

While I don't want to seem insensitive to your situation I want to make clear to you that you can't blame where you are because of the hand that you were dealt in life or because of the people that you have chosen to follow. When playing cards, my dad would always say it's not the hand that you were dealt, it's how you play the cards. We can also apply this same principle to life. It's not your circumstances that keep you from accomplishing your goals and keep your life going in the same cycles over and over again. It's how you handle your circumstances. This is especially true for a child of God. God doesn't have to boast the most favorable environment in order to make you prosper. In fact, God works best through adversity as you can see in the following verses of scripture:

But he said to me, "My grace is sufficient for you, for my power is made perfect in weakness." Therefore I will boast all the more gladly about my weaknesses, so that Christ's power may rest on me. That is why, for Christ's sake, I delight in weaknesses, in insults, in hardships, in persecutions, in difficulties. For when I am weak, then I am strong (2 Corinthians 12:9-10 NIV).

Paul made the statement that he would boast even more in his weakness because he understood now that his weakness allowed God's glory to be seen in its fullest. God specializes in turning what seems to be imminent defeat into a resounding victory. God loves using people who have been dealt what seems to be a bad hand in life, and causing them to prevail. When people see where you are, compared to where you came from, then they will know that it had to be God who got you there. God doesn't need the strongest person in order to accomplish his will. Neither does he need the wisest person. 1 Corinthians 1:27 let's us know that God chooses the foolish things of this world in order to shame the wisdom of the wise and he chooses the weak things of the world to shame the strong.

Simply put, God can use you with your issues. In fact the very thing you thought was going to hold you back God will use it to advance you into public notice in order for his Glory to be seen through YOU. You don't have to stay where you are right now. God is able to pull you out of whatever pit that you may be in. Not only that, but he said that he would take you out of the miry clay and place you upon a rock, and establish your goings (Psalms 40:2 KJV). When God establishes you, no one or nothing can hinder your progress. Even when you have dealt with a situation that has temporarily brought your forward progression to a halt if you reconnect to the "right source" you can begin moving forward again. However, this all starts with you making the right connection.

Check your Connection

There is great power in connection; however you have to make the right connections. Let's take a look at Ecclesiastes 4:9-12 which illustrates this principle.

Two are better than one; because they have a good reward for their labour. For if they fall, the one will lift up his fellow: but woe to him that is alone when he falleth; for he hath not another to help him up. Again, if two lie together, then they have heat: but how can one be warm alone? And if one prevail against him, two shall withstand him; and a threefold cord is not quickly broken (KJV).

Isn't it reassuring to know that when you face a difficult situation, you have someone to have your back? Doesn't it bring comfort to your spirit to know that if you fall, you have someone to pick you back up? No one ever wants to go into battle alone. Rather you want to know that there is someone that you are connected to who want allow any harm to come to you but will fight with you until the very end. That's why you have to make sure that you constantly check your connections to make sure you have the right ones.

Not What You Know, Who You Know

There is an old saying that states it's not what you know, it's who you know. It's this very reason that many people break their necks trying to get to know people who they feel can improve their social and economic status. They feel that if they can connect with certain people of a higher social and economic class, then it will improve their chances at success. Have you ever attempted to connect with someone just because of who they were? Take a quick stroll through memory lane to your first year in high school. Who you connected with that first year of high school would usually determine your peers for the remaining 3, or for some of us, 5 or 6 years of high school. These peers would be your "click."

You went out of your way to make sure you made the best possible impression on the click that you wanted to be a part of. You dressed like them. You talked like them. You signed up for all the same classes as them. Some of you would even disassociate yourself with the people who were once your friends in grade school just to be accepted by this new click. You did all you could to gain notice with the ultimate goal of being accepted by this click. Nobody wanted to feel like an outcast. Being a part of a click made you feel special. Unfortunately, the need to fit in would sometimes involve you acting out of your normal character and sometimes would steer you in a direction that wasn't beneficial for you. In other words you ended up compromising your integrity in order to improve your reputation.

These are the types of connections that you don't want to make in life as nothing good can come out of them. Regrettably this same concept has now migrated to the church. In fact there are just as many clicks in the church as it is in high schools. We have the "anointed click" who believes that nobody is as anointed as they are. We have the "holier than thou click" who believe that they are the only people in the church that are living a righteous life. We also have the "blessed like me click" who feel that nobody is quite as blessed as they are. With so many clicks in the church the most important connection that we need to have with God is sometimes lost in the shuffle. Instead of having a church who is working with one another in order to accomplish a common goal, we have a church that is divided against each other attempting to accomplish many different goals.

Teamwork Makes the Dream Work

The Bible makes it clear that if a kingdom is divided against itself, that kingdom cannot stand. It's time for the church, as well as us individually to restore our connection with God. If we stay connected to God it's nothing that can break our stride. If we stay connected to God then his Spirit will begin to lead us and guide us in the direction that we are supposed to be going. It's important that we don't allow anything or anybody to break the connection between us and God. The devil will use anything he can to try to break our connection.

David understood how important it was to stay connected to God when he stated in Psalms 73:28 (KJV), "But it is good for me to draw near to God: I have put my trust in the Lord GOD, that I may declare all thy works." Notice David didn't say that it was good for him to draw near to a prevalent group. He didn't say that it was good for him to draw near to affluent people. David understood that to have a connection with God was to have favor with God, and favor with God was the gateway to all of the other needed connections that he would ever need in life.

See when you are connected to God you don't have to worry about rubbing shoulders with those who you feel can propel you to the next level. When you have favor with God, He will open up doors for you that not even Donald Trump with all of his influence could begin to compare. Proverbs 3:3-4 (NIV) says, "Let love and faithfulness never leave you; bind them around your neck, write them on the tablet of your heart. Then you will win favor and a good name in the sight of God and man."

Connection Brings Direction

Maybe you are single in search of a spouse and want to make sure you connect with the right person. The way to know for sure is to first connect with God and let him lead you to the right person. Maybe you are torn in between two jobs and want to make sure that you choose the right one. First check your connection with God and then trust him to help you make the best decision. See when you think of connection you think of two things that are bonded together. If you are bonded together with someone then you both can't go in opposite directions. Someone has to be willing to submit to the direction that the other person is going.

When you are connected with God, don't try to steer God in your direction. Many times this is what we do. We try to make God go in the direction that we want him to go. He is telling us that we are about to head in the wrong direction but we are so sure that we are right that we keep trying to go in an opposite direction. When that happens God is not going to continue to fight with you to go his way. Rather, God will loosen up the tension and allow us to go our own way. John 10:29 makes it clear that no one can snatch us out of the hand of God, however James 1:14 let's us know that we can be drawn away by our own lust.

Some of us have been trying to connect to people who we thought could carry us to our destiny. However, God is saying I'm the only one who can truly give you the grace you need to reach your true purpose. Many of you have ventured away from your connection with God and now you have found yourself in a place of uncertainty. You have tried to trace back your steps and find out where you lost the connection but you feel as though you have made too many wrong turns to get back to God. I got great news for you, God never let go of the rope. Even when you have ventured away and let go of your grip, God still has his lasso of love wrapped around you and is able to pull you back if you are willing to come back to him.

God wants me to let you know that where you are right now is not your final resting place. Your ministry will begin to flourish again. Your current economic situation will change. The flame in your marriage will be rekindled. Don't believe what you are seeing right now. Reconnect to God and believe only what God has already declared about you in His word.

Don't allow your current situation to make you quit like the churches in Galatia had apparently done in Galatians chapter 5. The main hindrance of the Galatians' church was the fact that they had begin to connect more with the Law of Moses rather than the new Law of grace which is written on our hearts by the Spirit. They needed to check their connection. The churches at Galatia had caused their spiritual growth to stay at a standstill because they would rather debate meaningless arguments about the Law, rather than accept the liberty in which Christ had given them through his death.

I truly believe that this is also a problem that is being seen more and more in today's church. We have begun to argue and propose so many manmade laws for the church, that the true purpose to equip the church with the truth of the word of God in order to go out and make disciples of all men, is null and void. Many of you reading this book right now are part of churches that talk more about church guidelines, rather than the pure unadulterated word of God. We need to check our connection. Lamentations 3:40 says, "Let us test and examine our ways, and return to the Lord." Test your ways, and return to the Lord. Remember you can't do it your way. Your program is always subject to change.

Your Program is subject to Change

A lack of connection will cause one to stay stuck in a place where their gifts and abilities are going unexploited. A lack of connection will also lead one into becoming a programmed Christian. A programmed Christian goes to church week after week expecting to receive the same thing. They know what people are going to do in church even before they do it. They know who is going to sing. They know who is going to shout. They even know who is going to give what in the offering. Some of them are so good that they know what the Pastor's message will be and they even know how they are going to deliver it.

For many of you this is the only type of church you know. You don't know what it's like to have a supernatural encounter with God anymore because you have become so caught up in "programmed church." You can't remember the last time you witnessed the Spirit of God fill the atmosphere of the service. Many of you can't even remember the last time you experienced the tug of the Spirit weighing down on your heart so heavily to the point where you couldn't hold back the tears.

After you have been programmed for so long many times you will develop a preconceived notion of what church is supposed to be like. When you take on a preconceived notion of what church is supposed to be you will begin coming to church not expecting to experience anything different than what you have now grown accustomed to. This keeps you from experiencing the many different ways that God chooses to reveal himself because now you have put God in a box.

Take the Limits Off

What have you grown accustomed to? Have you grown accustomed to just church as usual without experiencing a divine move of God? Have you created your on agenda for your church, and even for your life? If so you have attempted to make God get with your program. This type of viewpoint usually stems from a misunderstanding of the word of God. Malachi 3:6 (NIV) says, "For I am the Lord, I change not..." Many read this and say well since God doesn't change then church should be programmed. They don't take into account, however, the many different attributes that reveals the nature of God. Isaiah 55:8-9 (NIV) says, "For my thoughts are not your thoughts, neither are your ways my ways, saith the Lord. For as the heavens are higher than the earth, so are my ways higher than your ways, and my thoughts than your thoughts." This lets us know that our human intellect could never grasp the richness and dept of God's vast imagination.

When we are programmed we place restrictions on what's possible for God. Ask yourself this question is anything too hard for God? While most would say no, many of these same people still operate in deficiency due to their inability to expand their thinking beyond their on customs. Don't miss out on what God is trying to do in your life because it doesn't fit your program. Isaiah 43:18-19 (NIV) states "Forget the former things; do not dwell on the past. See I am doing a new thing! Now it springs up; do you not perceive it?" What a powerful message. God is pleading to Israel, and even to Christians today, to forget the former things.

Forget how you use to come to church and just sit in the pew and do nothing. Forget how you use to worry about looking dignified and sanctified in church, rather than allowing the Spirit to have his way. Forget how much drama you had to deal with over the last year of your life. Forget about that relationship that didn't work out and now because of it you have grown accustomed with the ideal of having to settle for less than the best that God wants to give you. Forget about that job that laid you off and now you accept the fact that you are only qualified for minimum wage. You have to remember that your program is subject to change. God has the power to transform your situation. It's up to you however to begin the process of eliminating your past defeat from your memory banks. If you continue to hold on to past defeats, you will never experience future success.

Escape From Mediocracy

God goes even further by saying that we should not even consider the things of old. Some of you have been reconsidering old relationships that you know were not advantageous to you. Due to our economic climate many are considering working jobs that are far substandard in comparison to the qualifications that they possess. Many of you are even considering staying at an old church where your spirit man is going unfed all because that's the church that you have attended your entire life. You don't have to abide by that same program.

God affirms that I will do a new thing and it shall spring forth. The simple fact that it shall spring forth lets you know that when God does it, you will know that it had to be God. How many times have doors opened in your life that you knew that it was nobody but God who was working behind the scenes in order to bring it to past? When God blesses you many times you don't even see it coming. When is the last time God performed the unexpected in your life?

Everything that God does typically exceeds our normal expectations. In fact Ephesians 3:20 (NIV) states, "Now to him who is able to do immeasurably more than all we ask or imagine, according to his power that is at work within us..." You have to know that God is working in the midst of your life in order to accomplish the unimaginable. Unfortunately, life's issues have a way of making us think that it's no way God could ever do anything impressive in this "mess" that we call life. Isn't it funny how the devil can paint an excellent picture of your exterior? He loves to show you your moral flaws and defects. He loves to show you the fleshly freckles and blemishes that are in your life. He loves to show you how compared to others, your physique doesn't seem to measure up.

The reason why he does this is because if he can keep you focused on your exterior, then He can make you look past what he has deposited on your interior. There is something on the inside of you that the devil doesn't want to come out. Why? He knows that if you ever tap into what God has already placed on the inside of you that you will be a tremendous threat to his kingdom. So to keep you silent, he attempts to make you insecure. He wants you to focus more on your failures then your successes. He wants you to focus on the fact that you had a baby out of wedlock. He wants you to focus on the fact that you use to sell drugs. He wants you to focus on the fact that you use to be a whoremonger. The "fact" is, once you accepted Christ into your life, you became a new creature (1 Cor. 5:17).

You Are a New Creature

You are not that same person that you use to be. The Spirit of God is now working in your life in order to carry out a good work. As a result you can walk confidently knowing that he who begun a good work in you, will perform it until the day of Jesus Christ (Philippians 1:6). The simple fact that Christ begun the good work let's you know that your agenda didn't have anything to do with it. It wasn't because you were so good or so deserving of anything, it was all because of God's grace. The grace of God is so amazing. It has the power to reach you no matter where you may be in life. In fact if you look at the ladder part of Isaiah 43:19 (NIV).

God speaking to Israel decrees, "I will even make a way in the wilderness, and rivers in the desert." God was letting them know that even in that place of desolation that they had now found themselves in, He was about to make a way for them. Notice he didn't say a way out, however he said that he would make a way in the wilderness. What that means is that even in the midst of their bad situation, God was going to sustain them. God also said that he would bring rivers in the desert. In that place of drought that you may be in right now, God is able to bring some rain. Again keep in mind that God didn't necessarily say that he would end the drought immediately, but what God was saying was that He would give you a sufficient amount of "rain" to uphold you in your dry place until he does bring you out.

God Takes Care of His Own

Even when everything around you seems depleted, when you are a child of God He will still cause you to thrive. That lets you know that even if everybody else's bank accounts are in the negative, your bank account can still remain in the positive. Even if your neighbor's home was just foreclosed, God can still make a way for you to stay ahead on your mortgage. Even if everyone else's spiritual light seems to be dim, God can still cause your light to shine forth like the noon day. If you are willing to let go of the old, God can bring on something new. If you are willing to let go of your program there is no limit to what God will do in your life.

Some of you have been trying to hold on to some old baggage that God is trying to convince you to let go of. Some of you are still trying to offer God the same old routine praise. God is saying if you want to go places that you never been before then it's going to require you to do some things that you have never did before. You have to be willing to stretch beyond the ordinary and press towards a higher calling in Christ. Don't just sit there and allow your gifts to die. Don't choose to stay a "Programmed Christian" just because you have grown accustomed to being in that same place. When a person operates on a program over an extended period of time, eventually they will become susceptible to enemy attack. If your opponent knows your game plan in advance then he has an advantage on you because every move you make he can beat you there.

Change Your Game Plan

Many Christians are living a predictable life. This makes it easy for the enemy to keep them stuck because he knows exactly what he needs to attack in their life in order to make them uncomfortable. When we are uncomfortable we tend to complain. When we are uncomfortable we tend to be irritable and discontented. These negative emotions will eventually lead to doubt. In order to keep doubt from ruling our lives, we have to frequently change. If the enemy can make you doubt, then he can keep you from moving forward. The enemy is determined to make Christians doubt the legitimacy of the word of God in order to keep their destiny from manifesting.

Don't ever let yourself become comfortable in a place where your gifts are going unutilized and you begin to doubt God's word. The ultimate goal of the doubt that the enemy brings is to attempt to make us walk into our on program, which is usually in direct disobedience to the word of God. Ultimately if he can keep us from walking in obedience then he can prevent our destiny from ever coming forth. That's why it's so important that we don't carry our on agenda. It's time to change the program as his spirit will lead us to do so. This is usually easier said than done. A lot of times pride will keep people operating on the same program and therefore walking in disobedience. However, there is another factor that will keep a person from walking in total obedience and that is fear.

Fear: The Enemy of Purpose

For God hath not given the spirit of fear; but of power, and of love, and of a sound mind. (2 Timothy 1:7 KJV)

This is a very familiar scripture which you often hear quoted by a lot of Christians. When we quote this scripture it gives us a sense of security, however many times this feeling is short lived once we face an issue that seems unbearable. When fear grips us, instead of embracing God's guidance and being obedient to his commands, we often fall into exile and attempt to offer God a sacrifice. Have you ever found yourself in this position? God had instructed you to do one thing, and because you were afraid to step into the designated position that he had commanded you to be in, you attempted to satisfy God by doing something different. Most of us have been in this situation a time or two in our lives. In fact, some of you right now know that God has called you to a higher calling.

Some of you are singing in the choir, but God is calling you to be an evangelist. You are an associate minister, but God is calling you to be a pastor. You are working for a company, but God is calling you to own your own company. Some of you are so afraid of disappointment in life that you simply choose to do nothing. However, you are loaded with great ideas, which with a little effort could translate into big opportunities not only for you, but for others that are connected to you. Nonetheless because of fear you continue to operate out of position and anytime you operate out of position, you are being ineffective. Don't let fear keep you from stepping into your destiny. Don't let fear keep you in a place of hopelessness. Most of all don't allow fear to keep you walking in disobedience. You have to know that God has already made the way; He's just waiting on you to step out.

The Benefits of Fearing God

As I stated earlier, God is big enough and He is more than able to lead you through any circumstance, over any mountain, and through any valley in order to get you to your "end zone." Godly direction is just one of the many benefits of fearing God. Another benefit of fearing God is divine protection. The Bible says that his angels will encamp round about everyone who fears him (Psalms 37:4 NIV). Further more, the Bible informs us that the fear of God is the beginning of knowledge (Proverbs 1:7 NIV). Knowing this, why do so many people still operate in fear? This is because most of us possess the wrong kind of fear.

We fear failure. We fear not being loved by people. We fear rejection. Many of us even fear Satan. However, there are not a lot of people who fear God. Keep in mind that the fear of God should not be equated with the fear of man. To fear God means that we reverence Him. To fear God means that we respect and honor Him as deity. Fearing God is the way of obedience. Ecclesiastes 12:13 (NIV) states, "Let us hear the conclusion of the whole matter: Fear God, and keep his commandments: for this is the whole duty of man."

Fear vs. Love

As children of God, we have a moral obligation to fear God and we demonstrate this fear by walking in agreement with his word. In Ecclesiasts 12:13 the word fear can be equated to the word love. How do we know that? Let's look at another passage of scripture. John 14:15 states, "If you love me, you will obey my commands (NIV)." When we compare both scriptures we will see what appears to be two contrasting words, which require the same dedication, fear and love. A closer study however will show how these words are much more related than one would think. When a parent asks a child to do something they expect it to be done. One reason is because they know that the child fears the consequences of not doing what they were instructed to do.

The other reason is because they would hope that the child loves them enough to do what they had asked them to do. As a parent they understand that many times the child will not always do what they were instructed to do and will therefore have to face the consequences of their choices. This act of disobedience within itself didn't mean that the child didn't fear the parent or that the child didn't love the parent. On the contrary this was the innate nature of the child to sometimes be disobedient.

The punishment for this disobedience tended to be very passive. Paul stated in 1 Corinthians 13:11 that when he was a child, he spoke as a child, he understood as a child, and he also thought as child. Christ knows that in the infancy of our spiritual development we lack the aptitude to know everything that is initially expected of us. He also knows that sometimes we will stumble as we are transitioning from a crawl to a walk. His disciplinary approach in this case is one of love and instruction.

As you spend intimate time with Christ, he has time to nurture you and develop you into the man, or woman of God he has purposed you to be. As we take on more of the word of God then our fear and love for God should begin to increase. Our understanding begins to heighten. We are no longer stumbling as much as we use to. We have went through our infancy, continued on throughout the toddler years, endured the school-age years, and survived the pressures of adolescence. We are now ready to call ourselves an adult. Or are we?

When we become an adult in Christ, then it's time to "put away childish things." When I stamp that adult tag on me then that means that now my accountability has increased. The punishment for disobedience becomes more severe. Many of us want the adult tag however we don't want the responsibility that comes along with it. When one becomes an adult any deficiency in growth will be exposed. If you didn't learn how to count in your school-age years, then it will affect your adult life. If you wasn't potty trained in your infancy then it will affect your adult life. That's why we have adults still making a "mess" on themselves. All of the years of our physical development are connected. Therefore anything that was skipped can be detrimental to the final person we become. This is the same principle that applies to our spiritual life.

As it relates to love and fear, if you didn't take out the time to learn how to love God in your infancy, then it's no way that you will fear God in your adulthood. They are interconnected. A lot of people say that they love God however they lack the ability to treat their neighbor's right. There are a lot of people who say they fear God, but they don't walk in total obedience to his word. To know God is to love him, and everyone else, and to fear God is to revere him.

Obedience then will be the fruit of the love and fear, or reverent respect that you have for God. However, many of you are facing the consequences of your disobedience because of a learning disability that you faced in your childhood that was never corrected. This in turn forces God to have to deal with you more severely because you should know better. The good thing about it is God loves you enough to offer you a chance to get it right.

The Discipline of God

Hebrews 12:6 states, "...the Lord disciplines those he loves, and he punishes everyone he accepts as a son (NIV)." Just as a parent to a child, God offers discipline as an opportunity for you to see where you were in error with hopes that you want continue to make the same mistakes. Many heed this warning and turn their hearts back to God like David. However, if you continue to walk in disobedience God's discipline turns into severe punishment. Romans 1:18-19 (NIV) states, "The wrath of God is being revealed from heaven against all the godlessness and wickedness of men who suppress the truth by their wickedness, since what may be known about God is plain to them, because God has made it plain to them."

Don't ignore the discipline of God. When we completely ignore God's warnings with a total disregard for God's power, then we are setting ourselves up for failure and eventually destruction. In fact, we could actually step out of divine destiny and lose out on what God had in store for us. This is what happened to King Saul who chose not to obey God and was therefore rejected from being King of Israel. Don't miss out on your blessing because you refuse to obey. Fearing God makes way for blessings to begin to overflow in the believer's life. There are more blessings linked with fearing God, than in anything else.

As I stated earlier, the fear of God is the beginning of all knowledge (Proverbs 1:7). In other words, our fear of God births good decision making in our lives. If you don't have the fear of God in your life then you will not be able to make good decisions because you will constantly attempt to make decisions based on your own knowledge. The reason why many of us continue to go through cycles of bad decision making is because we don't fear God enough to accept his instructions. The only way to be Spirit led however is to fear God and obey his instructions.

Not My Will Lord

When a person fears God they live by the motto, "not my will Lord, but let yours be done." Do you fear God? I'm not just talking about saying we fear God with our mouths. I'm talking about allowing our actions to reflect our fear of God. A person who fears God will always live in subjection to the word of God. There are a lot of people who say they fear God with their lips, however if you look at their actions you will find that very hard to believe. Jesus put it best when he stated, *"These people draw near to me with their mouths, but their heart is far from me."*

This lets us know that the fear of God is a heart matter. It's time to check our hearts? Ask yourself the question, are my actions truly reflecting the fear of God? Am I living in total obedience to the word of God? If you can't answer those questions with a resounding yes then obviously you need some work. To be honest all of us could use some work in that category. If we were to survey our culture we would see that all of the depravity that we are seeing in our world can be traced back to a breakdown in the fear of God. When a society no longer fears God, then widespread chaos is bound to ensue.

Murders, thefts, adultery, lying, and so many other destructive habits all find their root in a lack of the fear of God. Even in the modern day churches we are seeing a replacement of the fear of God, with the fear of man. Many people don't mind sinning as long as they know they can hide it from the leaders of the church. This shows that the church has now placed the man of God in the position that God is supposed to be in. Sadly a lot of pastors are aware of this fact, however because of their desire for power they prey on the ignorance of many people in the church. They preach a self promoting gospel that further brings glory to themselves rather than God. Needless to say our greatest fear should never be in disappointing man. Our greatest fear should be in not pleasing God.

Just think how much better our world would be if we would shift our fear back to God. Individually, can you imagine how much better your life would be if you feared God more? If you allowed God to stamp his preapproval on every choice that you made before you made it. When you truly fear God you are willing to offer him your most precious possession to please Him. This shows God that He is the Lord over your entire life. Is God Lord over your life? Are you willing to give God your all? Abraham was. God instructed Abraham to offer his only son as a sacrifice to Him.

Abraham feared God so much that he was willing to offer his most priceless possession as a sacrifice unto the Lord. He didn't let people hinder him from being obedient. He didn't try to offer God anything other than what God required of him. In order for God to give you His best, you have to be determined that you are not going to give God anything less than your best. The Bible says that when Abraham stretched out his hand to slay his son that the angel of the Lord spoke to him and said, "Now I know that thou fearest God, seeing thou has not withheld thy son, thine only son from me (Genesis 22:12 KJV)." If we are willing to give God our all, then God will bless us with all that we need and more.

Blessed by Association

God richly favored Abraham with great power and wealth, but that's not what made him blessed. Some of you right now think that you can measure how blessed you are by how much you own. But that doesn't make you blessed. Abraham was blessed because he was obedient to the voice of God even when it hurt. God credited his obedience as righteousness. Through Abraham's obedience all of his descendents, including all future descendents who accepted Christ, would be blessed. Through the sin of Adam we were once "guilty by association," now through Abraham's obedience, and his future seed Christ, we are "blessed by association." The blessing was in the sacrifice.

The Blessing is in the Sacrifice

Just like in Abraham's day, the blessing is still in the sacrifice. Even though God didn't permit Abraham to sacrifice his son, he now knew that Abraham was willing to sacrifice his son and more in order to please Him. Abraham had given God total control over everything he possessed. Are you willing to sacrifice some things in your life in order to make it to your blessed placed? God is not asking you to sacrifice your child. God doesn't want you to offer him a goat or a ram as a sacrifice. But are you willing to offer your bodies as a living sacrifice holy and acceptable to God? Are you willing to cut the cord to relationships that are pulling you out of the will of God? Are you willing to spend time with God meditating on His word and seeking His face through prayer? If you are willing to humble yourself, then God will elevate you to places that you've never been before or even thought you could go.

Your Blessed Place

Abraham had made it to his blessed place. When you are in your blessed place your trust is not in money. When you are in your blessed place your trust is not in man. When you make it to your blessed place you are in a position that your faith can't be compromised. You have made the decision to put total dependence in God. The best part about that is that the enemy may attack your family, your job, or even your health, but He can never shake your faith. Why? Because now you understand that since you are in the will of God, that no matter what the enemy may attempt to do, no weapon formed against you will ever prosper (Isaiah 54:17).

No matter how bad your situation may appear you have to know that you are still blessed. David puts it best in Psalms 34:9 when he says "Fear the Lord, you his saints, for those who fear him lack nothing (NIV)." How refreshing it is to know that if you fear God and keep his commandments, that you will never have to want for anything. Yes that's right, nothing. You don't have to stay stuck where you are because of fear. Stop allowing fear to drive you. It's time to allow the Spirit to assume the driver's seat in your life in order to take you to your intended destination. The question is however, are you ready to submit to the Spirit? If so, then he's waiting to assume the leadership position in your life.

CHAPTER 3

What does it mean to be Spirit Led?

Everything that we talked about in Chapter 1 & 2 was all preparation for beginning to live a Spirit led life. However the question still lingers, what does it mean to be led by the Spirit? The definition of the word lead is to show the way to an individual or a group by going with or ahead. As it relates to the Spirit, He goes before you and surveys the path so He can prepare you for what's in your future. He acts as a messenger for the Father in order to guide you into all truth, seeing as though He never speaks in and of Himself, but rather only decrees publicly what God has already spoken unto Him privately.

St. John 16:13 affirms, "...when he, the Spirit of truth, comes, he will guide you into all truth. He will not speak on his own; he will speak only what he hears, and he will tell you what is yet to come (NIV)." We can rest assured that The Holy Spirit won't steer us in the wrong direction because He's already seen our future. He knows that our future is loaded with endless possibilities that we have yet to believe were attainable.

1 Corinthians 2:9 says, "...No eye has seen, no ear has heard, no mind has conceived what God has prepared for those who love him (NIV)." See many people read this passage and stop there. Therefore they assume that God chooses by some divine plan to keep secret the mysteries concerning His purpose for their life. Maybe you are a person who has been told that God doesn't desire to make known to you the predetermined agenda that

he has for your life. This way of thinking can lead to some very negative consequences.

Waiting on the Lord

The first problem that you usually see with this type of person is a lackluster approach to everything they do. They feel that since they don't know what to do and because they feel as though they can't know what God has for their life, then the easiest thing to do is to do nothing and just wait for God to move. Don't get me wrong, I'm a firm believer in waiting on God. However, we can't expect God to do everything for us. If I believe God for a new job, then I have to begin to look at job postings. If I believe God for a bigger home, then I have to start making preparations to obtain a bigger home. If I desire to grow in God spiritually, I have to take the initiative to pray and study the word. I have to apply action to my faith.

Some people though will just sit around and wait for God to drop the new job or the bigger home in their lap. They believe they can grow spiritually without any effort on their part. This is mainly because they feel that nothing they do will have any influence on what happens. These people tend to live by the creed, "what will be, will be." While certain things that happen in life are out of our control, there are many things that we control the outcome of.

I used the examples of a new job or a bigger home just for demonstration purposes. However, this approach affects more than just obtaining material things. There are many people who will hold back from a ministry that God has called them to fulfill because they are so afraid of being wrong. You never know how many people you are affecting, however, if you refuse to discover what God has called you to do.

Don't Guess God's Will

The second problem that you usually see with this type of person is the fact that they usually attempt to guess what God desires for their life.

Have you ever taken a vacation without the proper directions? You went on MapQuest to print off your directions but when you printed them you didn't print all the pages. Nevertheless because you were in such a rush you didn't take out the time to go print out the other needed pages. You make it through the first ten steps just fine and you begin to think that you may just be ok. However, after step ten you notice that your directions have ended.

You come to a four way intercession and you ponder which road you should take. Some of the people in the car say lets go back and find a store to get directions. However, if you do this you feel as though you would be admitting to the fact that you really didn't know where you were going from the start. So you confidently say, "I know which road to take" when in all actuality you don't have a clue where you are at. You then take a quick uncalculated guess and choose to go in a direction which later proves to be a completely different direction than where you needed to go. Instead of ending up in Florida, you end up in Kalamazoo.

As you probably noticed, I'm speaking from firsthand experience. Unfortunately many of us have taken this same approach in our everyday walk with Christ. The Bible says that we have to acknowledge God in all of our ways and he would direct our paths (proverbs 3:5-6). Nonetheless when it seems as though God is not answering us quick enough, or if the answer he gives us isn't what we wanted to hear we feel as though we haven't heard from God yet. Therefore we try to "guess" what the best choice is for many important decisions we have to make in life. How many times have you found yourselves in an awful situation because of a bad choice you made on your on without consulting God?

If you are like me then you have made this mistake many times in your life. This can be dangerous because when we try to take our future in our on hands, the final result ends up being disastrous. Proverbs 14:12, states "There is a way that seems right to a man, but in the end it leads to death (NIV)." Proverbs 16:2 goes on to state, "All a man's ways seem innocent to him, but motives are weighed by the LORD (NIV)."

Let's be honest none of us like to be told that we are doing something the wrong way, especially if we have been doing it that way for a long time. In fact we are usually content with doing things our on way even when our way is undeniably wrong. If we don't learn how to examine our actions against the word of God then we will always feel justified. The Bible is filled with men and women who were forced to deal with the consequences of bad decisions made on the basis of faulty direction.

Your Mistakes Effects Others

David thought it was a good idea to conduct a Census, but God was displeased. Because David chose to follow his own way, not only did God punish him, but 70K innocent people also had to deal with the consequences of his actions. David's sin brought "death." Just think about that for a moment. If you were to think through the passageways of your life, how many choices have you made that not only affected you, but also had an effect on others who were linked to you? How many fathers have made choices in life and now they are seeing the effects on their sons? How many mothers have chosen to go down the wrong paths in life and now they are seeing the fruit of their labor in their daughters? Many of you who are reading this book right now are experiencing some sort of death in your life because of the frequent attempts you have made to do things your own way instead of God's way. However, with God there is hope and a future.

Restoration in Jesus

No matter how many things we have let die in our lives, we can find restoration in Christ Jesus. Therefore, we can't spend our time focusing on stuff that we have let die in our life. There is restoration and redirection in the word of God. We just have to empty ourselves enough to receive it. Even when you have experienced death in your life, God is still able to impart life. John 12:24 states, "Truly, I tell all of you with certainty, unless a grain of wheat falls into the ground and dies, it remains alone. But if it dies, it produces a lot of grain (NIV)." Sometimes God has to allow some things in your life to die in order to fertilize the harvest that He is about to bring in your life.

There are some relationships in your life that have suddenly died and you didn't understand the reason. There are some jobs that ended prematurely, and you didn't know why. What God was doing was removing the temporary, in order to give you the permanent. God was controlling the circumstances of your life in order to prepare you for your next level. All of the things you lost were just temporary. If you would refocus on God, then He will begin to reveal to you some things that are eternal. Sometimes God will let things die for him to resume his place of importance in your life. So even though it may appear you lost everything, you really gained so much more.

The reason being is because when you come down to nothing, and all you have is God, it makes you look at God differently. God becomes the object of your affection again. It's almost like falling in love, with your first love, all over again. You begin to trust God more because you understand that He was with you even at your lowest point. You now understand that although other people had used and abused you God had never taken advantage of your love. You begin to feel unworthy of someone who would love you even when it wasn't reciprocated. This feeling of unworthiness softens the heart of a person. When our hearts are softened, then God can trust us in order to make an investment in our lives. The reason being is because now he knows that you wouldn't take advantage of His love because you understand how precious his love is.

Follow the Spirit's Lead

God wants you to know that even though you made some choices that might have carried you in the wrong direction; He is standing there to help you get back on the right path through the guidance of His Spirit. You don't have to spend all your time struggling to discover God's plan for your life. In fact, God desires to reveal it to you without the constant worry. In the ladder part of 1 Corinthians 2:10 is a passage of scripture that is literally full with so much possibility. The verse reads as follows:

> But God has revealed it to us by his Spirit. The Spirit searches all things, even the deep things of God (NIV)

This passage of scripture should help every believer breathe a sigh of relief as it assures us that our life is not a hazy maze which we have to feel our way through. We don't have to call the psychic network to find out about our tomorrow. On the contrary, we can know our tomorrow today. We can take a glimpse through the halls of time and see that God has a bright future for us. Jeremiah 29:11 says, "For I know the thoughts that I think toward you, says the LORD, thoughts of peace and not of evil, to give you a future and a hope (NIV)." The Spirit is telling the believer that in spite of all the darkness that may be surrounding them, God has a brighter day. The question still remains however, are we allowing the Spirit to lead us?

Who's leading you?

We learned earlier that the Spirit of God will instruct us in all truth, in order to carry us to a place of divine destiny. The question is however, are we allowing the Spirit of God to lead us or are we being led by other means? In a world that tends to be void of true leadership, many people attempt to find guidance in all the wrong places. Some people are led by emotions, others by people, and still others by personal ambition. We will take a little time to discuss all of these in greater detail.

Emotionally Led

Emotions are one of the worst types of leadership because they are based on "feelings." Feelings can't be a decisive type of leadership because they change so frequently. Do you recall the first time you "felt" like you were in love? She was the apple of your eye. He was the sugar in your Kool-Aid. The two of you never disagreed. The two of you never fought. The conditions of your relationship were exceptionally comfortable. In fact, in the beginning the two of you were virtually inseparable. That was until the circumstances in your relationship suddenly changed.

When the circumstances changed, so did your feelings. When at one time you were the apple of my eye, now you have become the reason my eyes cry. At first we hardly fought, and now we find ourselves fighting all the time. Now that the circumstances have changed, you quickly begin to look for something or someone else who can reproduce that original happy feeling. The love you thought you had wasn't unconditional. It was solely based upon certain conditions that made you feel the way you felt during that particular period of time in your life.

He Loves Me, He Loves Me Not

There are a lot of Christians right now who are facing this same situation. When things are going good in their life they are highly affectionate towards God. When the circumstances surrounding their life are favorable they can keep their focus on God. However, when turbulent times arise in their life they immediately get caught up in the emotion of the moment and begin to shift their focus to their issues, rather than God. In fact, they begin to doubt whether or not God even loves them. This allows depression to set in and where there is depression, there will be stagnation.

For this reason we, as Christians, should never be led by our emotions. If we are led by emotions, our guidance will only be as stable as the conditions we find ourselves in. Sometimes God will cause things to become uncomfortable in your life in order to see if your faith is authentic, or if you are just a "fair-weather friend." Let's take Israel for example. In the book of Numbers chapter 13, Moses is instructed to send some men to explore the land of Canaan in order to plan an attack against the city. Moses chose a man from each tribe to go out and explore this land. Upon returning from the exploration ten out of the twelve men who went, didn't bring back a favorable report. As a result, these men begin to plant fear into the Israelites by talking about how big the men of Canaan were. This caused Israel to magnify their obstacle bigger than the God they served.

Ironically, the two men who brought back a favorable report were Joshua and Caleb who would both go on to be prominent men in Israel. However, because of the bad report the Israelites received from the other men, they begin to grumble against Moses and Aaron. Even though God had already promised the Israelites the land of Canaan, now that they had heard this report, they allowed fear to make them doubt what God had already promised and they also begin to grumble against God.

Whose Report Will You Believe

Whose report will you believe? Can you still trust the guidance of God when your issues appear bigger than what you are able to handle? Or will your emotions get the best of you? Israel's emotions made them forget the very character of God. They forgot that he was Jehovah Jireh, the God who provided for them whenever there was a lack. They forgot that He was Jehovah Nissi, the Lord who had been their victory banner in battle. They also forgot that he was El Shaddai, the Lord who had shown himself mighty in bringing them out of Egyptian slavery. God had brought them out of bondage, carried them through the red sea, destroyed their enemies, and now they were saying that they would rather be back in bondage than have to deal with their present circumstances.

The fact of the matter is that they were being led by their emotions all along. They didn't have an unconditional faith in God. Their faith was purely contingent on how well their conditions were. Although they had been brought out of Egypt in the physical, mentally they were still in "Egypt." In other words their position had changed, but their mentality was still the same. Is that you? Are you being led more by emotions, rather than by the voice of God? Are you allowing your current situation to cause you to wish that you were back in a place that God had already delivered you from? If so, then you have yet to experience the beauty of truly being led by God. You are not seeking God's face, in order to hear his voice. On the contrary, you are only looking out for His hand.

The Road Less Traveled

The Bible says that my sheep hear my voice and I know them, and they follow me. When we listen to the voice of God many times He will tell us to do things that will inconvenience us. When we allow God to lead many times he will lead us places that we don't necessarily want to go. He will sometimes ask us to do things we don't really want to do. We have to understand however that he wouldn't lead us anywhere, or put us in any situation that he hasn't already equipped us to handle. Yes, it might seem overbearing right now, but God will not put more on you than what you are able to bare.

Never take an alternate route just because it seems more convenient or more bearable to you. This type of leadership will never allow you to stretch your faith beyond your on human limitations. You will always look for the short cuts in life even though sometimes it takes longer to do things the right way. Unfortunately this is the road most traveled. Jesus said, "… wide is the gate and broad is the road that leads to destruction, and many enter through it. But small is the gate and narrow the road that leads to life, and only a few find it (Matthew 7:13-14 NIV)." Sadly, most people will never truly discover God's true purposes for their lives.

This type of leadership also makes people focus on what they "feel led" to do. It's important that we be extremely careful about saying I feel led to do this or do that. We have to make sure that our instruction is a genuine conviction that falls in line with the will of God, rather than a fading moment of inspiration that was only based on our own personal feelings.

I Feel Led

How many times have we heard a Christian say, "I feel led to do this," however when they do it, they fall flat on their face? We rightly question whether or not this person has truly heard from God. There are many sincere believers who honestly thought they felt God leading them in a certain direction, or to do a particular thing. Later on, however, they discover they were misled. It can happen to anyone. If you take a moment to look back over your on life, most likely you will see that a large amount of the bad decisions that you have made stemmed from the emotions that you were experiencing at a particular time in your life. Decisions made on the basis of temporary feelings can lead to permanent damage. Let's look at an example in the word of God.

In the book of 1 Samuel chapter 8 Israel, in an attempt to be like the surrounding nations, requests that Samuel the prophet anoint a king over them. The request for a king within itself wasn't inherently bad; however it was the intent of the people's heart. Israel was looking to have a king over them that they could touch and feel, thus rejecting the covenant relationship with God who was the "King of Kings." How many times have life's issues cost you to replace the true God with another god trying to fill a void that you were then experiencing in your life? Some people try to fill this void with sex; still others try with material processions. Some people use drugs as a coping mechanism to help deal with the issues that they are facing in their lives. Still, others try to find other people to put their trust in rather than God.

Usually whatever makes you feel good for a moment, whatever offers you temporary relief from your pain, whatever promises a better tomorrow than your today is what you tend to "feel led" to pursue. This was the case with Israel. To have a king rule over them just felt right at the time. To have a king gave them a sense of security that the Judges, who they had previously had over them, didn't seem to compare to. In fact, the eagerness to have a king provided such an emotional uplift, that their judgment became skewed by their desires, rather than what they truly needed. Israel continued in their persistent nagging so much until God conceded and commanded Samuel to anoint a king over them.

Be Careful What You Ask For

When we are led by feelings many times we will covet certain things so much that as a result God will allow us to receive exactly what we were asking for. He does this to show us that we already had everything we needed in Him. There is an old saying that says, "You never miss your water, until your well runs dry." Many times we take for granted the grace and mercy that God has afforded to us. We fell to comprehend that it was God who enabled us the fortitude to do what we are doing, be where we are at right now in life, and it's still God directing where we are going. He had brought Israel out of Egypt, given them rest from their enemies, been their victory banner in battle, and ultimately taken them to their "Canaan Land." However now that they had reached a place of prominence, they felt as though they could make decisions on their on without the one who got them where they were in the first place.

Generation: Me

Sadly, this is also true for many of us today. Once we feel like we have made it we take on a sense of entitlement. Most people now judge what's right and wrong by what they feel is right and wrong to them, rather than what the word of God says is right and wrong. The word of God is no longer the measuring rod for life's decision. We now live in the generation of "me." I sincerely believe that this is the reason why we see so many different religions and church denominations in the world because everybody has their own opinions and no one wants to answer to the word anymore. Maybe I should say that no one wants to accept the entire truth of the word anymore. Now everyone wants to take different verses of scriptures that appeal to their situation becoming a religion to themselves.

This is idolatry at its greatest degree. People have even begun to say that there is no absolute truth in the world. They believe that truth is whatever convictions they believe to be true based on the information that they have taken in. Keep in mind however that if you haven't been taking in the right information your convictions will be biased and uncontested. While I am highly aware of this new enlightened age that we now live in, I choose not to indulge in this way of thinking. In fact even if I wanted to believe this to be true, if I'm a cautious reader of the word, I would soon discover that this way of thinking is in total contrast to the word of God.

> To the Jews who had believed him, Jesus said, "If you hold to my teaching, you are really my disciples. Then you will know the truth, and the truth will set you free (John 8:31-32 NIV)."

Continue in the Word

So is their absolute truth in the world? Yes. Where can we find absolute truth? We can find absolute truth in the word of God. Keep in mind, however, that we have to continue in the word. See what happens to many people is they will read a few scriptures and immediately feel as though they have received a special revelation. They then go out and spread this special revelation to others and they in turn spread it to someone else, and gradually a misinterpretation of the word of God begins to be preached and practiced due to a lack of true Biblical studying. This is becoming a domino effect in churches all over the world.

Freedom in the Word of God

Christ doesn't want us bound with these worldly traditions and practices that profit nothing. Christ wants us to be free. Free from what? Christ wants to free us from ourselves. He wants to free us from our own way of thinking. He wants to free us from our own opinions and idolizations. Christ wants us to be free from the bondage of a false belief system which leads to faith in tradition, but separation from God. Christ wants us to be free to step into a life full of abundance. The only thing that can free us is the word of God. Christ uses the word of God to purify our hearts and minds in order for his precepts to shape the way we live. Sanctify them by the truth; your word is truth (John 17:17 NIV). The rewards for walking in the truth of God's word are immeasurable.

In contrast however, as we mentioned earlier the punishment for disobeying God's word can be extremely severe. The apostle Paul lets us know that God's wrath is being revealed towards everyone who knows the truth, and chooses not to walk in it (Romans 1:18). To know the truth of the word of God, but choose not to obey it is the worst decision that anyone could possibly make. This was the snare that entrapped the king who was chosen to lead Israel.

Beware of Pride

The first mistake was made by Israel for feeling like they could replace God with a king. The second mistake was made by the king that was chosen to lead. God informed Samuel to anoint Saul from the tribe of Benjamin as the king. Saul came from very humble beginnings. In fact in 1 Samuel 9:21 Saul even appealed to Samuel concerning his election. 1 Samuel 9:21 reads, "But am I not a Benjamite, from smallest tribe of Israel, and is not my clan the least of all the clans of the tribe of Benjamin (NIV)?" Isn't it funny how God will take the person who is less likely to succeed and cause them to flourish? Some of you out there have been deemed less likely to succeed. Some of you didn't grow up living in lavish homes in great neighborhoods; rather you came from some of the worst neighborhoods and even more modest homes.

Also just like Saul many of you have had to deal with a negative stereotype that you gained due to your family association. But we have to remember that God can qualify even those who society has considered unqualified. The Bible says that he, who humbles himself, shall be exalted. Saul had been exalted to a place of significance that was bigger than his wildest dreams. If you are humble, God can take you to places you never thought you would go. God can cause you to do things that you never thought that you would be able to do. However, you have to make sure you retain the same humble mindset when God begins to elevate you, as you did when you didn't have anything. The same God that elevated you is the same God who is able to bring you back down.

Daniel 5:20 states, concerning King Nebuchadnezzar the King of Babylon, "But when his heart became arrogant and hardened with pride, he was deposed from his royal throne and stripped of his glory (NIV)." King Nebuchadnezzar's position had led to pride overwhelming him. This was also the same problem that Saul had. Saul didn't know how to handle being exalted. Saul's exaltation gave him a "feeling" of absolute power and he felt that he no longer had to answer to anyone. He felt like he could do whatever he felt was the right thing to do, even if it went against what God had already spoken.

You're Not as Smart as You Think

It's a dangerous thing to lean more on your own knowledge than God's. The Bible says that knowledge "puffed up." If you look at the landscape of the world today you will see that the number of people who are attending college is steadily rising. There are so many people now who are searching for knowledge. While I'm definitely an advocate for education, I'm also very aware of the fact that the knowledge of man could never begin to compare with the wisdom of God. When one's knowledge begins to replace the word of God as the final authority, then one's path becomes destructive.

II Timothy 3:7 states that they will be "ever learning, and never able to come to the knowledge of the truth." There are many people now who are gaining a lot of book sense and using it to formulate what they believe to be truth. Many Christians take this same approach to reading the word of God. They casually read the word and then formulate their own ideas based on what it means to them; however they lack true spiritual insight to gain a clear understanding of the word.

Clear understanding of the word of God only comes through careful study, accompanied by prayer. The sad part about it is when this happens people begin to create a religion for themselves, and ultimately begin to be led more by personal motivation, rather than the divine revelation of the word of God. Many times this motivation will prompt people to step into certain callings that God really hadn't appointed them to be in from the first place. This is the very thing that led to Saul's ruin as King of Israel.

Stepping Out of Position

In 1 Samuel chapter 13 the philistines begin to mount an attack against the Israelites. In fact the Philistines mustered together 30 thousand chariots, 6 thousand horsemen, and troops as vast as the sands on the seashore. The odds certainly seemed to be against Israel, and Saul, being king, was feeling the pressure. Saul needed to hear from God, and he needed to hear from Him fast. It was customary in times of distress that the priest would prepare a burnt offering to the Lord in order to inquire from God what the next move should be.

However, Samuel the priest had yet to make it to Gilgal where Saul and the other children of Israel were gathered. Saul became anxious and impatient about what decision to make concerning the battle because the children of Israel were afraid and many begin to leave. Therefore, instead of waiting on Samuel as he had been told to do, he chose to follow his feelings, create his own burnt offering, thus stepping out of his position as king, into the position of priest.

Can you remember how many times your personal feelings have driven you into stepping out of position? Just think back for a minute how many times, out of distress, you stepped over into an area of unfamiliarity to attempt to meet a need. When there is no way that seems right to you, remember, with God there is always a way. God has never met a situation in which He didn't know what to do. Don't ever make a decision out of helplessness. Nine times out of ten these decisions will have devastating results.

What Should My Next Move Be

Have you ever found yourself in a situation in which you didn't know what your next move should be? You needed God's help so in the midst of your despondency you prayed a little prayer that went something like this: "Oh, God, please show me what my next move should be! I don't know what to do and I need your help!" Have you ever prayed something like this? Many times when you pray this prayer, you already have in mind what decision you want to make. However, you are simply praying the prayer out of protocol. You are extremely quiet in the midst of your prayer. Then, out of the blue, a thought flashes to your mind. You truly think that the Spirit of God has just spoken to you. You feel good about the idea you have.

You then get up from your knees. You believe you have your instructions, but do you really? Saul thought that because there was a need for a priest at that moment that God would permit him to step into that position. He felt like he was making the best possible decision based on the circumstances. I'm sure you know people, and maybe even it's you, who have made decisions and then they say, "I feel at peace, this must be God." Are you sure that it is God who is leading you in that decision? Can you recall the circumstances leading up to you making your decision? Were you experiencing a moment of weakness when you made this decision?

Satan does not come to you when you are strong. He knows better. Like a roaring lion, he looks for weak, powerless prey. Satan did not come to Jesus until after He was hungry. At Jesus' weakest moment, Satan appeared. You have to remember that although the Spirit is willing, the flesh is weak and many times your flesh will lure you into making rash decisions that have very bad results. Saul made a temporary decision, which would have permanent results. I've seen more believers get misled during their times of weaknesses than anything else. They become so desperate for an answer; they will believe any impression they feel. Often what you felt God was telling you to do did not turn out as planned and you soon discovered that you missed God.

Don't Miss God

Perhaps it's a situation where you felt like time was passing you by and you would never find a mate. Therefore, you prayed and were sure that God had told you someone was coming to you soon that you were to marry. Sure enough you allow a person to sweep you off your feet. You feel good about marrying him, why? It might be because you feel desperate, and in your desperation you felt peace that someone was coming into your life. The person that has come into your life seems to fit all the qualifications of a mate you had been looking for. Later on you discover that the person you chose wasn't the person that you thought they were.

Maybe you are working a job that you really hate. You become discouraged about your job and you decide to seek God about your next move. In your distress you pray to God and you feel as though God is telling you to quit your job. Just to be clear if God has commissioned you to quit your job, then by all means do it. However, don't quit your job based on a feeling and then afterwards you end up sitting in the dark, eating peanut butter sandwiches every night because you moved out of season.

Maybe it's a situation where you are in a church and you are having problems in that church. In your distress you pray, however you pray to God with the wrong motives. All of sudden the thought crosses your mind to enter the ministry and start your own church. You are convinced that God is telling you to do this. Years later you see that there is a lack of growth in your ministry. Can you truly say that you heard from God earlier? Could it be that you felt God speaking because you were unhappy in your current church, so you decided to step into a position that you hadn't been called to, or maybe you moved out of season?

Can you see how the mistakes we make often stems from our frustrations? You have to understand that when you choose to step into the wrong position that not only are you hurting yourself, but you are hurting others. The reason being is because now you're operating in a position where you are not effective. Now all those who truly need deliverance in that particular position that you are preoccupying can't get it because the wrong person has assumed the position.

Make Your Election Sure

It's so important that we make our calling and election sure. If God is not calling you to be a pastor then don't step into that position. If God is not calling you to be a teacher, then please do everyone a favor and stay out of that position. Don't turn a temporary need into a permanent vacancy because you have stepped into the wrong position. Since you are out of position you are preventing the person who really needs to be there the opportunity to assume their rightful position. Because of Saul's hasty decision making, God rejected him from being King.

Saul regretted his decision after he understood the consequences of his choices, however it was too late. Saul stepped out of his destiny all because he let his feelings lead him, rather than God. Don't seek God's direction while in a state of unconsciousness. Get encouraged about where you are now, before you move into a new position. Seek the Lord through prayer and the Scriptures. If not, you may find yourself just like Saul, who because of his emotions forfeited the purpose that God had for his life.

People Led

The other type of leadership which is becoming more and more demoralizing in the world, as well as the church community, is the dependency on people. The world is constantly searching for that next great leader who can take us to our "manifest destiny." Every election we look to man to attempt to improve our world. We look for someone who can dig us out of the holes that we have gotten in with the previous leaders. We are always searching, however never finding, that person that can make everything all better.

Unfortunately no matter how much we look to man, no matter who that man is, no mortal man is able to make all your problems miraculously go away. Nevertheless we are constantly looking for a new "man" to pledge allegiance to. The world tends to look to the government for guidance. In the church world, many people would rather lean on what the preacher says, rather than seeking what God has to say. There are countless people who can quote to you all of the "rules" of the church as declared by the leader of that church; however they have trouble quoting even two of the Ten Commandments confirmed by God. With so much loyalty to man, it's not hard to see why so many people are being manipulated into regarding false doctrines.

Beware of False Prophets

Jesus was aware that in the last days many false prophets would arise. He gave us fair warning that this issue would arise. Matthew 24:11 states, "and many false prophets will appear and deceive many people (NIV)." If we take a look throughout history we can see the devastation that has been brought about due to this type of disparaging leadership. Perhaps the most famous in the secular world was Adolf Hitler.

Hitler is regarded as one of the greatest orator's ever. With such a strong persuasive voice, and a ruthless leadership approach, Hitler was able to direct one of the greatest mass slaughters of all time, the Holocaust. Hitler and his German counterparts were responsible for the death of over six million Jews. What's so amazing is the fact that one man was able to lead an entire nation to commit such a horrible offense against another nation. One man had such influence that people gravitated to him and were willing to do whatever he said was right.

Cult leader Jim Jones is also an example of this type of deceptive, persuasive leader. Jones was the founder of the Peoples Temple. Jones attempted and succeeded in forming a "safe haven" called Jonestown where all different nationalities could live in harmony with one another. However, over the course of time Jones treatment of his people became cruel and inhuman. In spite of his erratic behavior, because Jones was so influential with words, and even more brutal in discipline, he was able to manipulate the trust of hundreds of people. This all came to a halt on one dreadful day in November of 1978, when Jones convinced his devoted followers to commit a mass suicide by drinking cyanide. Over 900 people died that day, including 276 children making this the greatest single loss of American civilian life in a non-natural disaster until the events of September 11, 2001.

The Seed of Compromise

Do you see what can ensue if we listen to the wrong counsel? While the previous circumstances may be a little on the extreme side, there are still many people who are being led to believe incorrect doctrine even in many of today's churches. The Bible says that a little leaven, leavens the whole lump. All it takes is one hint of inaccurate doctrine to lead one into compromising the entire truth of the word of God. Compromising the word of God leads to disobedience and disobedience of any type is sin. The immorality that we are seeing in our world today can all be traced back to a seed of compromise. This seed has been watered, and has now begun to flourish in the hearts and minds of many people.

The Bible says that faith comes by hearing, and hearing by the word of God. On the contrary, if the preachers, who are supposed to be rightfully dividing the word of God, are continuing to compromise the integrity of the word, then this destructive seed of compromise will continue to grow. Right and wrong is now being determined by what's considered socially acceptable at the current time, rather than relying on the truth of the word of God. Homosexually has now been accepted in many churches and those who are living that lifestyle now believe it to be acceptable. Although we as Christians have to love everyone no matter what type of lifestyle they may be living, we still cannot condone any patterns of living that conflict with the written word of God.

There are many leaders who not only condone homosexual lifestyles, but actually practice these lifestyles either openly or behind closed doors. Some leaders are now teaching that they are the Messiah and we should follow them. Still there are other leaders, in the world and in the church, who are leading for monetary gain or for self entitlement. It's important that we test the spirits by the spirits. We have to reinstitute the standard of the word of God, rather than the opinions of man. Like David, we have to hide the word of God in our hearts so that we want be lured away by the deception of man's lips. Hosea says it best in Hosea 4:6 when he says, "My people are destroyed for lack of knowledge (NIV)." If we don't have the word of God in our hearts, then deception is inevitable.

Look to God, Not Man

We have to know who God is, and what his word says; therefore we will be more inept at identifying the "wolves" in sheep's clothing. Whether it's a friend, relative, pastor, or even a governmental official we cannot focus so much on man that we allow ourselves to be derailed from the track that God has destined us to be on. Remember that Satan will put anything in your pathway to make you shift your gaze from God. No matter where you go or what you do distractions will be a familiar element in your life. Distractions, if gazed on long enough, will cause us to lose our direction, even if that distraction is a person. Therefore, rather than looking to man, we have to keep our eyes on God. After all, it's better to obey God rather than man (Acts 5:29).

Led by Ambition

Perhaps the most destructive type of leadership is leadership fueled by selfish ambition. When a person is led by selfish ambition it usually means that they have a passionate desire for the "Big 3": money, power, and respect. A person with these desires will do anything to obtain them because they believe that they give their life meaning. In fact, if you take a look around, and I'm sure you wouldn't have to look very far, you will see that the desire for the "Big 3" is the gas that fuels the modern day world. Politicians lie to get them. Kings have killed to keep them. Even modern day preachers have used the power of persuasion to manipulate them. Philippians 1:17 supports the latter when it states, "The former preach Christ out of selfish ambition, not sincerely (NIV)…" This type of preacher is not looking to be a help unto others, but is simply focused on using their ministry as a means for financial gain and to bolster great power and influence.

Sadly, this often leads to a powerless, fruitless ministry that all but guarantees spiritual death to all those who are a part of that ministry. There are many ministries in the modern day church that are being led by this type of leader. A person, who walks in this type of selfishness, is a person who will not be able to walk into true Biblical ministry. True Biblical ministry is one that is birthed through servanthood. It's not rooted in selfishness, but rather selflessness. Philippians 2:13 states, "Do nothing out of selfish ambition or vain conceit, but in humility consider others better than yourselves (NIV)." Nothing that we do should ever be done just to benefit us. If so then we are probably being motivated by ambition rather than the Spirit of God.

Where is Your Treasure?

A person who possesses all three of the "Big 3" is typically considered highly successful; at least that's what society attempts to make us believe. In the hour that we live in, people are usually categorized by how much they have acquired or their rank, or by how much they will be able to acquire in the future. I believe that the desire for power and rank has been the perpetrator which has led to the demoralization of the fellowship between God and man. Let's look at Adam and Eve for example.

God had created them in His image and likeness. Since they were created in the image of God, they were already worthy of honor and respect. In other words they were permitted by God to represent His kingship over the rest of creation; therefore everything in the earth had to be in subjection to them. However, with great authority comes great responsibility. While everything in earth was theirs to subdue, God did give them one rule; but this one rule would be a test of the very character of Adam and Eve and disobedience to this rule would change the course of human history. God had instructed them that they could eat from every tree in the garden, but the day that they ate of the tree of the knowledge of good and evil, they would surely die.

Now one may say that the easiest thing to do was to just avoid the tree altogether. However, the tree would be forever before them because it was in the middle of the garden right beside the Tree of Life. So why would God make something that was so dangerous, so easily accessible? Simply put, to see where their hearts were. God was not being cruel or insensitive. God was not setting them up for moral failure. Sometimes God will leave obstacles in your life to see whether He's first in your life. It's not a divine test of will, but a test of loyalty. We see the perfect illustration of this in relation to the children of Israel.

In the book of Judges Chapter 2 God declared that he wouldn't drive out all of the nations from the land of Canaan, rather he would use them to test Israel and see whether they would keep His ways. God knew that if He found where their heart was, then he would ultimately know where their treasure was located (Matthew 6:21). Such was the case with Adam and Eve in Genesis Chapter 3. No doubt the snake was crafty in his presentation, and his exploitation of the word of God; however Adam and Eve's biggest problem was a hunger for supremacy, not a hunger for the "forbidden fruit."

Satan had assured Eve that if she ate of the fruit then she would be just like God knowing good and evil. The allure to satisfy a desire for power ultimately led both Adam and Eve to step out of a covenant relationship with God, and step into a place of shame and degradation. This has been a reoccurring theme which has been seen throughout the entire Bible from King Nebuchadnezzar who because of his desire for power and unrelenting pride was forced to eat grass from the field like a wild animal, to Judas Iscariot who being motivated by money, delivered our Lord and Savior Jesus Christ over to Roman Soldiers to be killed, only to commit suicide himself because of guilt. If we look at all of these stories from Adam and Eve, to Judas Iscariot we will see three aspects of temptation at work: the lust of the flesh, the lust of the eyes, and the pride of life.

The "Big 3"

1 John 2:16 states, "For all that is in the world, the lust of the flesh, and the lust of the eyes, and the pride of life, is not of the Father, but is of the world (KJV)." Understand that the world that is spoken of in this context is not the created world, but the world of sin in which Satan controls. Every sin in this world can be correlated to one of these "Big 3".

The lust of the flesh is basically anything that pleasures any of our outward senses whether it's taste, smell, or touch. The lust of the eyes pleasures our imaginations. When Eve saw how good the fruit was to look at, I'm sure her imaginations begin to run wild about how good it would taste. The eyes are the gateway in which the outward things of this world begin to capture our attention and cause us to gravitate towards what we deem attractive. The pride of life is the vehicle that drives us to answering the call of the lust of the flesh and the lust of the eyes in order to fulfill their desires. Pride makes a person overconfident giving them the assumption that they are right when they are really wrong. If pride goes unhandled it will give a person a false sense of security and invincibility that will lead them to making hasty decisions. Hasty decision making ultimately leads to one's downfall.

The Bible says that pride proceeds destruction (proverbs 16:18). Pride will eventually cause a person to be drawn away from God and cause them to be led by their own desires, which leads to sin, thus breaking fellowship with God (James 1:14). Can you think of some things in your life that may be causing you to break fellowship with God? Can you think of some desires that may be more self motivated rather than God motivated? If you were to be truthful, can you say that the career that you are currently in is what God wants you to do? Or does the attraction of money, power, and respect cause you to remain in your comfort zone?

Before You Do, Acknowledge God

It's important that we acknowledge God in every decision we make, BEFORE we make them. Acknowledging God is more than just telling God what we want to do, or what we want him to do for us. When you acknowledge God that means that you recognize his authority over your life and you trust whatever decision He chooses. Trusting God does not mean that you always understand what He has requested you to do; on the contrary, trusting God means radically realigning your purposes and desires toward His purposes and desires for us, even if it goes beyond our human comprehension.

God promised us in Psalms 37:23 (KJV) that if He delights in our ways then he would also establish our path. In verse 24 he lets the believer know that though we may stumble, He will never let us fall because He will uphold us with His hand. Isn't it reassuring to know that if your way is acceptable to God, He will keep you from falling? To have such a strong promise, one would have to wonder what causes people to take a different route. Is it that they don't believe the promises of God? Is it because their issues are so severe, they forget the promises of God? Or perhaps, is it the fact that the devil has diminished the promises of God by offering his own promises? In most cases the ladder tends to be the biggest problem.

Beware of Satan's False Promises

Just as God has promises for his people, the devil often attempts to counter God's promises with some promises of his own. He tried this tactic on Jesus after he had ended his forty day fast. He promised Jesus great authority and power if he would bow down and worship him. Doesn't that sound like the world we live in? It most certainly does. We have to remember that Satan is still the prince of this world. The same tactics that he used then are still being used today to cause people to seek created things, rather than the creator. Satan loves to attack us when we are at our weakest point, just like he did Jesus. He also loves to prey on our lust to tempt us into gratifying the flesh with worldly success, rather than spiritual success.

With today's resources and technology, promoting this message of worldly success has become more capable than ever before. Every time you turn on the television you see advertisements of big homes, new cars, designer clothes, and expensive jewelry. All of these things have polluted the minds of our culture and have contributed to the influx of people who are all in pursuit of the "American Dream."

Amazingly most of us fail to even realize how Satan is manipulating the media to appeal to our "lust" for more. Our youth now believe that in order to live the good life as portrayed in our media that they have to be movie stars, athletes, or entertainers. Because our culture has become so blinded by desire and greed, Satan has succeeded in diluting what the word "success" really means. To most people success is measured by how much they possess. This mindset has led to competition in the workforce, in the family, and even in the church.

To meet or exceed the success of the next man, more and more compromises are being made each and everyday. Even though God commanded us to be fruitful and multiply, married couples are choosing not to have children now because they want to focus more on their careers. While I'm not saying that pursuing a career isn't a good thing, you can't put the family on the back burner. If you do how else will the legacy of faith continue to the next generation when you're gone, if you have no family to spread the word too?

Also, even though God said that we should worship Him and Him only people have become so busy with their jobs, that they rarely ever have quiet time to spend with God in prayer and mediation. The stress to be able to acquire more and keep up with the Jones's has caused many people to volunteer church time, for work time. Thus they worship their jobs more than God. Even in the church world, Pastor's are now pre-occupying themselves with so many other obligations, that their true job of shepherding the flock of God and helping to equip the church to go out and win souls is going unfulfilled. This mindset is also beginning to affect the messages that are being conveyed.

Putting God in His Rightful Place

The church has replaced the doctrine of Christ which saves, with a prosperity doctrine which sounds and feels good, however isn't supported scripturally. We, the church, have become so ambitious about growing the building fund, that the people's spiritual development has become a thing of the past. While I'm not promoting a belief system that a Christian has to be financially challenged, I do believe that we have taken on the same mindset as the world and are now seeking riches and power prior to seeking God. God is a jealous God. He has to be first in our lives in everything we do and in every decision we make.

It's time for the people of God to check their motives. Nothing that we do should ever be motivated by what we can gain; rather it should be done to glorify God. It's time to put God back in His rightful place which is first in our lives. In Matthew 6:33 Jesus let's us know that instead of stressing about the material things in life, we should rather seek first the kingdom of God and His righteousness, and everything else would be added to us. How many people do you see that are concerned about seeking the righteousness of God? Also, how many do you see truly seeking the kingdom of God? Consider this a warning that it's time for the church to turn their hearts back to God. Let's look at a passage of scripture from the apostle Peter which discusses this in greater detail.

> Therefore, prepare your minds for action; be self-controlled; set your hope fully on the grace to be given you when Jesus Christ is revealed. As obedient children, do not conform to the evil desires you had when you lived in ignorance. But just as he who called you is holy, so be holy in all you do; for it is written: "Be holy, because I am holy." Since you call on a Father who judges each man's work impartially, live your lives as strangers here in reverent fear. For you know that it was not with perishable things such as silver or gold that you were redeemed from the empty way of

life handed down to you from your forefathers, but with the precious blood of Christ, a lamb without blemish or defect (1 Peter 1:13-19 NIV)."

Developing a Kingdom Mind

Christ is looking for those who have prepared their minds for spiritual warfare. He is looking for those whose concerns are not of this world in which we are only guest, but for those who have a kingdom mind. When you have a kingdom mind everything you do will be done with the kingdom in mind. You are not concerned about your status as it relates to the world's standards. On the contrary you are concerned with being holy just as your Father is holy in order to secure your permanent residence in Heaven. Your status in this world should never cause you to confirm back into the way the world views success which was the same way you viewed it when you didn't know any better. However, now that you are in Christ you understand that all of these material things are passing away.

Your home no matter how much you love it is not going with you into eternity. Your job, no matter how many figures you make will not have any bearing on your final resting place. Your main objective should be to live a life that glorifies God. You know you have achieved true success when worldly achievements no longer matters to you. When God sees that your mind is set on the kingdom then many times he will open up the doors for you to enjoy many of the material things in life because he knows that's not what you put your trust in. When you humble yourself before God and live a life that pleases God that's the greatest success in the world. Everything else that you achieve is just a bonus. That's the real key to success!!!

The Secret to Success

Many books attempt to reveal the secrets to success. However, true success is measure by neither your bank account balance nor the cost of your car. It isn't based on how many people respect you, nor is it determined by how much authority you have. True success isn't measured by the size of your wardrobe or your residence. The only way to measure true success is to know for certain that what you are doing pleases God. That's why we can't be led by selfish ambition because selfish ambition only hungers for what feels good to our flesh. God's purpose for your life is never a byproduct of selfishness. We have to learn how to consider others needs above our on. It would feel good to be a millionaire, but unfortunately that's not God's will for everyone. It would feel good to pastor a church with 40,000 people; however that's not God's will for every pastor. It would feel good to be respected by everyone however that's just not going to happen. You have to know that it's not about you, it's about Christ.

As we see in the case of Adam and Eve we are all selfish by nature. That's why the psalmist wrote, "Turn my heart toward your statutes and not toward selfish gain (Psalms 119:36 NIV)." This confirms that walking in selflessness is not something that we can do on our on. We should always ask God to keep our hearts entrenched in his word and to keep us from striving for what the world considers success. We can't base our level of success in comparison with where other people, who are in our same position, are. Stop letting your desire to keep up with the status quo drive you, or you may miss out on God's perfect will for YOUR life. What God has for you is for you, and no one can take it away. Don't compromise purpose, for pleasure. After all, there is no profit in gaining the whole world and then forfeiting your soul (Matthew 16:26).

CHAPTER 4

How Does the Spirit Lead?

We've learned the prerequisites for living a Spirit led life. We've learned what it means to be Spirit led. We've also learned about some of the other destructive forms of leaderships that are widespread in our society. Now we are going to discuss how the Spirit leads. It is one thing to say that the Spirit leads us. It is another thing to know how the Spirit leads us. The following verse tells us how: For ye have not received the spirit of bondage again to fear; but ye have received the spirit of adoption, whereby we cry, Abba, Father (Romans 8:15-16 KJV). This passage here speaks of the Christian's relationship with God. The word adoption signifies a legal action by which a person is brought into a family in which he has no blood relations. While this person may not have the exact physical presence as the other members of the family, they still are given all the privileges that the other members of the family hold.

Adopted Into the Family

As a Christian you have to know that no matter what you use to look like, no matter what your previous lifestyle was, when the Spirit enters your life he radically changes your persona for the good. You have to know for a surety that you have been adopted into Christ's family. The devil wants to make you think that you are still an outsider. He wants to make you feel like you don't belong. He will do everything in his power to keep you from realizing that you have now been endowed with Kingdom privileges that neither he nor his imps can ever take away. God first extended this adoption plan to the Israelites. However, now He has extended it to everyone who would accept Christ as their Lord and savior. So how do we know that we have been accepted into the family?

2 Corinthians 6:17-18 answers that question when it says, "Come out from among them, and be ye separate, saith the Lord, and touch not the unclean thing; and I will receive you, and will be a Father unto you, and ye shall be my sons and daughters, saith the Lord Almighty (KJV)." With that being said, the only way to be sure of your adoption is to separate yourself from sin and draw near to God. As we stated earlier, this is called the process of sanctification. Once you begin to follow God with your whole being, thus walking in the Spirit, then the Holy Spirit Himself will testify that you are a child of God. What great assurance? Not only to know God but to be known by God. Not only to have a familiarity with God but to have an expressed relationship with Him. To be able to call yourself a child of God is the greatest honor in the world and along with the classification comes some exceptional benefits.

Daddy's Got My Back

Growing up I was always a very small boy. Because I was so small in stature some of the other kids would pick on me. They wouldn't let me play with the good toys such as the Power Rangers and the Ninja Turtles. Instead I would be stuck with the GI Joe figurine that only had one arm and one leg. My dad however, while not a very big man, had a rather intimidating presence. If I said that I was going to tell my daddy on them they would quickly back away from me and let me play in peace. In fact sometimes it would even make them offer me toys that I hadn't even asked to play with. It wasn't that they were afraid of me. It was because they feared the person that I was related to.

Many of us let the enemy constantly pick on us and keep us from having the things that God has promised us. We allow him to make us give up on our dreams. We allow him to cause us to withdraw from places that God had promised us we could go in life. Worst yet we allow him to make us forfeit our destiny because we become intimidated by his threats. We have forgotten who we are related to. Although some of us may have forgotten about how powerful our Father is, the devil is still highly aware. James 2:19 lets us know that the devils believe in God and tremble. Mark 3:11 says that unclean spirits, when they saw Jesus, fell down before him and cried out that He was the son of God. The enemy recognizes the authority that Christ possesses. They recognize his deity. With that being said, why do we as Christians still struggle understanding just how powerful He is?

Do you know how powerful God is? Let me ask that in a different way. Do you understand how powerful you are? Yes I said you. You have to understand that when you have the Spirit of God on the inside of you, you take on certain attributes of God that certainly can't be denied. While the enemy is in no ways afraid of you, he is terrified of the power that lives on the inside of you. That's why the longer he can keep it suppressed, the better. He knows that because of your connection to God you have the power to drive him far away from you. He understands that since you are a child of the most high that you have the power to speak those things that are not as though they already were. Even the things that he has taken from you He knows that if you really tapped into your power source that you have the power to take your stuff back plus some more.

Just like I did to the kids who were picking on me, you can do in your spiritual life to the devil. Let him know that if He doesn't leave you alone you are going to tell your "Spiritual Daddy." There is a trick to this though. See the reason why I even thought to say I was going to tell my daddy is because I understood just how much authority he had. Because he had so much authority I took great pride in following him around no matter where he went since I knew that wherever he would lead me, He was tough enough to protect me. I was in total agreement with whatever choice he chose to make. Before you can truly be confident to call on the Spirit of God, your Spirit man has to be in agreement with God's Spirit. This is how the Spirit of God begins to lead us. He uses our own spirit to lead and guide us. Proverbs 20:27 confirms this:

> The lamp of the LORD searches the spirit of a man; it searches out his inmost being (NIV).

1 Corinthians 2:11 goes on to say:

> For who among men knows the thoughts of a man except
> the man's spirit within him? In the same way no one knows
> the thoughts of God except the Spirit of God (NIV).

God Sees All

In the Bible days a lamp was the tool used to guide someone along a dark path. In modern day uses a lamp is used to brighten up a darkened room. Therefore anything that was previously hidden from sight will now be made visible. This is what Proverbs 20:27 is saying. It's saying that God is using our spirits to guide us in our lives and to see everything that we are attempting to hide in our hearts. A lot of us are trying to figure out why God hasn't opened up certain doors for us.

We are trying to figure out why God hasn't given us some of the things that we have been asking for. The reason is because God still sees those secret things that nobody else knows about that you have yet to let go of. God sees the lust that you are trying to hide. God sees the hatred that you have for your neighbor. He sees the resentment you have towards your friend. He even sees the secret plans and devices that you are planning.

Can God Tell You a Secret?

God is saying before I can truly reveal to you my secrets, you have to clean up your heart. Before I can begin to lead you, your spirit man has to get in tune with my Spirit. There are a lot of people saying they want to be led by God but they have yet to prepare their hearts to make room for the Spirit of God to take permanent residence. Many are in search of the secret things of God but their motives for wanting them are not right. This begs the question; can God trust you with His secrets?

This is what 1 Corinthians 2:11 is saying. This scripture makes it plain that the spirit of the man knows everything about that man. Although you may choose to conceal your true self from others, your inner man knows all about you. While I do believe that we all struggle with something we have to be transparent before God about everything. The following verses let us know that nothing we do is hidden from God.

> Hell and destruction are before the LORD: how much more then the hearts of the children of men? Proverbs 15:11 (KJV)

> Shall not God search this out? For he knoweth the secrets of the heart. Psalms 44:21(KJV)

Your True Character

It is quite clear that it is impossible to screen our hearts from God. Why then do we still attempt to deceive God with so much hypocrisy? We live holy before people, but we live unholy when nobody is around. Don't you know that a true character of a man is determined by what they do when nobody else is around? David understood this principle very well as we can see from the following verses.

> O Lord, you have searched me and you know me. You know when I sit and when I rise; you perceive my thoughts from afar. You discern my going out and my lying down; you are familiar with all my ways. Before a word is on my tongue you know it completely, O LORD. You hem me in—behind and before; you have laid your hand upon me. Such knowledge is too wonderful for me, too lofty for me to attain. Where can I go from your Spirit? Where can I flee from your presence? Psalms 139:1-7 (NKJV)

David knew that God knew everything about him. God knew when he was going to get up and when he was going to lay down. He knew what path He was going to take before he took it. He even knew what David was going to say before he said it. David asked the question, "Where can I go from your Spirit?" This is a powerful question that we should constantly keep before us. Lord where can I go from your Spirit? The answer without a doubt is a echoing nowhere. We can't hide from the Spirit of God. What we can do however is get rid of the wrong spirits and receive the Spirit of God.

Developing the Right Spirit

The Bible says that his Spirit will not dwell in an unclean temple. Most of us attempt to clean up our outside appearance. We put on the nice suits and dresses in order to appear changed but deep down we still have the same filthy spirits that were in us before we accepted Christ. We still back bite. We still lie. We are still selfish. It's time for us to ask the Lord to renew the right Spirit within us. Once you do this then God can begin to lead your spirit. Once you become totally transparent to God and receive his Spirit, then God can trust you in order to reveal His secrets to you. 1 Corinthians 2:12-14 states, "We have not received the spirit of the world but the Spirit who is from God, that we may understand what God has freely given us. This is what we speak, not in words taught us by human wisdom but in words taught by the Spirit, expressing spiritual truths in spiritual words (NIV)."

God wants to reveal to you everything that he desires to give you. If you take a closer look at the scripture you will notice that the word "given" is in the past tense. This let's us know that there are some things that God declared was already yours even before the beginning of this world. Isn't it amazing to know that you were on the mind of God even before you were created? Some of you have grown up believing that you were just an after thought. Some of you have been told that you were a mistake. This scripture lets you know that God had plans for your life even before you were conceived. Notice, however, that before you can know these things you have to learn the right language.

The Spirit's Language

The scripture says, "These things we also speak, not in words which man's wisdom teaches but which the Holy Spirit teaches." The Spirit's language can't be taught to you by Rosetta Stone. You can't learn this language from a class in school. No matter how much you study you can't expect to learn this language with your own wisdom. The only one who can teach you this language is the Holy Spirit. The Bible says that our natural man cannot receive the things of the Spirit neither can he know them because they are spiritually discerned (1 Corinthians 2:16 NIV). The scripture goes on to say that these things are foolishness to the natural man.

Some of you right now have been looking at your situation through your natural eyes saying that it's no way God can get any good out of this situation. You have found yourselves constantly complaining about your current situations and have even thought about giving up on your promise due to your circumstances. Some of you are so concerned about what you use to be that you feel as though it would be foolishness to think that you could ever be used by God. This negative mindset will cause one to doubt the power of God. While they may have a form of Godliness, deep down they will deny the legitimacy of the power of God. That's why you have to be careful when you reveal secrets that God has shown you to others because everyone won't connect with nor understand your "language."

Never Doubt God's Promises

When a person doesn't understand the revelation that God has shown you, they will just consider it foolishness and will even try to convince you of the same. If you are not careful you may even begin to believe them. This is especially true when your current situation doesn't match the revelation that God has shown you. You may then find yourselves doubting God yourself. Have you found yourselves thinking this way before? Believe it or not we all have. Some of the greatest men and women of God have found themselves in a state of self-loathing and helplessness due to their circumstances. After Elijah had called down fire from Heaven to consume the sacrifice on Mt. Carmel, he then requested God to kill him so he wouldn't have to deal with Queen Jezebel who was determined to kill him.

Job after losing everything that he owned and physically suffering for so long had a moment of despair where he cursed the day he was born.

Jesus himself cried out to God and said can this cup pass from me sensing the agony that he would have to endure on Calvary's cross. While all of these men faced a discouraging moment in their life, their was something on the inside of them that just wouldn't let them quit. Aren't you glad that God didn't let you quit? When you thought that it was over for you the Spirit of God stirred up some hope on the inside of you to assure that it wasn't over until He said it was over. Although Jesus sensed the persecution that he would have to endure in the physical would be severe, he quickly shifted back to the Spirit man and he courageously proclaimed "Not my will Lord, but let yours be done."

Something happens when we shift from the carnal way of thinking to the Spiritual. I can imagine it being similar to Popeye the sailor man after he has been beaten up and beaten down, and it appears that he is on the brink of certain defeat. He senses that it might be over for him. I'm sure that if he were real, he would probably even contemplate quitting. But something supernatural happens when he gets his "spinach." All of a sudden he gains his strength back. In fact he becomes 10 times stronger than he was before.

I'm speaking from a carnal standpoint just for illustration purposes but we can use this analogy to explain what happens when we shift into our spiritual man. Suddenly what we once thought was impossible, now seems like a possibility as the spirit whispers in our ear, "You can do all things through Christ which strengthens you." When you thought your past was going to overcome you and your life was headed to sure defeat, as you shift into the spiritual man, the Spirit whispers into your ear and declares, "You are more than a conqueror through Christ who loves you." What happens after this is nothing short of amazing.

Undergoing Spiritual Renovation

As you begin to speak what the Spirit has been whispering in your ear, your faith begins to increase and it doesn't seem foolish anymore. No matter what your situation may look like, you still have assurance because now you have begun to change your language. This is how the Spirit leads your Spirit. He plants the word of God into your heart, which then begins to renovate what you accept as true, which then changes what you say, and eventually what you do. When your language changes, so does your attitude. When your language changes, so does your outlook on life. You don't find yourself complaining quite as much. You now begin to speak the word of God when it seems as though the odds are against you.

Just like Jesus did in the Garden of Gethsemane, you begin to declare, "Lord not my will, but let yours be done." You have officially been spiritually renovated. You now speak a new language. This new language transcends anything that you could have ever learned on your own. Solomon wrote, "Trust in the LORD with all your heart and lean not on your own understanding" (Proverbs 3:5). Your own understanding comes from your carnal mind, not your heart. He says to trust in the LORD with all your heart. Your heart is your spirit. Your spirit is the safe guide, not your mind. Your mind can get confused. Your spirit rarely can. You have begun to lose your mind and are taking on the mind of Christ.

Lose Your Mind

Following the guidance of the Holy Spirit is similar to a childhood game that we have all played before called follow the leader. In case you have forgotten how to play the game let me give you a quick refresher. In the game follow the leader there is one assigned leader and several followers. The leader has the unique ability to do whatever they choose to do and the followers have to do whatever the leader does, exactly the way he/she does it. Anyone who doesn't do exactly what the leader does is out of the game. Whoever makes it to the end becomes the leader. To effectively play this game it required all of the followers to lose their minds. In other words if you wanted to win you had to forget about what you wanted to do, forget about what you thought was right, and submit to whatever the leader was asking you to do. Not everyone was able to do this. In fact after a while many of the followers would become frustrated with the choices the leader was making and would choose to do something different, ultimately eliminating them from the game.

Follow the Leader

While life is not a game, the concept of "follower the leader" is very similar to following the Holy Spirit. Once we accept Christ into our lives we accept the Spirit of God as the undisputed leader. We can no longer do what we want to do, say what we want to say. Our life is no longer in our hands, however now we are required to be in total submission to the will of God. This is illustrated perfectly in the following verse.

> Even if Balak gave me his palace filled with silver and gold,
> I could not do anything of my own accord, good or bad,
> to go beyond the command of the Lord—and I must say
> only what the Lord says? Numbers 24:13 NIV

In the previous verse Balak, king of Moab hired Balaam, who was a non-Israelite sorcerer, to curse Israel who was king Balak's enemy. Balaam prepared a burnt offering before the Lord in order to see whether or not he could indeed curse Israel, however three times God put a word of blessing in his mouth, rather than cursing. King Balak was furious. However, Balak understood that he couldn't do anything, neither good nor bad, without the approval of God. Although Balaam would later in life be consumed by greed and ultimately come to be considered an evil man. He understood at this point in his life that he couldn't make any choices based on his on mind. The previous illustration was an illustration of someone who was obedient to God's leadership. Let's take a look at someone who chose not to obey what the leader had instructed.

The Consequences of Disobedience

In the book of 1 Kings Chapter 13 we are introduced to an unnamed prophet from the providence of Judah who had been instructed of the Lord to go to Bethel and prophecy against the alter at Bethel, which was used to make sacrifices to false gods. The prophet had been instructed by God not to eat any bread nor drink any water neither could he return back to Judah the way he had come. On his way home an old prophet of Bethel asked him to come to his home to eat and drink. The man initially declined the offer. However, after this the old prophet told the man that an angel from God had instructed him to come back to his home to eat and drink but he was lying. Nevertheless, the prophet conceded and went to the house to eat and drink only to be killed by a lion on his departure because he didn't abide by the initial instructions. That one act of disobedience caused him his life.

As Christians we have to make sure that we abide by the original plan that God instructs for our lives. There are people who would attempt to side track you with false counsel to pull you out of the "game." This is what the devil has been doing from the beginning. He plays tricks with the minds of God's people in order to get them to disobey God's word, and follow their own mind. That is why in order to properly follow the counsel of God you have to completely lose your mind. You have to lose your own way of thinking.

Some people will call you crazy. They will say that you are a holy roller. They will ask you questions such as how can you continue to love your neighbor when they are mistreating you? How can you remain faithful to one man or one woman for the rest of your life when there are so many other fish in the sea? How can you love God with all your heart and your entire mind when you have just been diagnosed with an incurable disease? How can you serve God when He has just taken one of your closet love ones? The reason is because you have lost your mind and you are following the leader.

The Sinful Mind

We must be careful because although we are now being led by the Spirit of God, the sinful mind is always awaiting an opportunity to take back the control. Roman's 8:6-8 (NIV) says, "The mind of sinful man is death, but the mind controlled by the Spirit is life and peace; the sinful mind is hostile to God. It does not submit to God's law, nor can it do so. Those controlled by the sinful nature cannot please God." When you allow your mind to be controlled by the natural mind, sin is inevitable. If sin is inevitable, then spiritual death is also inevitable because the wages of sin is death. The sinful mind will never submit to God's Spirit because quite honestly it lacks the power to do so. The Holy Spirit gives us the power to live a holy life. If we deny the Spirit of God access to our lives then any attempt to live a holy live on our on accord is useless.

When we are controlled by the sinful nature it is impossible to please God. Our carnal mind is not concerned with the cares of God. In fact it hates the concerns of God. In the KJV, Paul states in Romans 8:7 that the carnal mind is "enmity" against God. The word enmity means hatred such as one might feel for an enemy. A mind uncontrolled by the Spirit of God literally views God as the enemy. It hates everything about God. We can see this mindset operating in the minds of many groups of people today. Atheists are a prime example of those who feel this kind of hatred towards God. However, it's not just the atheists who operate in this mindset. Anyone who refuses to submit to God's will whole heartedly is also operating in this mindset.

Those who attempt to justify their wrong doing for truth. Those who live by the creed "it's my life and I will do what I want to do", yet they still say that they love God. Those in the church who continue to make their own choices without seeking God for guidance are all guilty of operating in this sinful mindset. Nothing good can come from this mindset. The only thing that will come from this mindset is death. It leads to death in relationships. It leads to death in your finances. It leads to death in your ministry. It ultimately leads to the death of your destiny. If you want to be led by God, you have to be willing to give God all of you and allow His word to transform your mind. You have to let go of your old mind, that sinful mind that leads to death, and you have to embrace the mind of the Spirit which leads to life and peace.

What Renews the Mind?

Paul lets us know in Ephesians 4:23 that we have to be renewed in the spirit of our minds. Our minds have to be reestablished in and by the word of God. Our way of thinking, our ideas, and our plans have to be replaced with what the Holy Spirit desires, not what seems good to us. This has to be intentional. We have to begin to take in more of the word of God.

A constant intake of the word of God will begin to alleviate the sinful mindset. We will become more acquainted with the mind of the Spirit.

To accomplish this we have to begin to pray more. The Bible says we should pray without ceasing. To pray without ceasing is not just walking around all day talking to God with our lips. There are many people who draw to God with their lips but their heart is far from him. Therefore it's not your lips, but you have to constantly utter prayers and thanksgiving from your heart to God without ceasing. It has to be a continuous formula in order to prevent the enemy from filling your heart with the wrong stuff.

When you are in a constant state of prayer, you leave no room for the devil to override the Spirit mind, with the carnal mind. Keeping your mind on God helps us sustain in life's most difficult times. This is what the prophet Isaiah was referring when he said that God would keep in perfect peace him whose mind is stayed on Him.

The Faithfulness of God

God will give you peace in no matter what you may be going through. No matter how bad the situation may appear, when you have the mind of the Spirit you know that "this too shall pass." I know it's seems crazy. You may be saying that I don't know what you are going through. You may even be saying I haven't walked in your shoes and if I had I wouldn't be so optimistic. However, when you take on the mind of the Spirit, it doesn't matter what you are going through, it's all about where you going.

The mind of the Spirit allows you to shift your attention from your issue, to God. It's not that I'm not cognizant of my issues. It's more of the fact that I trust God no matter what situation I may find myself in. So even when I want to complain, and even may find myself doing so at times. The Spirit is constantly letting me know that God is faithful. Jeremiah wrote the following to describe this:

> Yet this I call to mind and therefore I have hope: Because
> of the LORD's great love we are not consumed, for his

compassions never fail. They are new every morning; great
is your faithfulness. Lamentations 3:21-23 NIV

Jeremiah spoke passionately about how faithful God was. He spoke of
one who had been in desperate times, and had experienced the deliverance
of the Lord. He spoke of someone who had been down and out, yet
God still brought him through. Jeremiah goes on to make one of the
most powerful statements that one could ever make. He states that his
compassion renews every morning. That means that each day you wake
up God is granting you a brand new mercy. Each time you do wrong and
God spares your life, that's a brand new mercy. Each time God blesses you
and you really didn't deserve it, that's a brand new mercy. It's only because
of his mercies that we are not consumed. Often times we take for granted
the mercy that God has afforded to us. We need to learn how to thank
God for his mercy. After all, if it wasn't for his mercy none of us would
have been given an opportunity to experience redemption from Christ's
death on the cross.

A Worthy Witness

Jeremiah understood just how amazing God's mercy was. Jeremiah could
speak with so much fervor because he had dealt with difficult situations in
his life yet he had managed to come out on top all because of God's mercy.
Jeremiah was a prophet who was given a unique job of confronting Judah
and Jerusalem with a message of impending judgment that God would
bring against them. God's personal prediction to Jeremiah, "Attack you
they will, overcome you they can't," was fulfilled many times in the Biblical
narrative as Jeremiah warned of destruction of those who continued to
refuse repentance and its more moderate consequences. In return for his
adherence to God's disciplines and speaking God's words, Jeremiah was
attacked by his own brothers, beaten and put into the stocks by a priest
and false prophet, imprisoned by the king, threatened with death, thrown
into a cistern by Judah's officials, and opposed by a false prophet. Yet God
was faithful to rescue Jeremiah from his enemies.

God's People Always Come Out on Top

When Jeremiah's prophecies regarding the destruction of Judah and Jerusalem were fulfilled by Nebuchadnezzar's army in 586 BC, Nebuchadnezzar ordered that Jeremiah be freed from prison and treated well. You see Christ's people always come out on top even if they start out at the very bottom. Jeremiah's narrative is proof of this truth. It shows that God has genuine compassion for his people. He is a present help in the time of trouble for those who love and trust him.

You can have hope in the midst of difficult situations. If you keep your mind on him rather than your situations God will keep your mind in perfect peace. However you have to adapt the mind of Christ in order to still have faith when all seems lost. You can't develop this mindset by constantly complaining about life's issues. You can't adopt this mindset by lingering in doubt and self pity. The only way to take on the mind of Christ is to experience intimacy with the Spirit.

Intimacy with the Spirit

> Draw nigh to God, and he will draw nigh to you. Cleanse your hands, ye sinners; and purify your hearts, ye double minded. James 4:8 KJV

To truly embrace the guidance of the Holy Spirit, you have to first be intimate with him. Intimacy in this context is more of a close association with, detailed knowledge of, or deep understanding of a subject. You have to know how he works. You have to know what he likes and dislikes. You have to know what his concerns are. This allows you to better understand what He is going to lead you to do. The more you learn about him the more you are able to relate to him. You can please him better because you know what he likes and what he doesn't like. The more you learn about him the deeper your intimacy becomes.

You begin to shift from a familiarity with him, to an affectionate personal relationship with him. You begin to trust his decision making.

You begin to trust that He would never leave you alone. Even when the burdens of life seem hard to bear, you can find comfort in knowing that he's there with you to take you through them all. Isn't it reassuring to know that regardless of the storm clouds that may be brewing in your life, the comforter is standing their to shelter you from the rain? In spite of what's going on around you, the Spirit that's inside of you will give you the strength to carry on. That's what an intimate relationship with the Spirit does for the believer. He gives the believer hope. He gives them a since of security that nothing can shake. It's almost like being a kid all over again.

Shelter from the Storm

Do you remember the intense fear you felt when a bad thunderstorm suddenly emerged? The thunder roars outside so much so that it shakes the very foundation of your home. You peep through your window and you can see the lightning begin to strike. All of a sudden the rain begins to pour. You hastily jump out of bed to turn on the light but when you flip the switch it remains dark. The storm must have knocked out the electricity. You stand there in the dark terrified from the storm that is brewing outside. You contemplate making a run down the hallway to your parent's room but you fear tripping over something in the process because it's so dark. All of a sudden though you see a faint light begin to appear in your hallway. You suddenly hear light footsteps approaching you. With each step the light gets brighter and brighter, the steps louder and louder until all of a sudden you don't hear any more footsteps and your whole room is now illuminated with a white glow.

You cover your eyes to avoid the brightness of the light. As your eyes begin to adjust to the light because you have now been in the dark for a while, you notice that you mother is standing in the room holding a candle. Mama knew you were probably afraid because of the storm so she came to check on you. She quickly puts you back in the bed, but she doesn't leave you alone. She gets in the bed with you. She wraps her arms around you and you quickly cuddle up closer to her. You lay there for a minute still hearing the rumble of the thunder and seeing the ferociousness of the lightning, but you feel secure because mama has already assured you that everything will be just fine. You fall fast asleep resting securely in your mother's warm embrace never feeling safer. Why do you feel so safe? It's because you have been intimate with your mother for a long time now. You have been in situations like this before and she came to your rescue.

This type of relationship doesn't come overnight. See if my mother hadn't of grew up in the house with me and I hadn't spent much time with her, I probably wouldn't feel so secure. However, since I have spent a lot of intimate time with my mother. I know that she would sacrifice herself rather than see something happen to me. This is also the feeling that we gain from having intimacy with the Spirit. In spite of all the wickedness that may be going on around us the Spirit assures us that we are secure as long as we remain in him.

God: The Void Filler

Intimacy with the Spirit of God never comes without an investment of time. You have to be willing to lay aside your agenda and spend time with the Spirit. Most of us spend time trying to be intimate with the wrong things. We try to be intimate with a boyfriend or girlfriend thinking they can successfully feel a void in our life. We attempt to get closer to our job thinking that gaining more money will feel the emptiness that we feel. After we get the boyfriend, after we get the girlfriend, or after we get the promotion on the job, we still notice that the emptiness is still there. We thought we had found what was missing, but evidently not. Most people will in turn search for a different mate or a different job to try to satisfy their deficiency. Most people fail to realize that there is a special place in their hearts that nothing created could ever satisfy. Yet in still we continue to try to satisfy this area with the wrong thing.

We are forever searching for that "right" fixation that will take all of our problems away in hopes that we can live the rest of our life in total bliss. This will never happen until we change our affection. It's not that people are not seeking. It's just that they are not seeking the right things. You can't find everything else first and leave Jesus as the last treasure you find. Jesus has to be the first person that you seek before you seek a soul mate, a career, or any other material procession. These things feel good for a moment, but soon lose their attractiveness leaving you empty again. Jesus is the only one who can feel that void for good. Jesus said that he rewards those who diligently seek him.

If you look for God long enough, you will eventually find him. Finding him provides a satisfaction that lasts even after the climax of our sensual fulfillments. Only intimacy with God can truly fill your deepest levels of inadequacy. Only intimacy with God can give you clearer direction. The closer you get to him the more you learn about his character. The more you know about his character, the easier it is to discern whether or not the choice you are making is something that he has advised you to do, or if you were being motivated by your own desires.

Be Holy

The Holy Spirit is holy. With that being said it's no way that He could ever lead you to do anything unholy. That's why James gave the warning to purify our hands and purify our hearts. If you are feeling led to do anything that is contrary to the word, then the Holy Spirit has nothing to do with that. You have to cleanse your hearts from all of its wicked devices and schemes or else you may continue to be led by your own beliefs, rather than the Holy Spirit.

Remember there is a way that seems right unto man but ultimately it leads to death. If you feel as though the Spirit is leading you to take someone else's husband then you have obviously missed God. If you feel as though you are being led to steal then you have obviously missed God. If you feel as though you are being led to kill someone because they don't believe in your God then you clearly need psychiatric therapy. Oh yeah, and you have definitely missed God. Well how do I know the Spirit is leading me? The answer is rather simple. Everything the Spirit leads you to do will always be in direct correlation with the word of God and the character of God. The Spirit will not directly, nor indirectly lead you to do anything that is contrary to his word. Take a look at the passages of scriptures below:

Your word is a lamp to my feet and a light for my path.
Psalms 119:105 NIV

Direct my footsteps according to your word; let no sin rule
over me. Psalms 119:133 NIV

But the Counselor, the Holy Spirit, whom the Father
will send in my name, will teach you all things and will
remind you of everything I have said to you. John 14:26
NIV

As for you, the anointing you received from him remains
in you, and you do not need anyone to teach you. But
as his anointing teaches you about all things and as that
anointing is real, not counterfeit--just as it has taught you,
remain in him. 1 John 2:27 NIV

Remain in the Spirit

If you study closely you will see a direct connection between the Holy
Spirit and the scriptures. Why? It's because God moved on men's hearts
through the Spirit to write the scriptures. Therefore it's no way the Spirit
could ever lead you in opposition to the word in which he wrote. We are
tempted to go contradictory to the word when we are led by other means.
Notice in 1 John 2:27, John urges believers to remain in him. John is
using the word him to refer to the Spirit of God. So the scripture could
read, remain in the Spirit. If you don't remain in the Spirit then it's no
telling what you will say or do. The enemy loves to pull you "out" of the
Spirit. Keep in mind that the Spirit is still in the inside of you. Many times
however we will allow our Spirit to override the Spirit of God.

When this happens then you will immediately step into the carnal
man, and out of the spirit man. It's important to remain in the Spirit and
never allow anything to pull you back into your old carnal way of living.
By remaining in the Spirit you remain in the word of God. By remaining
in the word of God you remain in the will of God. By staying in the will
of God you remain in a place of security because you are pleasing God

with your submission to his word. Who doesn't want to please God? Most believers would say that they want to please God. A problem arises however when we move out of the Spirit and step into self. John knew this could be a problem and that's why he warned us to remain in the Spirit.

Many times with so many other voices speaking, the voice of the Spirit gets lost in the shuffle. That's why it's important that you don't allow anything to interfere with your intimate time with God. You can't let anything break your connection. All the enemy needs is a small break in connection in order to allow the wrong voice to enter your "frequency." Staying close to God helps you consistently recognize the voice of God. However, when you neglect your intimate time with God many times you will begin to be led by counterfeit voices.

Recognizing His Voice

Picture this. You are driving down the road listening to your favorite radio station. You can hear the station clearly while you are driving in your stations broadcasting area. However, as you go further and further away from the broadcasting area your signal begins to distort. You can still hear the station pretty well; however you can hear other stations starting to emerge on the same frequency. The further you move away, the more and more distortion you begin to hear. Before long you find yourself having to adjust your radio in order to hear your favorite station. By now, though, it sounds like three or four stations emerging into one, and you can't even tell which one is your favorite station anymore.

After struggling to find a clear station on the radio, you press scan on your radio in order to find any station available. This illustration is identical to what happens in our spiritual life. The more time we spend with God, the deeper our relationship becomes. The more we pray, the more we read our Bible, the more we praise God, the more we are able to recognize his voice. However, when you allow yourself to be drawn away from God and your channel begins to distort, then distinguishing his voice becomes extremely difficult. John 10:27 (NIV) states, "My sheep listen to my voice; I know them, and they follow me." This brings us back to the word intimacy. When you are intimate with God he identifies you as his sheep. It's almost like the two of you have become one.

Are You in to God?

I heard a preacher say that the word intimate could be interpreted as in-to-me. When you are into something, or somebody, that tends to be what you gravitate towards. You can be intimate with a lot of things but for illustration purposes I'm going to focus on a relationship between newlyweds in comparison to a new believer's relationship with Christ. I'm sure that anyone who is married, or who has ever been in a very serious relationship can agree that when you first unite with that person you attempt to stick as close to them as possible because you don't want to miss a single moment to be in there presence. You listen attentively to everything that comes out of their mouths even if what they are saying really doesn't interest you. When you are apart for even a short period of time it feels like forever and you usually can't wait until you can be in each other's presence again. You make it your personal business, even going out of your way at times to make them happy even if it requires you to sacrifice of yourself. When you have this type of affection for your partner intimacy isn't hard.

This type of intimacy though doesn't develop without effort. There are many scriptures that come to mind to describe this type of intimacy between a man and a woman. I'm going to focus on two in particular.

> A lovely deer, a graceful doe. Let her breasts fill you at all times with delight; be intoxicated always in her love. Proverbs 5:19 NIV

> Do not deprive one another, except perhaps by agreement for a limited time, that you may devote yourselves to prayer; but then come together again, so that Satan may not tempt you because of your lack of self-control. 1 Corinthians 7:5 ESV

While I'm aware that the contexts of both of these scriptures are sexual in nature, there is one key precept that can't be missed about intimacy. Speaking to the male companion, Solomon writes in Proverbs 5:19 let her breasts fill you at all times with delight; be intoxicated always with her love. Paul speaking to both companions warns not to deprive one another except perhaps by agreement for a "limited time." Both of these scriptures signify that intimacy should be continuous.

Continuous Intimacy

You can't be intimate with your spouse on Monday and then take a break on Tuesday. You can't appreciate your spouse today, and disregard them tomorrow. Don't you know that Satan will do anything he can to disrupt your intimate time? Any break in intimacy gives Satan the much desired opportunity to lure you into offering your affection to another. We can't be ignorant of Satan's devices. Many times he will use the smallest thing to disrupt intimacy. For the married couples who have children he will use them to cause the division. He will use arguments about finances to keep you and your spouse from being in agreement. It could even be something as small as your spouse not picking up after themselves. The devil is so crafty that he will use Religion to ruin relationships.

Many preachers and pastors who have wives forget to take out time with their spouse because they are spending so much time with their church. Many women who have positions in the church fail to realize that although they may be anointed, God has still commissioned them to be in submission to their husband. Even when it's a relationship where one partner is not a believer, intimacy still has to be a regular part of the marriage.

Whatever avenue, whatever angles the devil can attack your relationship, that's what he will do. As we stated earlier intimacy can be translated as in-to-me. As long as both partners are "in to" each other, intimacy comes natural. However if one partner feels as though they are being neglected, intimacy becomes very hard. If one partner feels as though intimacy is being forced just to please them or to silence their complaining, but not because their spouse really needs them, then it really doesn't feel like intimacy at all.

Lack of intimacy usually leads to abandonment in the relationship, physically and mentally. Conversation between the two becomes slim to non-existent. Hugs become cumbersome, kisses become few. Intimate moments which were once spontaneous and passionate, now become predictable, without excitement and without sentiment. All of a sudden they start leaving the house without their wedding rings symbolizing that they are no longer duty-bound to anyone. They form emotional attachments with other people often of the opposite sex, their jobs, material processions such as clothe and shoes, porn, anything that will temporarily satisfy their appetite for affection. Usually when this appetite goes unsatisfied then more drastic measures are taken such as adultery, which in due time leads to divorce.

Avoiding Spiritual Adultery

Although this is an illustration in the breakdown of a physical marriage, this is also usually what happens in our "spiritual marriage" with Christ. He is our shepherd, we are his sheep. As sheep we attempt to walk as close to our shepherd as possible. He is the bridegroom, we are the bride. When we accept Christ into our lives, the two of us become one (1 Corinthians 6:17). This new found relationship fills us with an inexpressible joy (1 Peter 1:8). In fact, in the infancy of our relationship to Christ our love for him exceeds that for anyone else. We communicate with him through prayer on a daily basis. We also spend time studying his word exploring carefully every word that has proceeded out of his mouth in order to get to know him better. We love telling others just how good our "man" is.

On the days when it appears as though He isn't around we long for him until he reassures us that he is right there and will never leave us. And everyday we leave the house with our spiritual ring on, which is the light that shines forth through our good works, signifying that we belong to the King. Our relationship couldn't be any better. That is until we run into a distraction. Distractions come in many different ways and with many different faces. A distraction could be a job. It could be family or it could even be friends. You yourself could actually be your biggest distraction. Anything that keeps you from following God with your entire heart and mind is a distraction. Distractions cause us to pull away from God and offer our affection to another, consequently causing a break in intimacy.

You might be saying, how can there be a break in intimacy when God promised to never leave me? Good question. You have to understand that God will never initiate the break in intimacy. However, as James stated every man is tempted when he is drawn away of his own lust (James 1:14). The allure of what the world has to offer often leads to destructive compromises in the believer's life. We begin to sacrifice our time with God, for time to fulfill our own lust. We adapt bad habitual lifestyle practices such as only praying when something bad happens in our life. We become subjective in reading the word of God, dangerously diluting the word to gratify our own desires, not to better ourselves. God no longer is the object of our affection, thus we find ourselves shifting our gaze from him, to other people and material things. We begin to substitute praise for complaining. We attempt to replace the word of God, with world news tonight. We become so blinded by the problems that are going on in the world, that we forget that God is the solution.

Keep in mind that in the midst of your spiritual adultery, God is remaining faithful. He continues to speak to you however the problems of this life have made it hard to recognize his voice. All of a sudden the "distortion" starts coming. You are listening to so many different voices that you don't know which voice to follow anymore. Spiritually you press the "scan" button and hope to find a clear station. Often times the station that you find is not the channel that you need to be listening to. You have now reached a state of bewilderment and desperateness in your life. Because of your confusion now everything you hear you believe that it must be God speaking to you as seen in the scripture below.

> For the time will come when men will not put up with sound doctrine. Instead, to suit their own desires, they will gather around them a great number of teachers to say what their itching ears want to hear. 2 Timothy 4:3 (NIV)

God's Coverage Area

The above referenced scripture lets us know that we should constantly check our hearts to make sure the instruction we are following is biblical. If we don't we are more than likely to be led by our beliefs rather than the word of God. We are more apt to fall into "spiritual adultery." We make an effort to get that old feeling back that we had with our relationship with God by surrounding ourselves with others who believe the same way we believe just to fill a void.

However, nothing or no one physically can satisfy a hunger that is birthed from your spirit. In all actuality at this point we can't remember the last time we heard the voice of God. We lost our signal with him a long time ago. When you lose your signal with the voice of the Spirit, you begin to accept the leadership of counterfeit voices. Often times you will feel pressured to do something or you may even feel obligated to complete a certain task but it's not really God that's leading you to do it.

When this happens you begin to fall for anything, tossed about by every wind of doctrine trying to find your way back to God. In reality you are simply moving further and further away from his "coverage area." Let me clear that last statement up. Unlike your cell phone provider and your local radio station there is no place that God's Spirit doesn't have coverage. He can reach you in the highest mountain and in the lowest valley.

However, the Holy Spirit is a gentleman. He will not force himself on you. On the contrary the Holy Spirit is very gentle. In fact the Bible sometimes describes him as a dove. He does not push. If you feel like you are being pushed to do something then most likely that's not the Spirit. The Holy Spirit gently guides. However it's up to you whether or not you choose to follow.

So if you are in a "non-coverage area" it's because you have isolated yourself from the voice of the Spirit to follow your own beliefs. Romans 1:21 (ESV) states, "For although they knew God, they did not honor him as God or give thanks to him, but they became futile in their thinking, and their foolish hearts were darkened." Don't allow your heart to become darkened and your thinking corrupted by allowing the enemy to seduce you with false promises and pretenses. The apostle Peter warns us to, "Be self-controlled and alert. Your enemy the devil prowls around like a roaring lion looking for someone to devour (1 Peter 5:8 NIV)." The devil is looking for any occasion he can to lure you away from God so that he can devour you. This is why intimacy is so important. The closer we stay to God, the closer he stays to us.

Come Back to your First Love

My point in all of this is this, when we are drawn away from God we give the devil an opportunity to wreak havoc on our lives. Many of us are actually feeling the effects now of some choices that we made on our own without God. Satan is destroying marriages. He is destroying ministries. He is destroying families. Still worst yet he is destroying people's destiny. If he can catch us without our covering then pretty much anything is up for grabs. We don't have to take this broad road which leads to destruction. Your first love is waiting with open arms anxiously awaiting his opportunity to rekindle the old flame that you thought had dwindled beyond restoration. God said that he is ready for a monogamous relationship. In fact God is the only person who will put up with your constant infidelity, put up with your waywardness, put up with your abuse, yet refuse to issue you a divorce.

He's also the only one who can put up with all of your mess, yet never waiver in his love for you. Paul illustrates this point in the following verses:

Who shall separate us from the love of Christ? Shall trouble or hardship or persecution or famine or nakedness or danger or sword? As it is written: "For your sake we face death all day long; we are considered as sheep to be slaughtered." No, in all these things we are more than conquerors through him who loved us. For I am convinced that neither death nor life, neither angels nor demons, neither the present nor the future, nor any powers, neither height nor depth, nor anything else in all creation, will be able to separate us from the love of God that is in Christ Jesus our Lord (Romans 8:35-39 NIV)

When you are a true believer in God, and therefore a true companion, nothing that happens can separate you from the love that he has for you. Christ loves the believer regardless of any circumstance, and even when they turn their back He longs to be reconciled to them. As you can see Christ's unconditional love for you goes beyond comprehension. In fact it's so amazing that many times we don't even feel worthy of this type of love. The question still remains if you are ready to commit to this type of relationship and accept the love that Christ is offering. You don't have to continue to say, "I think that God is leading me to do this or that, but I'm not sure." The Spirit is saying if you would only follow my lead, by obeying my word, then you wouldn't have to assume.

Whenever you're in doubt you should revert back to the word of God. The word want steer you wrong. For the most part instead of going back to the word of God many people will allow what they think the Spirit is saying to lead them. We often times forget however that the Spirit isn't the only one that's speaking in this world. If we are not careful we will find ourselves being led by the wrong voice. Intimacy opens our spiritual ear to the voice of the Spirit. Lack of intimacy however opens the door for various other voices to begin to guide us away from God's intended blueprint for our lives.

CHAPTER 5

Before I step out…is it you, Lord, who called?

Life is filled with lots of tough decisions. Who should I marry? After I get married where should we live? Should I go to college? Where should I attend college? What career should I pursue? What role should I fulfill in the church? These are just a few of the many questions that accumulate on the minds of people each day. The decision that you make in response to any of these questions will drastically alter your life, either for the good or the bad. Decisions of this magnitude should never be made alone. Before you step out and make any important decision in life, you need to have a relationship with God and know for surety that he is leading you to do so. This brings to mind a very familiar story from the book of Matthew. Matthew 14:22-29 (NIV) reads as follows:

> Immediately Jesus made the disciples get into the boat and go on ahead of him to the other side, while he dismissed the crowd. After he had dismissed them, he went up on a mountainside by himself to pray. When evening came, he was there alone, but the boat was already a considerable distance fro land, buffeted by the waves because the wind was against it. During the fourth watch of the night Jesus went out to them, walking on the lake. When the disciples saw him walking on the lake, they were terrified. "It's a ghost," they said, and cried out in fear. But Jesus immediately said to them: "Take courage! It is I. Don't be afraid." "Lord, if it's you," Peter replied, "tell me to

come to you on the water." "Come," he said. Then Peter got down out of the boat, walked on the water and came toward Jesus.

Besides the story of Jesus turning water into wine, Jesus walking on the water is probably the most well known story about the Savior. This is a story that has been repeated to most over and over again since their youth. We know most of the story by heart, however there is a hidden principle in this story concerning intimacy. Let's bring it all into perspective.

God's Sheep Know His Voice

The Disciples are on a boat heading to the other side other of the lake when their boat begins to sway due to the tremendous waves and strong winds that were blowing. Notice that the disciples didn't get afraid then. This is probably because many of them were fishers by trade before following Jesus and were used to dealing with turbulence on the seas. However, without warning they see what appears to be a ghost walking on the sea and they immediately become terrified. Jesus then speaks and says, "It is I, don't be afraid." Amazingly despite the wind, despite the waves, and even despite the fact that they didn't recognize his figure, Peter was still able to identify with his voice. This is because Peter had been intimate with God. As we stated earlier God's sheep know his voice and they follow him. Peter didn't step out of the boat until he was certain that it was Jesus that was speaking.

Many times in life our issues are so great that we find it hard to see Jesus. The great thing about it is if you have been intimate with God for some time, even if you can't see him in your situation, when he speaks you will recognize his voice. Without a doubt Jesus wasn't the only one speaking at this time. The wind was probably howling louder and louder with each passing minute. The wind was likely accompanied by the roar of thunder and the occasional discharge of lightning. I can imagine the waves crashing so loudly that it probably resembled the sound of hundreds of freight trains coming to a sudden halt. On top of all this Peter would have to deal with the disciples who at this point had to be whaling in fear as they felt like they were approaching their demise.

Peter was also dealing with the internal voices that were telling him it was no way he was going to make it through this alive. Nevertheless Jesus' voice managed to pierce through all of the other voices that Peter was hearing. This is because Jesus didn't just speak to Peter's ears, he spoke to his spirit. Connection of this type is only birthed from intimate time with God. What if Peter hadn't have been taking out time with God on a daily basis. What do you think would have happened if Peter hadn't of recognized the voice of God and chosen to listen to one of the other voices that were speaking?

The story possibly would have had a totally different outcome. Instead of Peter walking on the water maybe the whole boat would have sank in the sea. You may be saying that's a little far-fetched, but to be honest we really don't know what would have happened. This is a question that we all must consider when making tough decisions, "Lord is it you that are speaking?"

Finding Time to Hear God's Voice

If we step out at the request of any other voice other than Gods' then we may be setting ourselves up to sink. Have you ever really needed to hear from God about a very important decision that you had to make? Before you step out, you attempt to plan a day to be intimate with God in order to determine what choice to make. It seems as though however that every time you try to hear from God, you are abruptly interrupted by a bunch of distractions, nothing resembling the voice of God. You hear your spouse complaining to you about the bills. You hear your teenage children fussing about whose turn it is to play the game.

You go to your bedroom and shut the door hoping to get away from some of the madness. You haven't been in your room for two minutes when you hear a loud thump on the floor. You quickly leave the tranquility of your bedroom to go see what the noise was and low and behold your toddler has knocked over your very expensive vase that he manages to knock over every day no matter how high you put it. This time however it shatters.

By now it really doesn't even matter much that he shattered your vase. Besides it appears as though that any chance you would have had to hear from God that day was "shattered" anyway. At the end of the day you are so exhausted that you just go to bed hoping to get a chance to spend some time with God tomorrow. However the next day seems to be a repeat of the day before. Gradually your daily intimate time with God is being constantly disrupted by the unrelenting demands of life.

The choices that you need to make are steadily approaching and you have yet to find anytime to talk to God about which decision would be best. You manage to get alone for 5 minutes and you utter a quick prayer to God in the time allotted. During this prayer you are doing pretty much all of the talking and you never even give God a chance to respond. You make a bunch of request, inwardly already leaning towards what YOU want to do, and you leave thinking that you have heard the voice of God, but did you?

For many of you reading this book, this is the story of your life. Many of you have to wear a ton of different hats. You are a parent. You are a spouse. You are a student. Some of you may be business owners which consumes most of your time and energy. With bills to pay, children to feed, spouses to please, and taking out time for the occasional r & r, many times spending time with God moves to the bottom of your to do list. When intimate time dwindles, so does the ability to recognize the voice of God. When you fail to recognize God's voice not only will this drastically affect you, but it will affect many others who are depending on you.

For example, many people who are choosing to get married are making this choice on sheer feelings alone. Soon after they get married they realize that maybe they didn't make the best decision. To keep their marriage afloat they decide to have children feeling as though maybe this will provide an emotional vault to their marriage. Things get better for a while but eventually become even worst than they were before the new edition. The parents finally realize that they will not be able to make it work and decide to divorce amicably. While the parents may be able to remain on good terms through the divorce process, there is nothing amicable about making a child suffer because you the parent decided to "step out" and make a decision motivated by the wrong voice.

Many times when this happens the kids feel like it's their fault that the marriage didn't work and in turn grow up bearing emotional wounds that affect them even into their adulthood. This is also seen when parents of a child opt to give their offspring up for adoption because they are not ready for the responsibility of child rearing. While not all, many children who have been giving up for adoption grow up with a lot of anger, bitterness, and a sense of rejection because they feel as though they weren't wanted.

Be Sure of Your Election

This destructive pattern is even being seen more and more in the church. Many pastors' are so consumed by their on carnal affairs that they neglect taking out the necessary time to hear from God concerning how to direct the sheep. As a result the sheep are experiencing spiritual malnutrition and many are on the verge of spiritual starvation. There is also a sudden influx of people that are stepping into positions that God hadn't led them to be in. It's important that we make our calling and election sure when it relates to any type of ministry. If you are feeling a strong urge to go into any type of ministry ask yourself the following question: Lord is it you that called?

Often times now the calling of God has been replaced with the desire of man. Now people feel that if they desire something bad enough then God has an obligation to grant them want they want. If you are one of the ones who feel this way then sadly you have been misled. God is not indebted to us to have to give us anything. On the contrary it's us who are indebted to God to give him everything. God gave us all when he delivered his only son as ransom for our sins because we owed more than we could ever afford to pay. Yet for some strange reason many still act as if God owes them. I believe this outlook is due impart to a misinterpretation of a very common scripture.

Will God Give Me Everything I Want?

Psalms 37:4 (NIV) states, "Delight yourself in the LORD and he will give you the desires of your heart." Many people read this scripture and inwardly jump for joy. It's almost like a kid in a candy shop just given the permission to eat all the candy that he desires. After all, that is what's in our heart, the desire for a lot of "junk." There is one important word that is often overlooked, however when considered it significantly changes the meaning of this text. That word is delight.

In this context the word delight means to have or take great pleasure in someone. In other words if I delight in someone I'm not concerned about what that person can do for me, I'm concerned about what I can do for that person. Everything that I do will be done in the hopes of providing them with the upmost satisfaction. This goes back to what Peter did in the sea. Notice that Jesus tells Peter to come out on the water, rather than Peter telling him to come into the boat. Peter could have said if it be you Lord then come to me on the boat. If that would have been the case then it would have been Jesus delighting in Peter. This would have reversed the worship from God, to man. This would have been classified as idolatry.

Unfortunately, this is how most of us view our relationship with God. We tell him what we want done, when we want it done, and how he is supposed to do it. This is probably the reason so many of us keep falling flat on our face and then blaming God for our misfortunes. God doesn't work on your agenda. God is not going to worship you. You were created to worship him. This is why when Jesus told Peter to come to him Peter didn't hesitate he quickly "stepped out." Even though the storm was raging, and the wind was blowing, because Peter delighted in God he was determined to do anything he could to please him. What Peter did gives us the perfect illustration of what it means to delight in the Lord. When you delight yourself in the Lord he replaces your carnal desires with what he desires you to do.

Relationship Shifts Aspirations

Do you remember when you were in the world and had yet to except Christ? You had your own ideas and your own agenda of what you thought you were put here to be. When you accepted Christ into your life, the closer you got to him, the more your desires begun to change. When at one time you wanted to make the most money in the world to spend on your own desires, now you want to be blessed in order to help others who are in need. When at one time you wanted to be the greatest business man, now you're more concerned with Kingdom business. Your relationship to God shifts your aspirations.

All of us at one time or another aspired to be something whether it was being a professional athlete, or being the world's greatest singer. What we desired the most is what we worked the hardest to become. Those who wanted to play professional sports practiced hard everyday and attended sports camps in order to be able to perform under the bright lights. Those who wanted to be a great singer took vocal lessons and performed at every local concert in order to ensure that when they took the stage they would memorize the crowd and make a name for themselves.

Even for those whose aspirations weren't so high, they still worked towards becoming whatever they wanted to be whether it was a school teacher or a police officer. Some of you even had parents who wanted you to do something so they took the initiative to sign you up for different lessons to make sure you would be great. Many times though what they had paid so much money for you to do ends up being a waste of money and time.

Now I'm not in no means saying that God doesn't want people to be professional athletes or singers, nor am I saying that if you have a strong desire to pursue a certain career that God isn't the one that's leading you to do that. What I am saying is that many times what we desire to do can often conflict with what God wants us to do. This is why it's so important that we develop a relationship with God.

Relationship Shifts Direction

Not only does a relationship with God shift our aspirations, but it also shifts our direction. We may be going left but the closer we get to God, the more we hear him telling us that we need to go right. You have to continue to develop your relationship in order to consistently hear his voice. This is where most of us go wrong. We get to a certain level in God and feel as though we don't have to seek him quite as much as we use to. We feel as though that we have grown to a place where we are so spiritual that we can make decisions on our on. This goes back to why we see many people stepping into positions that they wasn't qualified to be in. They have stopped listening to the voice of the Spirit and they feel as though they can place themselves wherever there is a need.

If you look at this from a carnal perspective it doesn't sound like a bad thing. If there is a need for a deacon in the church, then why can't I fill the void? If there is a need for a pastor then why can't I fulfill that position? The reason is because if you are operating in a position that you weren't called to be in then you are being ineffective. We stated earlier that King Saul made the choice to step into the office of a Priest when God had anointed him king. Whatever position that God has for your life he has already anointed and equipped you to operate effectively in that position.

No matter what you do you can't replace anointing with education. Education can provide us with the know how to operate a certain position, but it can't give us the power to be effective in that position. We are effective when we are operating in the position that God has appointed us to be in. We are effective when we are following God's direction and not our on.

> And in the church God has appointed first of all apostles, second prophets, third teachers, then workers of miracles, also those having gifts of healing, those able to help others, those with gifts of administration, and those speaking in different kinds of tongues. 1 Corinthians 12:28 NIV

Your Appointed Position

When you have been appointed by God to operate in a certain position, no one can do your job better than YOU. When we operate in our appointed position it alleviates the temptation to be jealous of another's position. The reason being is because we understand that if I don't perform my position well then the entire body will be affected. In other words the efficiency of the body is dependent on how well I execute in my position. If the foot decides it doesn't want to walk, then the whole body is at a stand still.

If the eyes decide they don't want to open, then the body can't see where it is going. If the hands decide that they don't want to work today then I have no way to clothe the body, then the body will walk around exposed to the elements. This is why the church has been exposed because someone wasn't effectively working their position and now the world can see clearly the divisions within the church. I think you get the point.

Every single position is important and no one can do your job better than you. Once you become comfortable in your calling and are not trying to out do your brethren, then it's safe to throw education into the midst. When you are in an appointed position education can't make you more appointed, but it can enhance how effective you are in your position. For instance, although God gave us eyes, many of us have to wear corrective lenses in order to increase our vision.

Although we have legs, we still have to walk with them in order to increase their strength and to keep them from becoming stiff. Even if God has appointed you to operate in a certain position, you still have to increase your knowledge about your position in order to be effective. This doesn't necessarily require you go to some big school, while I'm not against that. The Holy Spirit himself will teach you if you are willing to take out the time to be taught.

> As for you, the anointing you received from him remains in you, and you do not need anyone to teach you. But as his anointing teaches you about all things and as that anointing is real, not counterfeit--just as it has taught you, remain in him. 1 John 2:27 NIV

When God has purpose for your life, not only does he appoint you to a certain position, but he anoints you to remain efficient in that position. God has a special anointing with your name on it but you have to make sure that you are constantly listening to the voice of God in order to be led to the right position and in the right season. As I have stated many times before, to consistently be able to recognize the voice of God, you have to be constantly intimate with God. You can't allow yourself to be distracted by many of the other voices that are speaking in the world. If you keep your spiritual ears in constant tune with the Spirit, then just like

Peter you will recognize his voice when he says "step out" no matter what the decision is.

Something on the Inside

When I was growing up as little boy going to church with my family every Sunday I would often hear them sing a song that I didn't really understand. The song said, "Something on the Inside, working on the outside, brought about a change in my life." This song would always seem to stir up a lot of emotions in many of the people at the church. Some would wave their hands. Others would jump up and down. Some would run around the church. Still others would just stand still with their eyes gazing towards the ceiling, mimicking the words of the song with their lips, however no words could be heard while tears were steadily screaming down their face. As a young boy I would often sit their dazed and confused trying to figure out what was wrong with these people.

I didn't realize that many of them had been broken. I didn't realize that they had been experiencing difficult issues in life that would have driven the normal person insane. However it was something on the inside that wouldn't let them quit. It was something on the inside that would bring comfort in times of distress. What was that something? Better yet, who was that somebody? That somebody was the Holy Ghost. He's also called the Holy Spirit. Some call him the Spirit of Christ. Still others simply call him the Spirit of Truth. The name you call him is not what's important. The main thing is to know that he exists and as a believer he lives in you.

The Holy Spirit lives to make intercession for you in your weaknesses. When we don't know what to pray, the Spirit that's in the inside of us speaks to God on our behalf concerning the state of our spirit (Romans 8:26). This is what the lady was doing in the church when her mouth was open, but no words were coming out. The Spirit was praying for her. The Spirit is also there to lead us and guide us into the truth of the word of God. The prophet Ezekiel writes, "I will give you a new heart and put a new spirit in you; I will remove from you your heart of stone and give you a heart of flesh. And I will put my Spirit in you and move you to follow my decrees and be careful to keep my laws (Ezekiel 36:26-27 NIV)."

Under the Influence

When we attempt to steer away from the truth of God's word, the Spirit seems to always "move" us back to the right path. When the Spirit fills us, we become intoxicated by his presence. Every move we make is influenced by him. It's almost like being under the influence of alcohol. In fact the world has actually adopted this concept. Beer and wine are limited to a maximum alcohol content of about 15% alcohol by volume. This means that a person would have to consume a larger quantity of these beverages in order to become intoxicated.

On the contrary, notice what a beverage with a higher alcohol by volume is called. In the world's terminology any distilled beverage that contains no added sugar and has at least 20% alcohol by volume is called spirit. This means that one is able to consume a lesser quantity of these beverages in order to become intoxicated. Generally speaking these beverages are considered better quality even with less quantity. Popular spirits include brandy, fruit brandy, gin, rum, tequila, vodka, and whisky. While many of you are not familiar with what these beverages are capable of, others know from first hand experience what these beverages are capable of doing once even a small quantity enters your bloodstream.

Your physical capabilities start to diminish. Your speech begins to change. Your balance and coordination start to decline. Your eyesight becomes dim. Many people who are under the influence of alcohol exhibit erotic behavior. Perhaps one of the most common side effects of being under the influence of alcohol is that it provides a new found sense of boldness that one wouldn't normally have. The drunkard tends to speak their mind without fear of what others will say or do to them. Their inhibitions go out of the window and nothing is off limits. If a person walks around constantly under the influence of alcohol, then they will constantly speak with great boldness and their actions will reflect the substance that is controlling them.

Be Filled with the Spirit

While there are many spirit beverages, there is only one Holy Spirit. What "spirit" beverages do to your physical body, the Holy Spirit does to your spiritual body. Paul warns in Ephesians 5:18 (NIV), "Do not get drunk on wine, which leads to debauchery. Instead, be filled with the Spirit." Paul uses strong imagery to compare being drunk with wine versus being filled with the Spirit. He urges believers to be filled with the Spirit. This was not a suggestion rather a command. Paul understood that to be drunk with wine would lead to sin and eventually death. Being filled with the Spirit in turn leads to obedience and life.

Just like being drunk with wine, when you are filled with the Spirit your actions begin to change. This usually begins with your speech. When you would once complain, now you rejoice. When you would once say what you couldn't do, now you begin to say what you can do. Your language begins to line up with the word of God. Not only does your speech change, but your walk also begins to change. When you were once walking down a road that appeared would lead to sudden destruction, when the Holy Spirit comes into your life he begins to lead you down the correct path which leads to a life full of abundance. He enables you to walk through the valley of the shadow of death, yet not fear any evil because you know that he is controlling your steps. What great assurance! If the Lord is deciding your steps it's no way you can go wrong.

An Expanded Vision

So we know that being controlled with the Spirit changes your talk. We also know that it changes your walk. One of the other major benefits of being controlled by the Spirit is the fact that your vision begins to change. Unlike alcohol, the Holy Spirit doesn't dim your vision, he expands your vision. You begin to see your wildest dreams coming true even when no one else does. Setbacks now look like setups for future success. Failures now look like achievements that are not quite mature yet. Disappointments even give the impression of being opportunities in disguise.

I would compare this new found sight to a person who has never been able to see. Their whole life has been spent living in darkness. In their mind they visualize things, but due to their disability they feel as though they will never be able to actually experience them. One day during their regular routine physical the doctor says that he has a cure for their ailment. They become very excited, yet very scared at the same time. What will it be like to see? What if I don't like what I see? What if my vision comes back for a short period of time, however then fades away because the procedure didn't work? All of these thoughts race through their mind however they agree to go through with the procedure. After all, what do they have to lose?

I Can See Clearly Now

When the procedure is over and the doctor takes off the blind fold the patient gingerly opens their eyes still squinting because their eyes have yet to adjust to the bending light rays. They feel their way over to the sink and feel for the mirror. After wiping the mirror off with their hands they gaze in for the first time ever at a reflection looking back at them. It's blurry at first but then all of a sudden everything starts to come into focus. The image in the mirror is doing everything they do. When they wave their hands, so does the image. When they touch their face, so does the image. How astonishing this must feel to see your appearance for the first time.

That's what the Holy Spirit does, he allows you to see past your exterior and see your true inward self for the first time. So many of you are still seeing what somebody else has called you. You are still looking at somebody that the world labeled a failure. You are still seeing the person you use to be with no real view of your true reflection. The Holy Spirit allows you to see the fine art that you truly are. He allows you to see through his eyes, and thus everything he does you have to mimic. The closer you become to the Spirit, the clearer your vision becomes. The clearer your vision, the closer you are to reaching your destiny.

Boldness in the Spirit

Last but not least when you are filled with the Holy Spirit you take on a boldness that you would have never had without him. Some of you right now are operating in positions that you would have never been able to walk in without the boldness of the Spirit. Some of you are in managerial positions on your job which require you to be very vocal; yet growing up you was always the quietest person in the room. There are many of you who were once so shy that you wouldn't even tell the gospel of Jesus to your family, let alone a stranger. Now you are not ashamed to tell it to anyone, anytime, and anywhere. Where did this boldness come from? It came from the enabling of the Spirit. It's the same boldness and same Spirit that enabled Peter and John to stand boldly and proclaim Jesus as Lord in front of the Sanhedrin court.

> Then Peter, filled with the Holy Spirit, said to them: "Rulers and elders of the people! If we are being called to account today for an act of kindness shown to a cripple and are asked how he was healed, then know this, you and all the people of Israel: It is by the name of Jesus Christ of Nazareth, whom you crucified but whom God raised from the dead, that this man stands before you healed. He is" 'the stone you builders rejected, which has become the capstone. Salvation is found in no one else, for there is no other name under heaven given to men by which we must be saved." When they saw the courage of Peter and John and realized that they were unschooled, ordinary men, they were astonished and they took note that these men had been with Jesus. Acts 4:8-13(NIV)

The men of the Sanhedrin court were astonished at the words of the apostles because they realized that Peter and John were just unschooled, ordinary men. They hadn't been trained at the best schools of their day. They weren't considered in any ways highly esteemed as some of the noblemen of their time were. They didn't have any degrees in Judaism or the popular mythologies of the day. Yet they were able to declare the wonders of God with great confidence and great power.

This shows us that Christ can use ordinary people to accomplish extraordinary things. While education is great, when Christ is in your life he can teach you things and equip you with ability that no formal education could ever provide. Even when someone else may be more qualified on paper than you to do a certain thing, God can give you the skill to "outclass" them and enable you to be promoted to a place that far exceeds your qualifications.

Walking Close to the Lord

Notice also that the men took note that the apostles had been with Jesus. When you walk close with Jesus, then people will recognize his presence in your life. Everything you do will stand out. People will feel uncomfortable around you and don't even no why. How many of you have ever been told that it's just something about you that they just can't put their hands on? Yes ladies, I know you probably thought that the guy who told you this was probably just using a pathetic pick up line, but he was probably telling the truth. How many of you have been told by someone, "I can tell that you are a Christian," and you haven't even mentioned your religious standings? There is something about Christ that is undeniable. There is something about his presence that makes people stop and stare in amazement.

The Spirit of Christ will give an average person with no significance public notice. This is the same appeal that was seen in Daniel. Daniel was a Jew who was taken into captivity with the rest of the Jews by the Babylonians. The Bible says that Daniel had a "spirit of excellence." Due to the spirit that Daniel possessed he was exalted highly as the ruler of the entire Province of Babylon in which he was a slave.

Many men of Babylon were jealous of Daniel, and I'm sure very confused about this. How could a Jew become so prominent in Babylon? When you stay humble under the voice of God and obedient to his word, God can cause you to excel even in foreign territory. What Daniel's haters didn't realize was that it wasn't anything special about Daniel. Rather it was what Daniel had on the inside of him that made him "stand out" from the rest of the crowd.

The Power to Stand Out

The Bible says that Christians should allow their lights to shine before men so in seeing this they will see our good works and glorify the Father. The great thing about Daniel was that he never attempted to take credit for the shine that was in him. Daniel always made sure that all the glory went back to God. After Daniel had interrupted a dream that King Nebuchadnezzar, King of Babylon, had the Bible says that the King said, "…Surely your God is the God of gods and the Lord of kings and a revealer of mysteries, for you were able to reveal this mystery (Daniel 2:47 NIV)."

Daniel didn't attempt to steal God's glory. He understood that it was no goodness of his own that these mysteries were revealed to him. He knew that it was the Spirit of God on the inside of him that had given him this great spiritual insight. It was after the interpretation of this dream that the king elevated Daniel above all his peers. When God can trust you with promotion, then he will give you a promotion. As long as your promotion brings him glory then God will continue to elevate you. Daniel was able to stand in front of the king with great confidence and hundreds of years later Peter and John would do the same thing when they stood in front of the Sanhedrin court.

While it was obvious that Daniel was promoted as he was made ruler in the Babylonian Empire. Due to the circumstances that Peter and John were facing many would miss the fact that these men had been promoted. However, if you study their story closely you will see that these men had definitely been promoted. Normally these men would have never been noticed by the Sanhedrin Court.

The Sanhedrin Court was the supreme religious body in the Land of Israel. Having so much authority and limitless influence would have no doubt contributed to very inflated egos within the Sanhedrin. They had the best education. Their fathers had been men of great esteem and wealth. This would have given them tunnel vision. They wouldn't pay attention to or recognize anyone else as being anybody but themselves.

All Eyes on Me

In the secular world I would compare them to a very popular fraternity. The fraternity is strictly reserved for the in crowd. In other words you have to be considered an important person, or the offspring of a bigwig to even be a part of this frat. These frats usually think they are the smartest. They usually think they are the most attractive. They also don't recognize nor respect anyone but those within their respective circle. Despite their arrogance everyone still gravitates to them. Everybody wants to say they know someone in the frat, or say that they are known by someone in the frat. All eyes are on them.

All of a sudden a smaller frat starts gaining a little attention. The large frat brushes it off because remember they are arrogant and they feel that no one could ever outshine them. Yet slowly but surely this new frat is becoming more and more popular. More and more people begin to gravitate towards them. The once popular frat all of a sudden doesn't possess the same magnetism that they once had. Now the smaller frat has their attention and they have to confront them. This is the same thing that happened with the apostles and the Sanhedrin.

Christ's Fraternity

The Sanhedrin became so intimidated because now a much smaller, unprivileged group of men were starting to steal their attention. That's when you know that God has given you a promotion. When people who had at one point didn't pay any attention to you now begin gazing your way because they don't understand how you are doing what you are doing, with what little that you possess. Sadly they fail to comprehend that the Holy Spirit in you is great. You are a part of "Christ's Fraternity."

You also know that this was a promotion for the apostles because not only did Peter and John stand in front of the Sanhedrin, but they weren't afraid to speak with great boldness. There are a lot of people right now who are intimidated to speak in front of certain people because they feel that these people are far more advanced than they are. Have you let

111

intimidation of someone else's ability cause you to keep silent? The devil uses intimidation as a weapon to silence God's people who truly have a powerful word in their belly. All Christians possess the power to have an affect on someone's life in a positive way with just a word.

Use Your Voice as a Weapon

As Christians, we have to learn how to use our voice as a weapon against Satan's army. We have to stand up and boldly proclaim truth in the midst of hypocrisy. As this relates to the Peter and John, these men would have never been bold enough to speak in front of these men of great power without the Spirit. Christ, the same man that Peter denied in order to save his life, is now the same man that Peter is defending with no regard for his own life. That boldness that Peter possessed to speak God's word even when it was unpopular and dangerous only came from the Spirit.

This is the same boldness that we as believers need today. These days a lot of people are watering down the Gospel message in order to assure that they want offend certain people who are of higher authority. Yet Peter, John, and Daniel were all committed to speaking the truth of the word of God even though it could have cost them their life. When God can trust you to continue to speak truth even when all odds are against you, then God can truly begin to elevate you. The higher you go, the more glory you are bringing to God. It's impossible to maintain this level of constant commitment, however, without constant relationship.

Preparation for Promotion

Your next promotion isn't going to happen because of your qualifications, but it's going to happen because of your relationship. God will continue to give you boldness to operate on levels that you may not have even thought you were capable of doing as you continue to draw closer to him. For instance, preaching God's word was never something that I thought that I would ever be able to do. Stand in front of people and proclaim the word of God, now you must be crazy. I knew that the call was on my life to minister, however I didn't feel like I was capable of carrying it out. I was very reserved and shy when it came to speaking in front of anyone, not to mention an entire congregation.

On top of that I had a speech impediment that had hindered me my entire life even when it came to reading in school. I was content with just playing the keyboard at my local church. The closer I got to God though, the more clearly I could hear the call to preach the gospel. I wanted to please God so bad, but how was I going to stand in front of people shy, reserved, and lacking the proficiency of speech needed to effectively engage a congregation? I was about to find the answer to this question in the word of God. There was a man in the Bible who dealt with a similar issue by the name of Moses.

Your Limitations Bring Glory to God

When God instructed Moses to go to Egypt and tell the Pharaoh of Egypt to let his people, the Jews, go Moses grumbled to God that he was slow of speech. God answered him and said, "…Who gave man his mouth? Who makes him deaf and mute? Who gives him sight or makes him blind? Is it not I, the Lord? Now go; I will help you speak and will teach you what to say (Exodus 4:11-12 NIV)." God was letting Moses know that not only did he know about his speech limitations, in which Moses viewed as debilitating, but he was responsible for him having this limitation and was still going to use him.

The greater your limitations the more glory it brings to God. God was attempting to stir up confidence in Moses to know that he could do all things through His strength. Just like Moses, many of us have been guilty of using our disability as an excuse not to do God's will. Never let your weaknesses hinder you from doing the will of God. It's not about your power but it's about the power of the Spirit which is in you. When people see you doing incredible things that far exceed your physical abilities, it lets others know that it had to be God working through you.

As long as your disability brings glory to God then that's all that matters. This is what God was telling me. The closer I got to God, the greater my confidence became. It wasn't a sudden arrogance that I had in my own ability. It was a confidence that I had in the God that was working through me.

I begin to speak boldly about the word of God to everyone who would listen. Many people knew of my speech impediment and thus were very amazed when I begin to speak in public settings. They knew that this couldn't have been that same boy who would only sing in front of his family if he was paid a dollar and even then would only do it if he could sit under the kitchen table. Now he is standing in front of the church with boldness talking about how good God is.

They knew that this boldness could have only come from the Spirit. When at one time I would stammer over my words, all of a sudden my speech became much clearer. Even when I would stumble over my words I would keep going like it never happened. Just as God had promised to help Moses speak, he was now doing the same thing for me.

The Spirit of God had given me such a boldness that not too long after this I accepted the call to preach and have been going from church to church telling the goodness of God every since. I sometimes wonder, however, what would have happened if I hadn't of tapped into the power of the Spirit? Maybe I would have continued to operate in a position of comfort, all the while people who needed my gift would have went neglected. There are some of you right now who have yet to allow the Spirit to completely intoxicate you.

You stand back timid and afraid to voice your input even when you may have great ideas. You choose to remain silent when the word that is in your mouth may well help countless people. You remain a member of the staff, when God has impregnated you with leadership capabilities. You continue to operate in a position that is below your ability all because you are not bold enough to boast about the God in you.

Don't Let the Enemy Steal your Voice

God's people should walk in the boldness of the Spirit in order to achieve everything that God has destined them to accomplish. God can't use people who refuse to use their voice. That's why the enemy desires to keep you speechless. In Mark 9:17 a man brings a child to Jesus who was possessed by a spirit that had "robbed" him of his speech. Don't allow the enemy to rob you of your voice. Remember he doesn't have enough fire power to rob one of God's children. He's only able to gain control over what you give him.

Stop giving him your voice. Stop complaining when you could be rejoicing. Stop speaking death when you could speak life. It's because of this wrong use of the voice or no use at all that so many of our neighborhoods are going unreached with the Gospel because now the church has giving the enemy its voice.

We have let everything cause us to either speak what is socially acceptable, or just choose to remain silent. We have let the government take prayer out of the schools. We have let the government begin reforms to approve same sex marriages. We have let false doctrines slowly creep into the churches and the real men and woman of God remain silent in order to avoid conflict.

Even in the homes the parents have allowed the enemy to keep them silent and now their children are doing whatever they want to do. It's time for the people of God to take their voice back. We have to cry loud and speak boldly the truth of the word of God even when people don't like it.

The Christian's Confidence

Your inhibitions have to go out of the door. We should walk with our heads hung high even when we face difficult situations because we are under the influence of the Spirit. Many people will call you crazy because of your optimism in the midst of such a pessimistic world. But your faith isn't from this world. You possess a supernatural power in which the world could neither give nor take away. Therefore, we shouldn't talk like the world does with their constant doubting and complaining. The immorality and dreadful conditions in this world should not cause us to shift our gaze away from God. In spite of our situation we should keep our eyes on God, looking to Jesus who is the author and finisher of our faith. As long as we keep our eyes stayed on God then we will stay under the control of the Spirit.

We do this by constantly meditating on the word of God. The word of God constantly reminds us that God is in control. The word let's you know that greater is he that is in you, then he that is in the world. Often times though we will allow our issues in life to detoxify us. We were once on a spiritual high but now we have lost our buzz. All of sudden our minds shift from a kingdom mind, to an earthly mind. Our issues at times appear so big that it will cause us to forget that the Holy Spirit is inside of us. You revert back to listening to those other voices that are speaking in your life. Let's take a brief look at some of these other voices.

CHAPTER 6

Which Voice will you follow?

In order for the Spirit to accurately lead man, man has to learn how to differentiate the voice of the Spirit from his own voice. Just like there are three different personalities to God: the Father, the Son, and The Spirit which ultimately all make one. There are also three different personalities which make up man. These three parts are the soul of man, the body of man, and the spirit of man.

> May God himself, the God of peace, sanctify you through and through. May your whole spirit, soul and body be kept blameless at the coming of our Lord Jesus Christ. (1Thes. 5:23 NIV)

Paul says may your whole spirit, soul and body be kept blameless at the coming of our Lord Jesus Christ. These are three different components that make up the entirety of man. Many people tend to get the spirit and the soul confused. They attempt to use them interchangeably as if they were one in the same. If we take a closer look at 1 Thessalonians 5:23 however we will see that they are not the same. In fact all three of these components operate in completely different ways.

The Voice of Your Soul

Hebrews 4:12 also goes on to say that, "For the word of God is living and active. Sharper than any double-edged sword, it penetrates even to dividing soul and spirit, joints and marrow; it judges the thoughts and attitudes of the heart (NIV)." It is important we do not confuse our spirits with our souls. The soul of a person is the mind. The word for soul in the Greek is the word *psuche*. This is the same word in which we derive our word psychology from which is the study of the soul or mind. Who a person is, their personality, their attitude, their emotions are all connected to the soul. Your soul can affect the rest of your being. David writes the following in Psalms 43:5, "Why are you downcast, O my soul? Why so disturbed within me? Put your hope in God, for I will yet praise him, my Savior and my God (NIV)."

Here you can picture David in a state of despair. He's probably moping around not doing anything because he has a lot of things on his mind which is affecting his overall mood and attitude. Their must have been a source of David's sudden depression. Yet as he begins to contemplate in his head he makes a decision to shift his mind from his issues to God. He rationalized within himself and discovered that his problems, although great, still didn't outweigh the goodness of God. This is called reasoning. Humans were the only created beings who were created with the ability to reason. Unlike animals we don't just live by instincts, but we are able to rationally think things through before we make a decision.

It Doesn't Make Sense

After God created man the bible says that he "breathed into his nostrils the breath of life; and man became a living soul (Genesis 2:7 KJV)." The fact that we became a living soul assures us that we have been given an ability to make rational choices on our own. However, when our reasoning interferes with the voice of God then we have a huge problem. That's what has happened to our world today. We live in a time where everyone wants to listen to the "voice of reasoning." Whatever makes sense in our mind is usually what we will believe to be true. This belief system can be seen in the religious philosophy called Thelema which was developed by the early 20th century British writer named Aleister Crowley.

This philosophy follows an ethical code which states, "Do what thou wilt shall be the whole of the Law." Essentially what this statement indicates is that people should seek out and follow their own True Will. Ultimately this mindset leads to idolatry and a seared conscience for millions of people who will believe that they can just do what they want to do, and not what is morally right. In fact this mindset tends to promote the idea that there is no set standard of morality. The people should be able to decide what is right and what is wrong thus becoming their own gods. Paul deals with a similar issue in his day. People were beginning to promote their own religions and ideologies which were beginning to transition into the church. Paul writes to Timothy in an attempt to warn him of these people who had allowed their conscious to be corrupted because of their own reasoning.

> These people are hypocrites and liars, and their consciences are dead (1 Timothy 4:2 NLT)

When a person's conscience becomes dead then they can no longer hear the voice of the Spirit. Even when the Spirit is speaking loud and clear they struggle to recognize his voice over their own beliefs. As children of God we have to make sure that we don't allow our beliefs to interfere with the plan of God. What God asks his people to do doesn't always make since in our own minds. That's why there are so many people who struggle to believe the simplicity of the Gospel because it boggles their mind. The fact that one man's death was sufficient enough to cover the sins of the world is just too amazing to be true in most people's mind. It seems as though it's just an old wise tail or a myth.

Redeeming the Soul

As long as we view life through our own souls, then we will never be able to fully embrace the destiny that God has in store for us. We have to literally die to our own ideals. Our souls are by nature evil. Therefore in order for us to accept the guidance of the Spirit, our souls have to be saved. Let's take a look at a passage of scripture which discusses this matter.

> Therefore, get rid of all moral filth and the evil that is so prevalent and humbly accept the word planted in you, which can save you. James 1:21 NIV

James warns us to get rid of all moral filth and the evil that is so prevalent. He then tells us to humbly accept the word that is planted in us which can save us. This lets us know that the only way to save our souls or minds is by constantly replacing our thoughts with the word of God. We will be filling our minds with the word of God and removing filth from our minds for the rest of our lives. We should never think that we are so advanced that we don't need to replenish our minds anymore. He, who thinks he stands, should take heed lest he falls. This renewing of the mind has to be intentional. Your mind will not clean itself up. You have to take out time daily to replenish your minds with the word of God.

It's ok to reason about certain things. For instance, God doesn't care what color suit you have on. He doesn't care what type of vinyl siding you have on your house. He only cares about what relates to His destiny for your life. Whenever your reasoning interferes with the purpose of God, and thus the plan of God, then you have made your own reasoning your God which is idolatry.

Don't Let Reasoning Over-shadow God's Plan

Looking at the situation from a pure reasoning standpoint, it wouldn't have made great sense for Noah to build an Ark. The rain that God was speaking of would be so great that it would cover the entire earth. Noah was building a huge ark, and apparently the weather was extremely fair. This wouldn't have made sense to many people. I'm sure the people laughed and made fun of Noah. Noah may have even thought to himself, "Why am I doing this?" Nevertheless, Noah wasn't going to let his reasoning interfere with the plan of God.

Don't ever let your reasoning place limits on what God is able to do in your life. When the Spirit speaks we have to listen even if it defies everything that we thought we knew. The Apostle Paul says that we have to hold the mystery of faith with a pure conscience (1 Timothy 3:9). What gives us a clear conscience is when we know that we are not allowing our own beliefs to guide us, but we are living a yielded life under the direction of the Spirit of God and allowing him to lead us to His purpose for our lives. When we don't put limits on what God can do then the possibilities for our life are immeasurable. When we continue to operate in a lack of faith we will eventually end up with a "seared conscience." A seared conscience lacks faith in God and without faith it is impossible to please God. Stop trying to prove God wrong with your intellect.

2 Corinthians 10:5 says "We demolish arguments and every pretension that sets itself up against the knowledge of God, and we take captive every thought to make it obedient to Christ (NIV)." Imaginations are images in the mind that come from worldly, carnal, ungodly thinking. All of these thoughts must be demolished because they are contrary to Christ. Your intellect lacks the ability to be able to comprehend on his level. We just have to trust God and know that his ways are far greater than our own. Romans 3:4 says "…let God be true, and every man a liar (NIV)." Remember if it's a question of who's right or wrong between you and God then you will always be wrong. That settles it.

The Voice of Your Body

Your soul deals with your personality and your mind. On the other hand, the body deals with your feelings. And just as your mind speaks to you, so does your body. We are not prepared to recognize the voice of the Holy Spirit, until we have identified the voice of our soul. The voice of the body is no exception. Many times we will think that the Spirit is speaking to us to do something, but in all actuality it's our body speaking. The soul (mind) and the body actually work hand and hand. Your mind usually tells your body what it wants, not the other way around. When you are hungry your mind tells your body to eat. When you are thirsty your mind tells your body to drink. These two work hand in hand as seen in the following verse.

> Among these also we all had our manner of living in times past in the lusts of our flesh, fulfilling the desires of the flesh and of the mind, and were by nature the children of wrath, even as others. Ephesians 2:3 NKJV

I'm not going to go into as great detail concerning feelings as we discussed this in a previous chapter. However, we have to make sure we are able to decipher between the desires of our minds and bodies, as opposed to our spirits. Many of the things that we desire are evil hungers that are birthed from our flesh rather than our spirits. We have to make sure that we bring our flesh under subjection to the word of God. As we stated earlier the Spirit is willing, but the flesh is weak.

Many times we will put things in front of our eyes for a long period of time and when our flesh desires to have it we think that it must be God speaking. God is not telling you to leave your spouse and commit adultery with another. That goes in direct opposition to his word. God is not telling people of the same sex to engage in sensual relationships. If we are having feelings like these then that means that we are still fulfilling the desires of the flesh and not the Spirit. Notice that Paul states that at one time we were all children of wrath.

By nature our flesh only desired what would please the flesh. The Bible says that if we walk in the Spirit we will not fulfill the lust of the flesh. The only way to overcome the lust of our flesh is to draw closer to the Spirit. If not we will continue to be tricked into following the voice of the soul and body, and not the voice of the Spirit.

Conquering the Flesh

Conquering the flesh is not an easy task, but it can be done. Peter states that we have been born again, not of corruptible seed, but of incorruptible, by the word of God, which lives and abides forever (1 Peter 1:23). I can't stress this enough. The only way to conquer the flesh is to constantly take in the word of God. The word of God slowly kills the flesh. The more you take in, the more of your flesh will die. Our Spirit man is at constant war with our flesh. Everyday it's an ongoing battle for who will reign supreme.

The one that we feed the most will be the one who constantly wins the battle. If you continue to allow the voice of your body to override the voice of the Spirit then you will never obtain everything that God has for you.

When we accepted Christ into our lives, we were crucified with Christ. However, because we are still in a fleshly body, then if not suppressed with the word of God our flesh will once again take dominion in the decisions that we make in life. Remember our mind and our bodies are working together against God. If we can conqueror the mind, then the body will have to follow. Romans 8:5-6 says, "For they that are after the flesh do mind the things of the flesh; but they that are after the Spirit the things of the Spirit. For to be carnally minded is death; but to be spiritually minded is life and peace (NIV)."

It's time to take control of our minds and all of the things that our flesh desires. If you are single and are waiting for a mate then stop watching sexually explicit movies which drive your passions insane. When you expose your flesh to things of this nature, afterword you can read your Bible all you want, but the seed has been sown. Eventually you are going to be led by the voice of your body to go out and satisfy your physical need. Yes I said need. The reason being is because after your flesh has gazed on something long enough it will fool your mind into thinking that you need it.

Shift Your Gaze to Christ

Some of you had a drug problem, however now that you feel that you have been delivered from it, you begin going around your friends who are still using. Sooner or later your mind will tell your body that you need a hit and you will experience a relapse. This can happen with any addiction that you thought you had beat whether it be alcohol or sex. If you continue to make provision for your flesh, then your flesh will get the best of you. If you don't want to continue to be led by the flesh, then you have to change your focus. You have to shift your affections from the things that are on the earth which are only temporary, to those things that are above which are eternal (Colossians 3:1-2).

Sure I know that if you are single you will get lonely. I know that many times you will feel like going back and doing the things you use to do. However whenever you are tempted to go back, just remember the future that Christ has for you. You don't have to continue to live in the past making the same mistakes over and over again. Christ wants to give you power over the flesh so you can receive everything that he has for you. Stop putting yourself in situations to be tempted to go against God.

Paul states in Romans 13:13-14, "Let us behave decently, as in the daytime, not in orgies and drunkenness, not in sexual immorality and debauchery, not in dissension and jealousy (NIV)." Paul urges us not to make any provision for the flesh. Don't make a decision just because it feels right to our flesh. Usually when we make decisions that feel good to the flesh, they usually end up with devastating results.

Just ask King David when he impregnated Bathsheba and then had her husband Uriah killed to cover his steps. David wasn't even thinking that God saw everything that he had done and because of David's sin and misdirection, his baby would have to die. Even though David lay before God fasting and crying out for mercy, the baby still died.

Often times we think that when we do choose to follow the wrong voice that we can go back to God and get it right and there will be no consequences. Galatians 6 let's us know that whatever man sows he will reap. If you sow to the flesh then you will reap corruption. Are you tired of reaping the harvest of the bad seeds you have sown, all because you chose to follow the wrong guidance? We have to recognize when we are being lead by the flesh, rather than the Spirit. The only way to do this is to take in more of the word of God. It's only then we will be able to differentiate the voice of the mind and body, from the voice of the Spirit.

The Voice of Your Spirit

The voice of our spirits is called conscience. Paul speaking concerning the Gentiles who followed the law even though they weren't trained in the law states, "…since they show that the requirements of the law are written on their hearts, their consciences also bearing witness, and their thoughts now accusing, now even defending them (Romans 2:15 NIV)."

In this scripture Paul was pointing out to the devout Jews, who believed that salvation was largely connected to observing the law, that when the Gentiles, who didn't have the law, did by nature the things that were contained in the law then they had become a law unto themselves. In other words all mankind must have possessed an innate ability to be able to determine what was right and wrong, and have the moral reasoning to be able to determinedly choose between the two.

The Gentiles didn't have the written law, but their spirits or consciences had an inward ability to be able to identify what was morally right and what was wrong and to decisively choose right. God imparted this ability to us when he breathed the breath of life unto man. James 2:26 goes on to say, "As the body without the spirit is dead, so faith without deeds is dead." In the physical as long as a person has a mind then his body can still function.

In the spiritual, when a person has a mind, but lacks the spirit, then that person is considered spiritually dead. The spirit of the man is what brings conviction of what is right or wrong. We see this correlation between the spirit of the man and morality many times over. When David cut off a portion of Saul's robe then the Bible says that David was "conscience-stricken" for having done this because Saul was still the anointed of God (1 Samuel 24:5 NIV).

David knew that this wasn't the right thing to do. If you go over just one chapter in the book of Samuel you will find David "conscience-stricken" again after he has conducted a census even though God had told him not to (1 Samuel 25:31). The Holy Spirit uses the conscience of man to convict him of his wrong doing. In this aspect the mind and the spirit work together. If a person has a renewed mind, then he will be able to test and approve what God's will is. When your mind and your conscience are in agreement, then hearing the voice of Spirit becomes so much easier. With that being said a renewed mind and a conscience can be a reliable guide; however, we have to make sure that we are putting the right information into our mind.

Your path in life is a summation of the information that you receive. This information begins the formation of your destiny. Your path becomes crooked when you take in the wrong information. There are many people who have a weak conscience because they have filled their mind with the wrong information, and thus their convictions are not in line with the word of God, rather what they believe to be right and wrong. Paul mentions this in 1 Corinthians 8:7 when he talks about the people who wouldn't eat foods that were traditionally sacrificed to idols. Of course we know that person was operating with a lack of knowledge because all things that God made were good.

However, Paul asserts that for the sake of that person's conscience then those who have the knowledge that there is nothing wrong with eating this meat shouldn't eat it in front of them as this would be a sin against Christ and your brother (1 Corinthians 8:12; 10:28-29). While there was nothing sinful about the person choosing to abstain from meat, this weak conscience could eventually lead to deeper issues. Titus 1:15 states, "To the pure, all things are pure, but to those who are corrupted and do not believe, nothing is pure. In fact, both their minds and consciences are corrupted (NIV)."

If a person continues to operate in a weak conscience then eventually this could lead to a defiled conscience. A defiled conscience will keep you from walking into your destiny due to unbelief. This is a very sinful and dangerous mindset to have because it affects purpose. When a person's mind becomes corrupted, and he's not even adhering to his conscience which lets him know what's morally right and wrong, then he is in danger of developing a seared conscience. It doesn't take long for a person to develop this type of conscience. That's why Paul used the word seared to describe it.

A Seared Conscience Brings Condemnation

The word seared literally means to burn, scorch, mark, or injure with or as if with sudden application of intense heat. It's so important to be careful of the doctrine that you receive. Nothing corrupts the mind like the incorrect application of the Word of God. It doesn't take long to do either. In fact it can happen quite abruptly. If you are not rooted and grounded in the word of God then you are more easily duped into believing the deception that many false prophets are teaching. The un-renewed mind is also subject to condemnation. There are many preachers and teachers now who are preaching for gain the Gospel of Jesus Christ. They use their wit and persuasive rhetoric skills to make you feel guilty about things that have no bearing in the word of God. This is not how the spirit leads. He doesn't look to bring condemnation.

Paul reassures of this in the following verse of scripture: There is therefore now no condemnation for those who are in Christ Jesus, who walk not according to the flesh, but according to the Spirit (Romans 8:1 NIV). The Spirit doesn't bring condemnation; he brings correction and instruction in righteousness. The Holy Spirit teaches us the truth of the word of God which frees us from the guilt of our past. If you are being led to do something because of guilt, then you know that it's not the Spirit leading you to do this. Don't allow the enemy to corrupt your thinking in an attempt to corrupt your conscience. Instead we have to guard our conscience.

A Clear Conscience Brings Freedom

Just like Paul we should try hard everyday to keep a clear conscience before God and man (Acts 24:16). The Holy Spirit will identify with your conscience when you are doing right. You might find yourself in a situation where something feels good (voice of our body) and seems reasonable (voice of our soul) but your conscience (voice of our spirit) tells you not to do it. As I stated earlier the Bible says that the lamp of the Lord searches the spirit of the man (Proverbs 2:20). Let God search your innermost parts and remove anything that's not like him and replace it with more of His Spirit. 1 Corinthians 2:14 states, "The man without the Spirit does not accept the things that come from the Spirit of God, for they are foolishness to him, and he cannot understand them, because they are spiritually discerned (NIV)."

If you want to know the deep things of God, the plans that he has for your life, the mysteries in his word, then you have to receive his Spirit.

Verse 15 states, "The spiritual man makes judgments about all things, but he himself is not subject to any man's judgment." When your spirit is one with the Spirit of God then no man can ever judge you again. Paul goes on to state in 1 Corinthians 4:4, "My conscience is clear, but that does not make me innocent. It is the Lord who judges me." Paul knew that no man could judge him. Even though Paul had persecuted so many Christians in his past, Paul's conscience still managed to be clear for his future. Why? It's because Paul was now walking in the freedom that the Spirit of God provided. He was no longer following the voice of his body nor was he any longer following the voice of his soul. Paul had crucified his flesh, renewed his mind, and his spirit man had been made new by the Spirit of God.

So many believers are walking around today with their minds un-renewed. They haven't allowed the word of God to seep deep into their hearts and penetrate deep into their minds. They are still holding on to old beliefs, and are even still fulfilling the desires of the flesh. This is why the Spirit can't lead you, because you have yet to listen to his voice. The Bible says that the day you hear his voice harden not your heart. He is speaking to you. Don't continue to reject him. Don't continue to ignore his voice in order to satisfy your flesh. This could be your last chance to walk into your destiny. Quit allowing the precepts of man to formulate your thinking and damage your conscience ultimately leading to an untransformed life.

The Dangers of a Seared Conscience

Paul encourages Timothy to hold on to faith and a good conscience as some of his fellow brothers in Christ had rejected these and in turn shipwrecked their faith (1 Timothy 1:19). Paul is talking about two people in particular in this scripture. These are Hymenaeus and Alexander who had rejected the truth of Jesus Christ and thus ship wrecked their faith. We have to make sure that we don't allow our faith to become ship wrecked and our conscience seared by constantly doing things our on way. As we stated earlier it's not about your program. You have to get with the program that God has already planned for your life, not the one in which you envision. Don't build up a callous for the voice of God in which you refuse to submit to his will in any area in your life.

As Paul stated, the wrath of God is being revealed from heaven against all the godlessness and wickedness of men who suppress the truth of God by their wickedness (Romans 1:18). Even though you may think that you are getting by, God sees all and will eventually judge all. Never think that God isn't conscience of the wrong that you are doing. Think God for grace and mercy because if it wasn't for them most of us would be dead for continuing to do things our own way.

Developing a Good Conscience

So how do you develop a good conscience? You develop a good conscience by constantly replenishing your mind or soul with the word of God. Your thought process has to experience a complete transformation. Transformation of any type never occurs instantaneously. Transformation usually signifies changing from one form to another. The first step in the transformation process is gaining knowledge of what you are transforming to. Contrary to the movie transformers, we are not able to change from a human to some other type of life form. The transformation that we experience is a spiritual transformation.

Paul writes in Romans 12:2, "Do not conform any longer to the pattern of this world, but be transformed by the renewing of your mind (NIV)." This suggests that the first component of man that has to experience change is the mind. If we don't change our mind, then we will still be in bondage to the desires of our sinful flesh, and we will only be able to hear whatever our carnal mind and fleshly body speaks. We have to clean our minds and purify our hearts because by nature we are all children of wrath.

We have wicked devices and wrong motives that have to be changed into integrity for uprightness and proper intentions of the heart that please God. A constant intake of the word of God will begin to change our minds, which will gradually change our actions. This is why Jesus told the Pharisees to first clean up the inside of the cup and then the outside would follow. It's because once the inside becomes a clean place for God's Spirit to reside, then he will come in and take residence in your heart.

When God is on the inside of you he begins to affect your other senses. He affects your sense of feel because he will no longer allow you to touch the things you use to touch. He keeps you from putting your hand into the wrong "cookie jar." He affects your sense of taste by taking away your appetite for "unwholesome food." He let's you know that man can not live by bread alone but by every word that proceeds out of the mouth of God. You have tasted and now you see that the Lord is "Um Um good." He affects your sense of smell by killing the bad things that use to lure you in by their aroma. Ecclesiastes 10:1 states, "...dead flies give perfume a bad smell..."

Everything that smelled good to your flesh before, now gives the smell of a cheap perfume to your spirit. We talked earlier how Christ affects your sense of sight by giving you a new set of eyes. At one point you had eyes but you couldn't see the destruction that you were headed to. You didn't see the traps that Satan had placed in your path in an attempt to detour you from your purpose. Now our eyes have been opened. We have shifted our eyes to the Lord and now he is leading us through his eyes. Psalms 123:2 says, "As the eyes of slaves look to the hand of their master, as the eyes of a maid look to the hand of her mistress, so our eyes look to the Lord our God, till he shows us his mercy (NIV)."

Even though through our carnal eyes we may see a lot of chaos and trouble in this world, through the eyes of the Spirit we see the grace and mercy that God has given us. Our future no longer looks dreadful, but now we look forward to the blessed hope of seeing our Savior face to face.

Last but not least, our sense of hearing begins to change. A relationship with God gives the believer spiritual "hearing aids." When at one time you could only hear the voice of the body, and at one time you could only hear the voice of your mind, now you are able to hear clearly the voice of the Spirit. He begins to tell you which way to go. He begins to instruct you what you should do. He changes your direction. John 8:47 states, "He who belongs to God hears what God says. The reason you do not hear is that you do not belong to God (NIV)." The word belong signifies ownership. Before the spirit can accurately guide you without the constant interference of the other voices that are within you, you have to give up your rights to yourself.

Giving Up Your Ownership Rights

Many of us said God I will give you my mind but you can't have my body. God I will give you my body, but you can't have my spirit. If you have yet to give yourself totally to God then you will not hear him because you don't belong to him. When you continue to listen to these other voices that are speaking and you are continually using your body as an instrument to do wrong, then you have given Satan "ownership" of your life. 2 Corinthians 1:21 says, "Now it is God who makes both us and you stand firm in Christ. He anointed us, set his seal of ownership on us, and put his Spirit in our hearts as a deposit, guaranteeing what is to come (NIV)."

As you can see you are not your own. Christ purchased you with the shedding of his blood on Calvary. When you draw closer to the realization of this simple yet powerful truth and welcome the Spirit into your heart, then you can rest assured knowing that God has a "guaranteed" future for you. You need to believe and know the truth. Once you have gained the knowledge of this truth, then you have to continue in his word. You can't quit.

You can't approach the word of God with your own ideologies and philosophies. Our own philosophies can eventually lead to a "seared conscience" that has its own idea of truth, which rejects the truth of the word of God. As they continue to act against their conscience eventually their personal convictions becomes their religion and not only will they not accept truth, but they will not even be able to recognize truth beyond their own beliefs.

We just discussed that those who belong to God hear his voice. If your conscience has been seared then you can no longer hear from God. If you can't hear from God, then the Bible says that you don't "belong" to God. This is a dangerous place that no one wants to be in. That's why it's important that you have a good conscience, one in which the Spirit can communicate with. The more you read God's word, the deeper your faith will become, the purer your heart will become and the better your conscience will become. Now the Spirit can begin to lead you. As Paul writes, "The goal of this command is love, which comes from a pure heart and a good conscience and a sincere faith (1 Tim 1:5 NIV)."

The Voice of the Devil

We have talked about the three different voices that are all part of the makeup of man. However, there is one voice that we left out that is constantly speaking to God's people. This is the voice of devil. The devil has a way of manipulating all of the other three voices that are at work within us in order to steer us away from the plan of God. This is the same tactic that he attempted to use on Jesus. He tried to appeal to Jesus' voice of body, his voice of soul, and even his voice of spirit.

After Jesus had been baptized by John at the Sea of Galilee, and the Spirit had lightened on him, immediately he was led by the Spirit into the desert to be tempted by the devil. However, the "tempter" didn't come to Jesus until after he had fastened forty days. No doubt at this time the Spirit within him would have been strong, but his physical man would be exceptionally weak.

Doesn't it seem as though the devil speaks to you most when you have had to endure a very tough battle in the physical? When you are busted, disgusted, and on the verge of physical exasperation, then he comes and attempts to push you completely over the edge. Many times the Spirit will allow this to happen intentionally. He wants to make sure you can still recognize his voice when the other voices of the body have increased their volume. Let's take a look at the dialogue between the devil and Jesus as recorded in the book of Matthew.

> After fasting forty days and forty nights, he was hungry. The tempter came to him and said, "If you are the Son of God, tell these stones to become bread (Matthew 4:3 NIV)."

Satan loves to come to you when you are at a weak point in your life and tempt you with the very thing that you have been lacking. For instance, Jesus had been without food for 40 days and night. His body would no doubt be yearning for some sort of physical nourishment to fill the emptiness that he been experiencing. Satan was appealing to two of Christ's voices: the voice of the body and the voice of the soul. Stomach growls and hunger pains were speaking louder now then ever before. A morsel of bread would go a long way when you haven't eaten in 40 days. The hunger pains in his stomach were probably telling him that this must be God making a way for him to satisfy a hunger.

As it relates to the voice of the soul, or the voice of reasoning, it would make perfect sense to turn the rock into bread. After all, he hadn't eaten in 40 days. His body and his soul were now working together in an attempt to trick him into satisfying their desires, rather than satisfying the Spirit of God. He would have been settling for less than the best that God wanted to give him.

Beware of Satan's Deception

Don't be fooled in your time of weakness within your flesh. The devil is very crafty and he plans accordingly for the right time to make his move. He's like an army general strategically studying his opponent in order to find a weakness that he can exploit. Some of you have been praying for a spouse, and because your flesh is at war within you, and your hormones are raging out of control you choose to settle for the first person that tickles your fancy. You say to yourself, "It must be God because he knows I "NEED" a companion. We so often confuse our wants for our needs. God said in his word that he would supply all of our needs according to his riches in glory (Philippians 4:13). However, when we fell to differentiate need versus want then we are more susceptible to the deception of the enemy.

You have to understand that your adversary is at work studying your every move. He knew that you had been looking for a spouse for a long time. To make matters worst he knew exactly what qualities' you were looking for in a companion. Therefore he found the perfect person who fit your personal preferences on the external, but inwardly they were full of manipulation and deceit. Matthew 7:15 says, "Watch out for false prophets. They come to you in sheep's clothing, but inwardly they are ferocious wolves (NIV)." Just because a person looks the par, says the right things, and comes to you when you feel like you are in dire need of companionship, doesn't mean that is the person that God has for you. As children of God we have to learn how to wait on God's timing and not allow our emotions and intellect to lead us.

No matter what it is you have been lacking, as long as you are satisfied with Jesus, then he will sustain you until you receive what he has for you without you having to compromise. As hungry as Jesus was he knew that he needed the word of God more than anything else. Jesus overcame the temptation to cooperate with the enemy, by abiding in the word of God. Jesus answered the devil and said, "...It is written, Man shall not live by bread alone, but every word that comes from the mouth of God (Matthew 4:4 NIV)." Jesus ignored the voice of his body and the voice of his soul. He was also able to ignore the voice of the devil by following the voice of his spirit which was in harmony with the Spirit of God. The devil didn't stop there, he kept on speaking.

Maintaining Your Defenses

Whenever you successfully ignore the voice of the devil then he goes back and reevaluates his strategy in order to successfully prepare a counter attack. This is why you have to make sure that you don't dwell on past success. Whenever you allow yourself to become too satisfied with a past success, then you are more prone to lower your defenses. Often when the enemy comes back for round two of the battle he catches you with your guards lowered and he delivers a blow which could potentially be a knockout. The children of God should always retain their guard even after great triumphs in order to defend against the enemy's constant onslaughts.

After Jesus had avoided the first temptation that the devil attempted to use against him, he came back twice more, only this time he centered predominantly on the voice of the spirit. The first thing he tells him to do is to throw himself down from the top of the temple reminding him that because he is the Son of God, God wouldn't permit not even his feet to dash against a stone. Satan attempted to distort the meaning of the word of God against the son of God. If Satan would attempt to distort the meaning of the word of God against his own son, then we know that we are no exception. In fact Satan has been doing this since the beginning of time.

The Bible calls Satan the father of all lies (John 8:44). He told Eve that she wouldn't die by eating the forbidden fruit. On the contrary he promised her that by doing so she would become like God. Adam and Eve made a conscience decision to believe Satan rather than the word of God and as a result brought death not only to themselves, but to every person that would be born to woman thus after. This may seem extreme compared to him telling Jesus to tempt God. However, if Satan can get you to compromise in a small matter, then he can also do the same in the bigger matters. Notice the formula.

Understanding Satan's Battle Strategy

He begins with information. He quotes the word of God to you, while purposely leaving out important details. He knows that your conscious will only convict you based on the information that you have taken in. This is vital because any distortion of the word of God can give us a false sense of security in the decision that we are making not knowing that we are in error heading for sure destruction. As I have stated numerous times before, we have to constantly fill our minds with the truth of the word of God in order to avoid the lies that Satan is attempting to tell us. If he can take away your convictions then he has you right where he wants you.

He can then tell you anything and you will believe it to be true. I truly believe that this is the reason why so many people are calling right wrong and wrong right. Satan has deceived and is still deceiving many people by misrepresenting truth. He loves for us to focus on the love of God and make us blind to wrath of God. Psalms 50:22 states, "Consider this, you who forget God, or I will tear you to pieces, with none to rescue (NIV)." How does one forget God? We forget God by not abiding in his word. God will judge disobedience of his word whether it's in this life, or in the judgment, you want be able to escape his wrath.

Satan doesn't want you to know this though. That's why he tells us it's ok to commit certain sins because God is faithful to forgive us. He loves to harp on the longsuffering and forgiveness of God. He loves to remind us how God's grace is surely sufficient for us. He doesn't want you to know that any misuse of God's grace will be punished to the fullest extent. Although the grace of God is sufficient for us, this doesn't give us a license to habitually sin against him. Premeditated sins will eventually lead to imminent judgment. All the ways of man are before the Lord and he gazes deep into the heart to see man's true intentions. In spite of this fact many still abuse the grace of God and continue to sin against God having a clear conscience not knowing that they are storing up wrath for themselves.

Don't Put God to the Test

The Bible says that our sins will find us out. We have many examples in the Bible of people who have put God to the test by sinning against him only to face sudden destruction. The very thing that you are doing to tempt God could be the very thing that leads to your demise. When the children of Israel were in the wilderness, many of them begin to tempt God by participating in satanic religious practices which involved placing snakes on their bodies as a form of occult worship. This direct sin of idolatry led to the lost of many lives due to snake bites (1 Corinthians 10:9).

Another example of blatantly tempting God was the tragic story of Ananias and Sapphira recorded in Acts 5. Ananias and Sapphira sold a piece of property and kept back part of the money for themselves. Ananias then carried the remaining money and laid it at the Apostles feet, however he informed them that what he was given them was everything that he had made from the sell.

Not only was this lie premeditated but it was unnecessary. The money belonged to him. The Apostles hadn't made any claims to any percentage of the money. Ananias and Sapphira had the right to do whatever they wanted to do with the money. Yet in order to appear to be something that they weren't, they concealed how much they really made and lied to the Holy Spirit with no shame. They conspired to tempt God with a lie and suffered an untimely death because of it. While the last two examples were obvious examples of tempting God, many times the temptation is not as obvious.

In Exodus 17 the children of Israel begin to grumble against Moses because they had been led to a place where there was no water. They lacked the faith to trust God to provide like he had done so many times before. They didn't realize that there complaining was not just a disrespect to their leader Moses, but worst yet they were guilty of tempting God. The mere fact that they were grumbling and complaining showed that they questioned whether or not God was even with them. This may have very well been what Satan was attempting to do to Jesus, make him question whether God was really with him in his "wilderness experience."

Have you ever complained against God because of a situation you were going through? In all fairness all of us have at some point in our life. What we fell to realize however is that our complaining could be tempting God. We should never tempt God by complaining so much about our situation that we begin questioning whether or not he is with us. When we do this we are guilty of questioning the faithfulness of his word because he has already promised us that he would never leave us nor forsake us. Jesus was determined that he wouldn't let Satan corrupt his conscience. No matter what his situation looked like, he knew that God was with him and he didn't need to tempt God to make sure of this fact.

Satan's Last Stand

Satan had tried twice, with no avail, to get Jesus to listen to his voice instead of the voice of the Spirit. He tried to get Jesus to turn stones into bread. After failing with this plea he attempted again, this time in an attempt to convince Jesus to tempt God. This attempt was also unsuccessful. He had one more trick up his sleeve. His last crack at breaking Jesus was to offer him all the kingdoms of the world if he would bow down and worship him. At this point you can see that Satan is becoming irritated with Jesus. He has tried two consecutive times to break Jesus and has failed miserably. Satan now has no choice but to pull out the big guns.

As I stated earlier each time that you successfully resist the devil, he will go back and rethink his approach, and come back stronger than ever before. While Satan is coming back loaded with more ammo, physically Jesus is becoming weaker and weaker. Keep in mind that each second that goes by is another second that he has gone without food. This is how the enemy attacks believers still today. He is constantly studying your every move trying to find one Achilles' heel that he can use against you.

As I stated earlier Satan, just like any enemy, is not going to attack you when you are at your strongest, he wants to attack you at your weakest point. This is a common combat tactic used by everyone from war generals to the common everyday street fighter. If I can hit my opponent when and where he least expects it then I can gain the upper hand. While I'm on the opposing team, I must admit that what Satan did was very clever and profound. In Jesus' weakness he offers him something that he already has procession of. Think about that for a second. Satan offers Jesus dominion over all the kingdoms of the world and great glory. Jesus, while in the outward appearance of a man, was beyond doubt God. David had already written in Psalms 24:1 that, "...The earth is the LORD's and everything in it, the world, and all who live in it..."

The entire universe and everything that encompassed it already belonged to God. All the glory, all the dominion, and all the power were at his disposal. Wait a minute. Since Satan knew this why would he attempt to offer Jesus something that already belonged to him? That's just like someone borrowing my shirt and then attempting to sell it back to me. Was Satan losing his mind? The answer is no. In fact it was a brilliant effort on his part. What Satan was hoping was that due to Jesus' current circumstance, being devoid of nourishment, that he wouldn't be "conscience" of the fact that everything, including Satan, belonged to him. He was hoping that Jesus wouldn't be thinking clearly and would jump at this once in a lifetime opportunity.

Don't Compromise in Times of Distress

Satan is attempting to persuade the believers in this day to accept his many offers. In your distress, in your lack, and in your desolation he whispers to you and tells you that I can make it all better. He promises wealth and power. He offers to give you public notice all if you would just worship him. Most people say that they will never worship Satan no matter what he offers. What happens, however, when the mortgage and the car note are both due, but you just lost your job? Your mortgage provider has called your home and informed you that if you don't have the money within a month that they will foreclose. The car dealer has already come back and repossessed your car and you only had 7 more payments left on it.

You try to stay optimistic and believe that God has given you dominion, however right now your circumstances are telling you something different. Your spirit man feels as though it is at the brink of depletion. Even your physical body is declining due to the constant stress of worrying how you are going to maintain in your season of drought. Nevertheless you remain faithful to God and to your local church assembly. You submit your resume to your local temporary agency and you also submit resumes in your respective job fields hoping to land a job.

You pray and ask God to open up a door for you to gain employment. One day you get a call about a job. The job is for an office administrator at a clinical facility. Your job responsibilities would include typing, preparing charts for patients, and answering incoming phone calls, while making some outbound calls. With your extensive background with computers and excellent organizational skills you more than exceed the qualifications for the position.

You then ask the question, what about weekends, in particular Sundays, since you don't want to compromise church time? They tell you that the office is closed on Sunday, but you may work occasional Saturdays but it would only be for half a day. That sounds more than reasonable to you. Also they inform you that this job will pay 30% more in salary than what you earned on your previous job and would include a 401K plan, an excellent benefit package, and a paid vacation package that trumps that of any job you have ever worked. They tell you if you want the job then you can start immediately.

This seems too good to be true. Nevertheless, you jump for joy believing that all of your prayers have been answered and your season of drought is now over. You go to the job the beginning of the following week to begin your training. Once there, you quickly see that they left out some very important details concerning the job. This wouldn't be your normal clinical job. This is an abortion clinic which goes strongly against your pro-life standing.

To add to that they tell you that you will be on call on Sundays' in case an emergency came up. So you may have to leave church to go prepare a chart for someone who was going to commit murder. This is a stark contradiction to the word of God and you know it. Nevertheless, you quickly revert back to the fact that you would be making more money than you have ever made in your life. You believe that this job would no doubt position you to be successful.

Temporary Compromises Will Have Permanent Consequences

As I stated earlier the world views success by how much "stuff" you possess. If you have a good job, nice home, nice car, and money in the bank then you are considered successful. Many people will stop at nothing to be successful. What's worst is that many will sacrifice anything even if it means compromising their relationship with God in order to be considered successful. All it takes is one compromise to take us out of the plan of God. All it takes is one of seed of compromise to cause us to give our faith to things rather than God.

Satan is aware of this fact and he preys on people's greed. He tells us all the things that he will give us if we would only just bow down and worship him. When you choose to pursue material processions before you pursue Christ then you are bowing down to Satan. Also, when you choose to compromise your walk with God in order to gain status in this world, then you are bowing down to Satan. It's not always easy to recognize when we are compromising. That's why Jesus told his disciples, "…Take heed, and beware of covetousness: for a man's life consisteth not in the abundance of the things which he possesseth (Luke 12:15 KJV)."

The word covetousness used here literally means an extreme desire for material wealth. It can also be translated as an excessive desire to acquire or possess more, especially more material wealth, than one need or deserves. One of the biggest problems with most people is that they can't be content with what they have. A common saying among many is, "I want more." They want more money. They want more clothes. They want more cars.

They want more women. They want more men. They believe that if they have more then this will solve all their problems.

The longing for more is the oil that keeps our culture's lamps burning. The lottery lines are loaded with countless people all trying to strike it rich. Publishers Clearing House is getting new subscriptions each day from people who believe they could be their ticket to a stress free life. Drug dealers are perpetually recruiting more and more of our youth to employ in order to make them rich. Our youth are falling victim to their proposals because of the glamour that this lifestyle promises. The church is not exempt either from compromise.

Great singers in the church are being enticed to sing different genres of music because of the money and fame that it will provide. Pastors are watering down their messages because some of the people who are doing wrong are giving the biggest tithes. There are also many people who are choosing to work tons of overtime at work or get second jobs just to satisfy their hunger for the best things in life. In the process their church attendance has become slim to nonexistent. The debt crisis, the crime rate, and even the increased stress in our world can all be attributed to compromises that have been made. Compromises of any type can usually be traced back to a lack of contentment.

Godliness with Contentment

A person with a lack of contentment is an easy target for the devil's attacks. When he knows that you are not content with what you have then he can easily trick you into accepting what appear to be blessings but are really just counterfeits. A true counterfeit will resemble the real thing, but if you look closely you will begin to see inconsistencies. Being content is not something that comes easy. It takes discipline, it takes trust, but it yields great rewards. Hebrews 13:5 says, "Keep your life free from love of money and be content with what you have, because God has said, 'Never will I leave you; never will I forsake you (NIV).'"

We are given a stern warning from the writer of the book of Hebrews to keep ourselves free from the love of money. This is because the love of money is one of the main vices Satan uses to ensnare God's children. He wants us to have more faith in money than we do God. Therefore when he attacks our money and material possessions he can at the same time attack our faith. This is why many have lost hope and they walk around with their heads hung down constantly complaining about what they don't have. Some people are so wrapped up in their money and possessions that if they lose them they would also lose their reason to live.

Your possessions should never be the definitive reason that you choose to live. When you are satisfied with Jesus then you know how to be content when you have money and when you don't. You have reached a placed to know that no matter what it looks like God is still faithful, and he has promised never to leave you. You might not see how things are going to turn around, but you know that even though you may be jobless, God can and will make a way. The world hears this mindset and calls it crazy. They say that only the poor people have this mindset. Obviously they never read the book of Psalms. King David said in Psalms 37:25, "I was young and now I am old, yet I have never seen the righteous forsaken or their children begging bread (NIV)."

David surveyed his entire life from his youth to his senior. This survey would include the days from him being in the field tending to the sheep, to the days he spent hiding in caves and being fed from his enemies tables, to the days of his Kingship. Not once had David seen the righteous forsaken or God's children begging for bread. Many say that you can't use this as a blanket statement to cover all believers. They say that this story is only relevant from the perspective of David's eyes. I beg to differ from this perspective. To suggest that this particular scripture reference only applies to David would be admitting that God at times forsakes his children.

We know that's not true because he promised never to leave his children. Even if you have to miss some meals sometimes, even if you lost your job, even though they may have foreclosed on your home, as the righteousness of God you still have the assurance that God is right there with you and it helps you count all of your loss as gain, knowing that the trying of your faith is producing patience within you. At the end of all of this, if you remain faithful and thus content, you will be perfect lacking nothing. Just like God sustained the children of Israel forty years in the wilderness with no lack, he will do the same thing for you. Contentment is the key. When we, as the children of God, learn how to be content, we will never have to want for anything again. Let's examine what Paul told Timothy concerning being content.

> But godliness with contentment is great gain. For we brought nothing into the world, and we can take nothing out of it. But if we have food and clothing, we will be content with that. People who want to get rich fall into temptation and a trap and into many foolish and harmful desires that plunge men into ruin and destruction. For the love of money is a root of all kinds of evil. Some people, eager for money, have wandered from the faith and pierced themselves with many griefs. 1 Timothy 6:6-10 NIV

Paul was warning Timothy to be aware of the false teachers among them who were preaching a prosperity gospel, rather than the Gospel of Jesus Christ. These men were equating godliness with how much a person possessed. The more a person had, the godlier that person was considered to be. Paul painted a clear picture to contest this incorrect view of godliness. He tells Timothy that we brought nothing into this world and we wouldn't be able to carry anything out of it. Therefore we should be thankful for the fact that God clothes us and gives us food to eat. That is true godliness. True godliness is being thankful for the small things that we sometimes take for granted.

I use to hear the old people say in church, "I think him for a portion of my health and strength." I didn't understand it when I was younger, but it makes perfect sense now. They were saying that although they may have had a few aches in there body, they were still thankful because it could have been a whole lot worst. They would go on and say, "I'm thankful for having food on the table and clothes on my back." They might not have had filet mignon on the table every night, but they were thankful for the homemade bread and fried chicken that they did have. They might not have had the most expensive clothes, but they were thankful that the clothes they did have on kept them warm.

They had learned the secret to being thankful in whatever situation they found themselves in. To have this positive outlook on life is the greatest gain in the world. It gives you peace in the midst of chaos. It gives you joy in the midst of sorrow. It takes away the stress of trying to keep up with the Jones'. It gives you the patience to wait on God's timing. You will stop trying to figure out how to do things on your own. Rather you will be able to rest patiently and contently until God comes through for you. Most of all it helps you keep your heart fixed on those things that are eternal.

Build Your Hope on Things Eternal

As believers, our main goal in life should be to get as close to God as we possibly can. When God sees that your heart is not concerned with gaining worldly success then he will impart the true riches of his word to you. God will open up your spiritual eyes and begin to impart divine revelation to you. Often times God will even gift you with wisdom and knowledge and with talents that will enable you to acquire great wealth just as he did for King Solomon because his heart was right. The favor of God will posture you to accomplish great deeds and possess belongings that money could never grant you. However, you have to make sure that getting rich is not your primary aim.

As we see in the text above those who desire to be rich will fall into a snare that leads to temptation and foolish and harmful lust which will lead to destruction. Satan is not just seeking to destroy people's lives with drug addictions, sexually transmitted diseases, or murders due to terrible acts of violence. Satan is using the world's lust for riches against them. The love of money is the root of all kinds of evil. Satan is using something that God never meant to be sinful as means to steer people away from God. Notice I didn't say that Satan forces you away. Satan couldn't force you to do anything. He can only show you the bait, but you don't have to take it.

Don't let your love for money lead you away from your faith. Learn how to be content with God and him alone. Remember everything that you need has already been given to you. God has already promised you that you would be the head and not the tail. He already promised you that you would be the lender and not the borrower. He already declared that you would have dominion in this world. Don't let Satan's counterfeit blessings rob you of the authentic blessings that God has already given you. It might not look like it right now, but God has already declared that you were blessed.

Jesus knew that he already had the key to abundant life. Satan couldn't trick him in his wilderness experience to bow down to him. He knew that if he resisted the enemy, with the word of God, that Satan would have to flee. That's why when Satan offered Jesus all the cities of the world if he would worship him Jesus could boldly say, "Be gone, Satan! For it is written, you shall worship the Lord your God and him only shall you serve." Satan had no choice but to leave at that very moment. Jesus would let nothing the devil said cause him to give God's worship to another. All the devil wants is to be able to rob God of his praise. He feels as though that praise belongs to him. Everything that he says to you will always be in an attempt to revert praise back to him. Nothing makes him happier than knowing that he caused someone to listen to him, rather than God.

Victory over Satan

We fight a very realistic battle against the enemy. As long as you live he will be continually speaking to you trying to make you deter from God's preordained plan for your life. You have to learn how to distinguish his voice from the voice of the Spirit. Remember everything that he tells you to do will always in some form or another shift glory to him rather than God. You should always examine the motives for any decision that you make in life. You do this by making sure it's in accordance with God's word.

As in the case with Jesus everything that Satan tells you to do will go in stark contrast with the word of God. Meditate on his word day and night. Safeguard it in your mind and in your heart. Pray the word of God everyday. When you pray the word of God, you pray the will of God. In fact the word of God will begin to align your prayers to be in accordance with His word. Then when Satan begins speaking to you, even in your time of weakness, you will be able to resist him and put him to flight with the word that's hidden in your heart. Then and only then will you truly have victory over Satan.

The Voice of the Spirit of God

We have talked about the other voices that are at work in man. We discussed the voice of the body, the voice of the soul, the voice of the spirit of man, and lastly the voice of the devil. Yet the most important voice that we should all be striving to hear is neither one of these voices. Our main goal in life should be to effectively interpret the voice of the Spirit of God from all the other voices that are at work in us and around us. This is the voice that will give us instruction. This is the voice that will determine our direction. This is also the voice that will lead and guide us into the purpose that God has for our life.

With that being said this is the only voice that all of us should be striving to hear clearly everyday. While this may be true, modern psychology will tell you something different. It tells us that the voice of reasoning and human understanding should be the primary voices that we listen to. Sigmund Freud, the father of modern psychology, speculated that there were three main forces in man's life: the *id*, the *ego*, and the *superego*. According to Freud's model of the psyche the id is the set of uncoordinated instinctual trends; the ego is the organized, realistic part; and the super-ego plays the critical and moralizing role.[2] For illustration purposes I want to focus particularly on the id.

Overcoming Our Selfish Natures

The id encompasses the unorganized part of the personality structure that contains the basic drives. The id is responsible for our basic drives such as food, water, sex, and basic impulses. It is amoral, selfish, seeks pleasure and never pain, needs immediate satisfaction, and doesn't take no for an answer. Doesn't that sound just like us? For starters by nature we tend to be selfish people. Case in point Adam and Eve who had access to every tree in the garden accept for one and lost it all chasing the only one that they couldn't have. For the most part we also hate taking no for an answer and usually require immediate satisfaction. This lack of patience leads us into

2   Snowden, Ruth (2006). *Teach Yourself Freud*. McGraw-Hill. pp. 105–107. ISBN 9780071472746.

making hasty decisions which usually only offer temporary gratification to our flesh and does little to nothing for our spiritual man.

This brings me to my next point. By nature we usually seek pleasure and do everything we can to avoid pain. This is a common fact that is shared between all humanity. As it relates to the Spirit, he doesn't always speak through pleasure. Neither does the Spirit always offer immediate gratification. The Spirit doesn't lead us in ways that are always pleasurable to us; neither will his answer always be "yes" to all our demands. Therefore, to effectively recognize the voice of the Spirit, we have to be conscious of the many ways that he speaks. If we are only looking for him to speak through pleasure then we will never be able to accurately recognize his voice. If we only expect him to speak in ways that fit into our prearranged agenda, then we will miss him every time. As it is written, "For my thoughts are not your thoughts, neither are your ways my ways," declares the LORD (Isaiah 55:8 NIV).

Since his thoughts are not our thoughts, nor are his ways our ways, then there is no way to effectively determine exactly how God will speak. Instead we have to realign our thinking to be in accordance with His word to make sure that when he does speak we don't miss it. We have to learn the many ways that God's Spirit speaks and trust him enough to follow him even if it doesn't make sense to us. Let's take a look at some of the many ways the Spirit speaks to his people.

The Spirit Speaks through Trouble

"The Beginning of purpose does not start out with fulfillment, it starts out with pain." -Thomas Dexter Jakes

A lot of people believe that the Spirit of God always chooses to speak to us through the favorable times in our life. When doors are opening up then we normally equate this as a sign that the Spirit is speaking. Through the years I have discovered that success is not always birthed through good times. In fact perseverance and successes are more often than not born out of trials and out of pain. Douglas Moo states that various kinds of sufferings will come to us, but we can rejoice in them when we recognize that they serve a purpose: to develop our Christian character.[3] 1 Peter 4:12 says, "…do not be surprised at the painful trial you are suffering, as though something strange were happening to you (NIV)."

Self-consciously we tend to attribute trials and tribulations as punishment for our wrong doing. That's not always the case. Whether it's the death of a love one, the dissolution of a relationship, or the lost of a job, pain will be a prevalent part of all of our lives. Pain is an unavoidable bridge that we will frequently have to cross. 2 Timothy 2:3 says, "Endure hardship with us like a good soldier of Christ Jesus (NIV)." Paul was writing to his protégé Timothy to give him fair warning that just like him, he would have to endure hardships. As a result Timothy wouldn't think that his suffering was a response to his wrongdoing. Rather it was a "shared" burden that all believers would have to bear. The writer of the book of Hebrews writes the following:

> And you have forgotten that word of encouragement that addresses you as sons: "My son, do not make light of the Lord's discipline, and do not lost heart when he rebukes you, because the Lord disciplines those he loves, and he punishes everyone he accepts as a son."(Hebrews 12:5-6 NIV)

Suffering, in doing right, identifies you as a child of God. It shows that God loves you and accepts you as a child. That's why we can't give up during tough times because your perseverance during tough times will yield great results. Don't let life's adversaries stagnate you. On the contrary, you have to keep pushing through the many adversaries that life will throw at you. The devil wants to make you quit. He wants to make you believe that the pain that you are facing is too tough for you to handle. As a student of the Bible however we should know that God wouldn't put more on us then we are able to bear. The discipline that we are experiencing is not because God doesn't love us. It's also not because he get's enjoyment out of seeing his children suffer.

---

3   Moo, Douglas J. "Encountering the Book of Romans." (Grand Rapids:: Baker Academic) 102.

Contrarily the discipline of the Lord shows his love for his children. While no pain feels good, some pain that we have to endure is good for us. The only enjoyment that God get's out of disciplining his children is having the reassurance that his discipline is making us better. His discipline is providing instruction that will in turn shape your direction and if you learn to embrace it, it will lead you to destiny. A father doesn't always discipline a child because they have done wrong. A father disciplines a child in order to give them proper instruction on how to deal with certain issues in life usually before the child has to encounter that specific issue. Therefore, when you do make it to that bridge in life you won't be stuck on the opposite end not knowing how to cross.

The Discipline of the Lord is Shaping Your Future

The discipline that you're enduring in your present is preparing you for what you are going to have to handle in your future. If we can endure the pain, then there is a reward waiting for us. That's why the woman in labor continues to push, because she knows that her perseverance through the temporary pain that she has to endure will give birth to a reward that she can enjoy for a lifetime. The reason why the athlete continues to push, even though the pain is sometimes severe, is because he knows that his persistent will yield great results. You have to make up in your mind that no matter what you may have to endure, you will continue to push forward toward the prize that God has for you. The Apostle Paul puts it best when he states, "For our light and momentary troubles are achieving for us an eternal glory that far outweighs them all. So we fix our eyes not on what is seen, but on what is unseen. For what is seen is temporary, but what is unseen is eternal (2 Corinthians 4:17-18 NIV)."

You have to approach your problems with a state of optimism knowing that this too will pass. Your issue that you are going through is not eternal. It was not intended to be your end. There is always joy connected to your problem. David lets us know this in Psalms 30 when he declares, "For his anger lasts only a moment, but his favor lasts a lifetime; weeping may remain for a night, but rejoicing comes in the morning (Psalms

30:5 NIV)." This is a very common scripture that most Christians can quote from memory. However, many times we fail to look deeper into the meaning of the text. Most people believe that because the scripture declares that joy will come in the morning then that means that their problem must be over. We usually only get excited because we believe that our trouble is about to come to an end, however that's not what the text says.

How Much Longer Lord?

The scripture says his anger lasts only a moment, but his favor lasts a lifetime. Moment and lifetime each indicate a period of time. One of these is an exact period of time and the other one is open for interpretation. If someone says give me a moment then that could mean anywhere from a couple minutes to several hours. However, when something is for a lifetime then that signifies the remainder of one's life. For example let's say for instance a guy is interested in dating a specific young woman. He asks her if she will be interested in going out with him and her response is, "you would have to wait a lifetime to go out with me." Naturally this response would provide a feeling of rejection in the guy. He would pretty much know that the two of them wouldn't have much of a chance of developing a more serious relationship.

Let's look at this same scenario from the other end of the spectrum. Let's say he approaches the young woman and proposes the same question and her response is, "let me take a moment to think about it." This response would invoke a great feeling of optimism in the young man. Even though she didn't immediately say yes, there is a possibility that she may say yes considering the fact that she didn't instantaneously answer no. The young man has a great feeling of hope because he knows that it could be any second, any hour, any day before she actually does say yes.

Again, if she wanted to say know she would have done so already. The young man tries to keep his emotions in tack but he can't help but rejoice even though it's a painstaking process to have to wait, however he has hope that this pain will bring about great results. In all actuality he is rejoicing for something that hasn't even happened yet. The truth is she could still say no. However, with each passing moment that goes by without her saying no, his anxiety is slowly changing more to hope because the possibility for a yes seems more and more likely.

It's Just Temporary

We have to learn how to rejoice even in the midst of our problems knowing that our issues are only temporary but his favor endures for a lifetime. Let's use a Biblical example in order to bring this point full circle. In the Book of Daniel we are introduced to three young Jewish men from Judah by the name of Shadrach, Meshach, and Abednego who have been taken captive by the Babylonians during the first deportation of the Israelites. King Nebuchadnezzar, king of Babylon, erects a statue of himself and makes a decree which commanded all to fall and worship the monument when the instruments played. Anyone who didn't bow down and worship the statue would be thrown into a fiery furnace.

Shadrach, Meshach, and Abednego refused to bow down and worship the statue. The king called the three men in to give them one more opportunity to worship him or else they would face sudden destruction. The three men replied, "...If we are thrown into the blazing furnace, the God we serve is able to save us from it, and he will rescue us from your hand, O king. But even if he does not, we want you to know, O king, that we will not serve your gods or worship the image of gold you have set up (Daniel 3:17-18 NIV)." In spite of the imminent danger that awaited the three young men because of their refusal to bow down to the image, they were still able to give God praise. Why? They understood that their situation would only last for a moment, but the favor of God that was on their life would last a lifetime. Therefore, they could approach their situation with great joy not because God had already delivered them, but because they knew that he could.

As Christians we should learn how to rejoice even in the midst of life's most difficult circumstances. Sure their will be nights when we will cry. Their will be times when we will feel like giving up. Yet if we would just stop and consider the grace and mercy of God, then our entire disposition will begin to change. God said in his word that He will give us a garment of praise for the spirit of heaviness. When we consider the pain that Christ had to endure on the cross just so we would have a chance to receive salvation then it will make our mere light afflictions seem obsolete. Instead of complaining it will make you say "thank you Lord." David said, "But I have trusted in thy mercy; my heart shall rejoice in thy salvation (Psalms 13:5 KJV)."

A Heavenly Trust

The key word behind David's rejoicing was "trust." This wasn't just an ordinary trust, but this was a heavenly trust. This type of trust is only born through relationship. David could rejoice in the salvation of the Lord because God had "saved" him so many times before. Even from David's youth he knew God as his savior. God had protected him in the wilderness when the wild animals attempted to attack his sheep. God delivered him from the Philistine giant Goliath who had defied the armies of Israel and attempted to take his life. Even when Saul attempted to kill David on many different occasions, God delivered him from his hands every time. David didn't just have a familiarity with God as savior, he personally knew God as his savior. Shadrach, Meshach, and Abednego possessed this same "heavenly trust."

A heavenly trust allows you to focus on those things that are eternal and not so much on those things that are temporary. The three young men were able to look past their pending death sentence and focus entirely on God. They knew that even if God didn't deliver them that he was still able and they would continue to praise God no matter how bad their situation looked. As children of God we have to maintain this heavenly trust even through great pain and distress. Often times God will use our pain as an avenue to speak his will into our life. Let's look at Paul for example. Paul was imprisoned several times, three times he was beaten with rods, once he was stoned, three times he was shipwrecked, and at various times throughout his life he had to go without food and without sleep, but through all of this he never became bitter towards God.

Instead, Paul understood that as long as his pain was bringing glory to God then it would be all worth it in the end. Paul also knew that through his pain, through his trials, and through his often public humiliations that

God was going to speak his divine purpose for his life. Looking at Paul's situation from a carnal mindset one could easily say that Paul had a right to question God concerning everything that he had to go through when you compare it to everything that he had accomplished for God. After all Paul was, and is still recognized today as the greatest of the Apostles. He is the author of thirteen out of the twenty-seven books of the New Testament. Great signs and wonders followed Paul's ministry.

Paul accomplished all of these great deeds and he wasn't even one of the original twelve disciples who walked with Jesus while he was on earth. Nevertheless, Paul walked so close with God that he was given a vision where he was caught up into the third heaven. Paul describes this life changing experience in 2 Corinthians chapter 12. He says that he was "caught up into Paradise and heard inexpressible words, which it is not lawful for a man to utter (2 Corinthians 12:4 NKJV).

In spite of everything that Paul had accomplished and despite the divine revelations that God had given him, Paul still managed to stay humble. Paul always shifted all glory and honor back to God. To make sure that Paul stayed humble in light of the vision he was given, God put a thorn in Paul's flesh. Paul describes it as a "messenger of Satan sent to buffet him… (2 Corinthians 12:7)" Webster's dictionary describes the term buffet as a word used in the 13th century meaning to strike repeatedly.

A Thorn in My Flesh

Therefore, this thorn was a "constant" reminder that it was no goodness of Paul's, but it was all about God. Now we don't know for sure what this thorn was, but we know that it caused Paul a lot of discomfort for the simple fact that he asked God to take it away from him on three different occasions. God had to make sure, however, that Paul didn't get so elevated that he would no longer be able to hear from God. Can you imagine having to deal with some sort of pain that never ceases? It repeats itself over and over and over again.

Whether you know it or not all of us have some sort of "thorn" in our life. While your thorn may not be as severe as Paul's considering all that he had accomplished, God sometimes chooses to keep some sort of pain in our lives to make sure that we are constantly aware that it's all about Him. God will use a thorn to keep the lines of communication open between you and him. When things are always pleasurable to us many times we don't try to hear from God. When things are going good we don't feel as though we have to pray like we use to. We tend to cut back on our studying and fasting because we feel as though we are now on a level that doesn't require us to do all of this anymore. The time that we use to spend with God has now been replaced with time to take care of our worldly affairs.

Now we are on such a spiritual high that we feel as though we can make decisions based on our own intellect because we have received a "divine" touch from God. During your time of bliss God continues to try to reach you, however every time he dials your number he keeps getting a busy signal. The times when you do answer the phone are often short lived because you quickly have to click over to catch the other line. This is until you experience some type of pain in your life. Now instead of God trying to reach you, you make it your personal business to reach him. You are desperate to find out if he has some sort of remedy for this pain that you are going through. Now he has your undivided attention. Now the lines of the communication are wide open and he can impart to you his divine will for your life.

His Grace is Sufficient

Some of you need to take time right now to thank God for the pain that you have had to endure because if it wasn't for your pain you would have missed out on what God was speaking to you. Paul's pain was very severe and for a brief moment in time he was in a state of despair and self-pity. Like most of us, he probably felt like he didn't deserve to be going through this situation. Maybe he even asked God why me. However Paul didn't stay in this state of depression very long. In the midst of the pain God spoke to Paul an awesome truth. God told Paul, "...My grace is sufficient for you, for my power is made perfect in weakness (2 Corinthians 12:9 NIV)."

Paul's pain quickly shifted to pleasure, knowing that his suffering was bringing glory to God. Paul understood that how he responded to his suffering would determine his overall attitude and outlook on life. If he focused predominantly on his suffering then he would probably become depressed and begin a downward fall into discontentment and self-pity. This would ultimately lead to Paul becoming a negative, bitter Christian—always complaining about how bad life is and never taking out the time to recognize the goodness of God. Paul was determined that he wouldn't take on this sort of pessimistic attitude which causes people to take on a wrong view of themselves and most of all of God.

Paul knew that if he learned how to embrace suffering as a means of fellowshipping with Christ and as a part of every Christian's road to spiritual maturity then it would ultimately make him a better Christian and not a bitter Christian. For that reason Paul concluded that he would take joy in his infirmities. This is a statement that will baffle the mind of most people. Who in their right mind would take joy in suffering? Paul now understood that the weaker he became in flesh, the stronger God would become in him through the Spirit. What an awesome revelation? To know that when I'm physically exasperated and can't carry on, the Spirit that's on the inside of me is at His strongest and will not let me give up.

Unconditional Faith

How many times in life have you felt like you couldn't go on but just when you was about to throw in the towel you discovered some untapped strength that you didn't even know you had? That was the Spirit of God standing up in you. In our times of weakness, we learn to rely on God's strength and He takes great delight when we trust in Him. Paul would have never been given this awesome revelation if he hadn't of experienced some pain in his life. Now I'm not saying that if you are experiencing some pain in your life that it's because you have committed a trespass against God. You may actually be doing everything right, yet your right doing doesn't exempt you from having to go through trials in life. Just ask Job.

The Bible says that Job was a perfect and upright man. He walked in total obedience and total fear of God. One day Satan came to God and God asked him, "Have you considered my servant job? There is no one on earth like him; he is blameless and upright, a man who fears God and shuns evil (Job 1:8 NIV)." In spite of Job's faithfulness God asked Satan if he had considered bringing some trouble in his life. At first glance this may seem unfair of God. Was God being disloyal to one of his faithful servants? Absolutely not—Satan believed that the only reason job was faithful to God was because God had a hedge of protection around his life and his possessions. Satan believed that if God removed the hedge of protection that he could make Job curse God to his face. God wanted to prove to Satan that Job's faithfulness was not contingent on his great possessions or his good health. He wanted to show Satan that Job's faith was in him and in him alone. Through pain God would also speak a new purpose into Job's life.

Turning Trouble into Triumph

Satan begins his onslaught by attacking Job's oxen and donkeys. In the same day Job's sheep and the servants that were tending the sheep were consumed when fire fell from the sky. Still later on in the same day Job's servants were attacked and killed by the Chaldeans and all of his camels were taken. To lose so much in one day would take its toil on anyone. However, nothing could prepare Joseph for the emotional pain that he will soon have to endure. Job's children were all eating dinner at the oldest son's house when a strong wind blew, possibly a tornado, and collapsed the house killing all of the children. Everything else that had proceeded this devastating lost had yet to move Job. He had lost his oxen, donkeys, sheep, camels, and even his servants and remained unshaken.

However, Satan presumed that taking his children would be the final straw that would drive him to the verge of insanity. Satan was convinced that the pain of this act would cause Job to curse God. No parent wants to ever have to bury any of their children. Can you imagine the pain of having to experience the demise of all of your children at the same time? The emotional strain associated with this kind of loss would be enough to shake anyone's faith. Job's initial reaction to this tragedy appeared to be the making of a man who would wallow in self-pity and of a man who had become angry with God. The Bible says that when Job heard what had happened that he got up tore his robe and shaved his head (Job 1:20) as if he were on the verge of throwing his hands up to the sky and saying that he was done with God.

I'm sure that this was Job's worst nightmare coming true. What do you do when your worst nightmare has now become a reality? How do you continue on when you have experienced a blow that knocked you off your anticipated track? Do you just sit there and do nothing? Do you curl up in a corner and just wait to die? No. You have to understand that nothing happens to you that God hasn't already equipped you to handle. When we recognize this, we can find joy in the midst of sorrow. We can find hope in the midst of despair. We can find the strength to continue pushing forward even when we have received a blow that had the potential to stop our progress. Sure, the blow that you received might have knocked you down, but it didn't knock you out. Through the power of the Spirit you can get back up again.

The Bible says that after Job had torn his robe and shaved his head that he then fell to the ground and begins to worship. Job declared, "… The LORD gave and the LORD has taken away; may the name of the LORD be praised (Job 1:21 NIV.)" Job understood that he didn't have ownership rights to anything that he possessed. Instead he was just a steward of what he had been entrusted with by God. Job wasn't making permanent connections with temporary belongings. It's not that he didn't care what had happened, but he trusted God above all else. Despite Job's pain, he never charged God with any wrongdoing. Job had passed this test, but this was just the beginning of a long sequence of issues that Job would have to deal with.

Bless God and Live

In chapter 2 of the book of Job, Satan once again presents himself to God, only this time he asks God to stretch out his hand and strike Jobs flesh and bone. God grants Satan access to afflict Job's body, however, Satan must spare his life. Job had made it through the emotional pain, but Satan was confident that if he could afflict Job's body that Job would surely curse God. Satan immediately went to work afflicting Job's body with painful sores which covered his entire body from the top of his head to the soles of his feet. The sores were so irritating that Job used a broken piece of pottery to scrape them. You know that you are experiencing tremendous pain when you have to use something, which in normal cases causes pain, to soothe your pain.

Job's wife told Job that he might as well curse God and die. The very person who should have been there for Job in his time of need, was the very one telling him to give up. When life's issues appear to have gotten the best of you many times the people who you love the most, instead of encouraging you to keep pushing, will make preparations to bury you. They will tell you that you might as well give up. They will tell you that it's over. In these moments of helplessness it's imperative that we don't listen to these wrong voices. Remember God put you in that situation for a reason. Often people who have become gravely ill feel the need to question God concerning their condition. What did I do to deserve this? If God loved me why would he allow this to happen to me? Have I did something wrong?

As I stated before God rarely ever speaks in the way we thought he should have spoken, but there is a message connected to the pain. Instead of complaining about the situation, we should listen to hear what God is attempting to tell us in the midst of this situation. This will require great discipline. It requires you to be able to ignore everything else that is speaking. In Job's case he had to block out his wife, his friends who were telling him to repent and he hadn't committed any transgression, his flesh which was constantly reminding him of how great his pain was, his voice of reasoning which was jogging his memory not only concerning his present physical pain, but of all the emotional pain that he had been through previously, his spirit which was telling him that he didn't deserve this, and the voice of Satan which was using all of the other voices collectively in an attempt to persuade Job into giving up.

Although the desire to complain probably crossed Job's mind on more than one occasion, Job persevered in his faith. His enduring faith through pain is what makes Job the poster boy for resilience even still today. In response to his wife's plea to just curse God and die Job states, "You are talking like a foolish woman. Shall we accept good from God, and not trouble (Job 2:10 NIV)?" What a remarkable statement of faith. Normally we consider it foolish to accept trouble, Job considered it foolish not to accept trouble. This shows that Job understood the very character of God.

If you looked back throughout the Bible you would see that God revealed a different attribute of his divine nature by the things that he did. The actions that God performed were usually a reaction to a problem that needed a solution. In other words, God was going to use trouble to reveal something about himself to Job.

Problems with Benefits

For instance, we wouldn't have known God as Jehovah-jireh, the LORD who provides, if Abraham hadn't of needed a sacrifice to offer to God in place of his son. We wouldn't have known God as Jehovah-nissi, or the LORD who is a victory banner, if Moses wouldn't have needed him in the battle against the Amalekites. We wouldn't have known God as Jehovah-rapha, or the LORD our healer, if God hadn't of promised the Israelites in Exodus 15:26 that if they would diligently hearken to his voice and keep his commandments then none of the diseases that he brought upon the Egyptians would ever affect them for he is the LORD that heals them. One that we can all relate to is Jehovah- Tsidkenu, or the Lord our righteousness.

When Adam and Eve sinned against God all humanity would be declared unrighteous sinners because of it. We would forever be separated from a righteous God because he could never allow sin to dwell in his presence. No bull, no goat, or no ram would ever be able to satisfy the debt that we had incurred. We were doomed to go to hell and there was nothing we could do about it. God could have just let us stayed in our sin and condemned us to hell where we belonged, but due to his love for us he offered an alternative. Therefore, a righteous God gave his only begotten Son so that unrighteous sinners, who accepted his Son as Lord of their life, would be declared righteous. As you can see God's very nature is built around being a problem solver. Although no issues feel good in the present, many times God uses our present issues to show a definitive characteristic of his divine nature for the first time which will extend a lifetime.

Therefore, when God brings trouble in your life it's not always just for you, but God will use your trouble to give others a new revelation of who he is. When people see what God has done for you then a sudden hope will spring up in them concerning their situation. Maybe your family has struggled financially through multiple generations, but when God delivers you out of poverty your immediate family will never have to struggle with that situation again. Maybe no one in your family has ever attended college and has had to endure the pain and frustration of working dead end jobs.

However, when God opens up that door for you, you will influence other members in your family to do the same. You may have to struggle to attain this victory, but if you can press forward through the struggle there is a reward with your name on it. Job knew that God was using this trouble to birth something in his life. He didn't know what it was, nor to what extent he would have to struggle to get it, but he knew that his pain would ultimately lead to a purpose.

Though He Slay Me, Yet Will I Trust Him

Job experienced many low points during this trying time. He got so low that he even cursed the day that he was born (Job 3:1). Behind Job's complaints was an inner faith however that surpassed every inclination of doubt that ever reared its ugly head. Through anguish and through pain, through times of self-loathing and through moments of immense frustration, and even through what appeared to be sure defeat Job was still able to make a statement that was loaded with certain victory. Job 13:15 (KJV) states, "Though he slay me, yet will I trust in him." By the time Job made this statement he was at a place of severe hopelessness. Yet, he was determined to find some hope in what seemed to be a hopeless situation.

However, as the story of continues Job begins to progress into a dangerous descent of self-righteousness. Job felt like he didn't deserve everything that was happening to him. Concerning the trials that Job was going through and what appeared to be injustice on behalf of God, Job makes the following statement, "Does he not see my ways and count my every step. If I have walked in falsehood or my foot has hurried after deceit—let God weigh me in honest scales and he will know that I am blameless—(Job 31:4-6 NIV)." Job was so caught up in self-pity and disillusion that he even asked the question what profit it was for him not to sin. He felt as though that he was receiving punishment that was due unto a sinner, and he hadn't even sinned.

Job arrogantly attempts to justify himself by condemning the justice of God, and he wasn't alone. As the old saying goes, misery loves company. Job went and found three of his friends who would listen to his venting, yet wouldn't let him know just how foolish he was talking. This is typical of most "church folk" today. When they face a difficult situation they love to get a pit party together and talk about how bad they are having it. They love to tell how they do this right and do that right, but yet they have to go through these difficult situations. Usually no one within the pity party is willing to speak up and say God is still good. None of them will say that this situation isn't permanent it's just preparation for a greater calling. None of them will tell you not to complain because God is going to bring some good out of this situation.

Again I Say Rejoice!

You have to be careful who you connect with when you are going through a difficult time. You don't want to connect with faithless, complaining people who will only push you deeper into self-entitlement. The more we complain about our situation, the more power our situation will have over our life. We all have trouble, but trouble should never have us. Unfortunately the reason why so many Christians are still living a defeated life is because they haven't learned how to gain power over their situations. The only way to gain power over our circumstances is to recognize that God has everything under control.

Instead of tempting God by complaining, we should begin rejoicing in the Lord knowing that no matter what we might be going through we are still in his care. The Bible says rejoice in the Lord always (Phil. 4:4). You might say, how do I rejoice in the Lord in the midst of all the suffering that I have to go through? I could make an effort to answer this question, but I think that my answer would pale in comparison to the Apostle Paul's answer which can be seen in the following verses of scripture.

> Not only so, but we rejoice in our sufferings, because we
> know that suffering produces perseverance; perseverance,
> character, and character, hope. And hope does not
> disappoint us, because God has poured out his love
> into our hearts by the Holy Spirit, who he has given us
> (Romans 5:3-5 NIV)

The Christian is not rejoicing because of his suffering, but in his suffering because he knows that there are some benefits that are connected with suffering for Christ. First, God is producing perseverance in you through suffering. Perseverance is defined as a steady persistence in a course of action, a purpose, or in a state. This is a good definition, however, this may give one the impression that they are maintaining on their own. The theological definition of the word perseverance means a continuance in a state of grace to the end. What makes this a better definition in this context is the word grace.

Thankful for Grace

Have you ever been through a tough situation that could have killed you, but some how you made it through? As you think back over the situation you wonder how you ever made it through without losing your sanity. Maybe it was a bad relationship. Maybe it was a terminal sickness. Maybe it was the lost of a love one and you never thought that you would be able to continue on without them. Yet somehow you are still alive, still have your right mind, and are still moving forward despite the lost. It wasn't any goodness of your own, but it was the grace of God that kept you. It was the grace of God that wouldn't allow you to quit. To bring this point full circle, it's still the grace of God that is keeping you even right now and it's the grace of God that will carry you on until the end of time.

Once you realize that it was only the grace of God that kept you, even though you didn't deserve to be kept, then your character begins to change. You become more and more thankful no matter what situation you may find yourself in. You become more humble. Your attitude towards others begins to change for the better. You even take this same attitude towards those people who have misused and abused you without any cost. The character of Christ gives you the ability to forgive. The character of Christ gives the believer the ability to walk in selflessness always considering the needs of others even above their own. This is the perfect illustration of Biblical servant hood. As you can see in the scripture above the character of God also gives the believer hope, and this hope does not disappoint.

The Bible says that hope deferred makes the heart sick, but this hope will never be deferred because it is a heavenly hope. I like the way the Zondervan NIV study Bible describes this type of hope. It states that the believer's hope is not to be equated with unfounded optimism. On the contrary, it is the blessed assurance of our future destiny and is based on God's love, which is revealed to us by the Holy Spirit and objectively demonstrated to us in the death of Christ. This hope assures every believer that God has a future destiny in store for them. It doesn't matter what you have done in your past. God has a hope and a future for you. It's not awarded to us based on our human efforts, rather it is decided based God's love for us, in which the Holy Spirit has revealed to us, and this truth was further established by Christ's death on the cross.

The Importance of Godly Connections

This is a hope that can't be shaken because it doesn't rest in things that are temporal--it rests in those things that are eternal which have been disclosed to us through the word of God. This is why, as believers, we have to make sure that we connect with other "likeminded" believers or we might miss out on this blessed hope that has been promised to us. Although it was commanded that we be, all believers are not likeminded. In Job's distress he reached out to friends who lacked the Godly counsel needed to pull Job out of his present state of depression and self-entitlement. Therefore, Job continued on with his boasting and complaining until one friend stepped up and dared to silence Job.

The other friends had found no answer to refute Job in his attempt to vindicate himself as being innocent, yet God still finding guilt in him as if it were a harsh injustice. His friend Elihu had heard enough and he was about to give Job a rude awakening. Elihu was a man of great wisdom and knowledge, but he was much younger than Job and his other friends.

When the Spirit is trying to get your attention he will sometimes send you a word by someone you least expected. In response to Job's claims of his blamelessness and God's refusal to answer his prayers Elihu reminds Job that God speaks one way or another, although man may not always recognize that it's him speaking. He goes on to remind Joseph that God speaks through dreams, through visions, through calamities, through his intricate design in nature, and through many other great warnings in order to turn men away from wrongdoing and keep them from pride (Job 33:17).

Sometimes we may have pride in our heart that needs to be dealt with. He who humbles himself God will exalt, however, sometimes God has to influence events in your life which will ultimately lead to the humbling. We have to repent from all pride and self-entitlement that we harbor in our hearts before God can truly exalt us in life. Amongst many other ways, Elihu also reminds Job that sometimes God speaks through affliction (Job 33:15). God is not unjust because he has allowed an affliction to come into your life. How can he who was created charge the creator with wrong doing?

If God allowed something to happen in your life then it must have been for a reason. God uses trouble to gain people's attention and commands them to examine every inclination in their heart. Elihu reminds Job that God has promised that if he would only listen to God's correction and obey and serve him even in the midst of his situation that he would spend the rest of his life in prosperity and contentment (Job 36:11). This type of contentment is an overall appreciation and acceptance with whatever God allows. True direction comes when we learn how to just go with God's flow. Don't complain about the direction that the Spirit is leading you, just trust that he will get you to the correct destination.

God is Faithful

Elihu was able to remind Job just how unsearchable God's ways and methods were. Most importantly he reminded Job that in spite of what God allows, he is faithful to see his people through. Thank God for friends who will put you back on the right track of thinking when you have wondered off course. This is when you know that your friend has your best interest in mind. Although these were great words of encouragement to Joseph from a true friend, they must have been very bitter words to swallow considering the fact that the young man who delivered these words was very much Job's subordinate. Just to put an explanation point on all that was said, God broke his silence and spoke to Job out of the storm.

He immediately begins to ask Job a series of questions which would paint a vivid picture of who was in control. He asked Job was he there when he laid the earth's foundation or when he marked the dimensions and boundaries of the earth which would keep the sea from covering the land. He asks him who controls the weather and who endows the heart with wisdom and gives understanding to the mind. He asked him who provides food for all of the animals of the earth and who had the ability to humble the proud man. God continues asking Job many more questions in an effort to prove one inevitable point: everything under heaven belongs to him and everyone in it.

God controls the vast expanses of the universe. Nothing happens that he doesn't approve. God was reminding Job of His omnipotence and omniscience. Job had spent so much time accusing God of ignoring his pleads for justice and for punishing him for doing no wrong that he had forgotten just how powerful God was. Job now understood that he was speaking as a man without knowledge. He was speaking as a man devoid of true understanding. He was questioning God about things that were beyond the scope of what his human comprehension could grasp. God's ultimate aim was to show Job that just like he had a plan for the structural makeup and constant sustaining of the world, he had a plan for Job's life and he would sustain him through the pain in order to reveal a divine purpose in Job's life.

There is a Purpose in Your Pain

While Job was still experiencing great pain, God sent three of his friends to him in order for him to pray for them. Job could have been selfish and refused to pray for his friends until God had delivered him. However, Job was obedient to God and interceded for his friends even when he was in a worse situation than they were. God used Job's pain in order to birth a spirit of intercession through him. All that Job had gone through was preparing him to speak to God on behalf of others. The Bible says that as soon as Job prayed for his friends that God restored to him everything that he had lost. Not only did he restore what Job had, but he multiplied Job's processions by double. This was not given to him because he was a man without sin, but because he had been obedient to purpose.

As you can see from the story of Job, the Spirit of God will sometimes use pain as a way to speak a new ministry into your life. I have read countless stories of people who have turned their experiences of great pain, into even greater ministry opportunities. Many formally abused women have used their story of hurt and turmoil as a way to help other women who are now facing domestic abuse. Many former drug abusers, who now by the grace of God have overcame their addiction, are advocating a message of hope to current addicts to let them know that they can be drug free.

Many Aids victims who have since given their life to God are spreading the good news to others who have suffered the same fate letting them know that although the doctor's may have given them a certain death sentence, through Christ they can have eternal life. Never think that you are suffering for nothing. There is a purpose behind the pain. It may have taken you a long time to break an addiction or bad habit but now God is going to use your victory in this area to help someone else who is struggling with the same issue, come out in a shorter period of time. You never know whose deliverance is connected to your perseverance in suffering. That's why you can't give up.

Even when you get down in dumps and begin to drown in self-pity like Job, you have to quickly change the way you look at your situation. Don't look at it as being unfair. Don't view it as being your final state. Recognize that someone's deliverance is connected to your faith during the struggle. Your issues are not just for you, but God will use your situations as a way to reach many people that you didn't even think you could help. That's why you have to stay faithful through the pain of the process. Also note that your faithfulness in suffering will make you a better person. God will use your trouble to make and to mold you into the person that he has destined you to be.

God doesn't want us to complain every time there is an obstacle in the road that causes painful detours in our life. Instead God wants us to turn to Him and trust Him with our whole heart knowing that our life is in his hand and this situation will eventually work out for good. There is light at the end of the tunnel. You might not be able to see it, but if you learn how to listen to the voice of the Spirit even in pain, then you will truly discover the purpose that God is trying to shine forth through your struggle. Make thankfulness your response to difficult situations. Remember it's not the pain that will hinder your purpose; it's how you respond to the pain.

The Spirit Speaks through Rejection

In the last chapter I talked about how the Spirit speaks to us through trials and tribulations. Did you know, however, that the Spirit will also speak to us through rejection? Everyone wants to feel as though they are accepted. Acceptance gives us a feeling of belonging. It gives us a feeling of accomplishment. No one likes to be rejected. However, sometimes God will allow rejection in order to speak a new direction in our lives. Rejection from this stand point implies the perversion of an intended action or plan. In other words the plans that you had desired to carry out were rejected by God in order to keep you in the will of God. There are many examples of this sort of rejection throughout the pages of the word of God. Briefly, let's explore a few examples of this type of rejection. The first example I want to discuss is the story of the sorcerer Balaam.

God Blocked It

In Numbers 22 we find Balak, the king of Moab, as well as the Moabite people in a state of fear because of what the Israelites had done to the Amorites. They feared that the sudden destruction that had been brought upon the Amorites by the Israelites would soon become their fate. In an attempt to avoid being overtaken by the Israelites, Balak sent messengers to Balaam the sorcerer and informed them to let him know that a people has come out of Egypt and they are so great that they cover the face of the earth. He requests Balaam to come to Moab and curse this great people since they are too mighty for him. Why Balaam? Balaam had a great track record and everyone who he had blessed was blessed and everyone who he had cursed was cursed.

Balaam inquired of the Lord to see if he should go back with these messengers to Moab in order to curse this great nation. The Lord came to Balaam and informed him not to go with these men to Moab to curse this people because they were blessed. Although God had rejected Balaam from going with these people, Balak wasn't through with his persuasion. Once again Balak sent for Balaam, only this time he sent noble princes to persuade Balaam with great honor, glory, and whatever else he could ever ask for if he would come to Moab and curse this great people. Balaam informed the men that he could not go with them unless God granted the approval, however he said that he would inquire of the Lord again to see whether or not he could go.

The mere fact that Balaam would approach God again for something that God had already forbade him to do, proves that Balaam was now being influenced more by greed than by him. This time God permitted Balaam to go with the men back to Moab but he strictly warned Balaam to say only what he instructed him to say. Balaam got up the next morning, saddled his donkey and went with the princes of Moab but God was very angry with Balaam for going with them. Now you may say, wait a minute, didn't God just tell him to go? Yes he did. However, God knew that Balaam's choice to go was not based solely on the fact that he had given him permission to do so. Balaam went to God with a prearranged agenda which was predominantly motivated by his love for money more than his desire to do God's will.

How many times have you approached God for guidance concerning a situation knowing in your heart that you had already decided exactly what you were going to do? Many times the desires of life will eclipse the will of God in our life. We talked earlier about the dangers of being led by selfish ambitions. Selfish ambitions will keep you from fulfilling the plan and purpose that God has for your life because you are too focused on what you want to do. James 3:16 states, "For where you have envy and selfish ambition, there you find disorder and every evil practice (NIV)."

When selfish ambition has blinded your judgment then you may be doing something that seems good when in fact it's completely evil because it's out of the will of God. Balaam had allowed selfish ambition to corrode his heart and thus alter his course. So much so, that his intent was no longer to follow the plan of God but to satisfy his own material comfort. God had a plan, however, that would get Balaam back on the right track.

Thank God for the Detour

Balaam continued on his journey to Moab riding his donkey. The angel of the Lord was standing in the middle of the road to oppose Balaam but he was too blinded by greed to recognize this. Therefore, he continued on his journey not even realizing that the angel of the Lord was standing in the road to confront him. Sometimes when we are headed in the wrong direction God will put an obstacle in our way to put us back on the right course. Often times because of our "spiritual blindness" we want even recognize the obstacle. Even in our blindness, God has a way of getting our attention.

Although Balaam couldn't see the obstacle, his donkey that he was riding on did. When the donkey so the angel of the Lord he became so afraid that he detoured off the intended course that would have taken them to Moab. Balaam hit the donkey in anger; however he didn't even realize that it was a detour that saved his life. No one likes to detour on to a different road when they are headed towards an intended destination. We feel as though this will make our journey longer than what it needs to be. The question is however were we going the right way from the start?

Picture this. You are riding down the road headed to your job and you have to be there at a specific time. The ride is progressing smoothly and actually at the rate you are going you will get to your job with a few minutes to spare. As you are getting closer and closer to your job, it just so happens that road workers are working on the road that you needed to turn on in order to reach your job. They tell you that they will be finish in about twenty minutes if you didn't mind waiting, however you know that twenty minutes would make you about five minutes late to work. You grumble and complain because you have been "rejected" from going the way you intended to go and now you have to find a different route which will take more time.

You hesitantly turn around to attempt to find a different route, all the while you're still complaining because you know that you are going to be late to your job. About thirty minutes after you make it to work the company announces that a terrible car accident occurred on the road that you would have taken and two of your coworkers were pronounced dead at the scene. Your heart drops and you begin to sweat profusiously. You become disorientated and confused. For a minute you detach yourself from everyone who is in the room with you as your mind tries to take in everything that has just happened. A couple minutes ago you were complaining to a coworker concerning the "stupid roadwork" that you had encountered earlier. Now you are in a state of emotional shock realizing that you could have easily been one of the ones who lost their life that day. It was a detour that saved your life.

God's Divine Intervention

Think back to some past rejections that caused you to take a detour in your life. That boyfriend that you thought you were going to marry, only to find out that he had another girl on the side. In your rejection and pain you reached out to God and you made him the center point of your life. As you drew closer and closer to God he begins to give you new direction. At one point you were only content with just having a high school diploma and working a job that paid minimum wage. However, the closer you drew to God, the more you felt a strong urge that he had more for you to do.

Through the tugging of the Spirit you decided to enroll in college to pursue a degree in social work. God showed you that he was going to use you to help children who were being misused and abused in their homes. Now you are saved, you have a college degree, and you have been blessed with a career that reaches hundreds of abused kids. To top it all off God has also connected you with a man of God who treats you like a woman deserves to be treated. In a situation like this, when you look back over your life and think about the choice that you were going to make before, you can't help but to thank God for your rejection. It was through this rejection that the Spirit spoke new direction in your life.

Maybe you applied for a job with a fast growing company that promised great pay and excellent benefits. You anxiously checked your email everyday to see if you had heard anything from the company, however it seemed like nothing would ever come. You opened your email box one day and you saw an email from the company. You were excited, yet apprehensive at the same time. Could this be the email that you had been waiting for? You opened the email and begin reading: The email reads as follows:

> "Thanks for your interest in our company. We appreciate the time you've taken to share your background and experience with us. After careful consideration, we have selected a candidate whose qualifications more closely match the requirements of this position."

This unexpected response hit you like a ton of bricks. Your brief moment of joy had quickly turned into sorrow. You had previously been rejected by several other companies; however you had high hopes that this time would be different. By this time you felt like all hope was gone. You had a family, you had rent due, and you didn't know how you were going to get it done. You had submitted your resume to a temporary agency some weeks prior however you hadn't heard anything from them. Frankly, you weren't even concerned about hearing from them because you presumed you had this other job in the bag.

One day the temporary agency called you and informed you that they had a temporary position open at a company. You could start on Monday if you liked, however, they made it clear to you that this would only be a temporary job. You have bills to pay so what other choice do you have? You begun working the job and time quickly went by. Before long you realized that your temporary position had expired, however, because of the great job that you had done they offered you a full time position. This job paid more than the job that you had been previously rejected from, the benefits were much better, and because you were already familiar with this job, the learning curve wouldn't be very steep.

What's so amazing is that the job that you had previously been rejected from closed their business entirely. God influenced the rejection of the previous job because he knew that if I took it I would have missed out on the job that he had for me. Yes, I did mean to say "I" in the previous sentence. This situation actually happened to me. I was rejected by several companies before God opened up the door for me to be able to work at a Fortune 500 company. I didn't realize it at the time, but as I look back over the entire situation I can't help but thank God for the rejection. While I was scratching my head trying to determine my own path to take, God was working behind the scenes influencing certain events in my life that would lead me to his purpose for my life.

The Deceptive Blessing

The pursuit of prosperity often leads us down roads that look good to us, however are not always good for us. Getting back to Balaam, it appeared to be a good thing and not to mention profitable for Balaam to go to Moab with these men. He would receive very healthy pay for doing what he did best, yet he would have been out of the will of God. Therefore God used the donkey to change Balaam's course. Balaam struck the donkey so many times that finally God opened the mouth of the donkey and allowed it to speak. He informed Balaam that out of all the years that he had been riding him, he had never rebelled against him. Balaam knew then that it had to be some reason why this donkey was so afraid.

God then opened Balaam's eyes to see that the angel of the Lord was standing their waiting to kill him because of the impure motives of his heart. Now Balaam knew that God meant business. Gaining wealth was no longer his objective. He simply wanted to do the will of God. I'm sure that Balaam thanked God for the rejection on that day that spared his life. If the donkey would have kept walking, Balaam would have lost his life. For this reason we should always examine our hearts and minds and make sure that they are pure. What we can profit should never be our motivation for doing anything. That's why when we are rejected we shouldn't always look at it as a bad thing.

In fact it may actually be the best thing that could have happened to you. The way to divine destiny will sometimes take you through severe hardships. Yet it's not the hardships which will determine your outcome, it's how you handle the struggle. Don't be down on yourself because something didn't work out how you thought it would. Don't lose heart. You have to know that God is causing everything that you are going through to work together for your good. Sometimes what we think are setbacks, are really just divine setups in order to keep us in the will and timeline of God. Often times God will purposely hold back what you were requesting from him, because he knows that you can't handle what you are asking for or it isn't a part of your destiny.

Holding back what we are asking for in order to keep us in His will is the best thing that God could ever do for us. The story of Balaam also shows us that just because you possess an ability to do something, that doesn't mean that you can use your ability whenever you want to. Balaam had an ability to bless and curse however his motives for doing so had to be right. Our gifts and abilities should always be in subjection to the will of the Spirit of God. Just look at King David for example.

Accepting God's Rejection

David desired to build a house for God's presence to dwell in. David was a very astute man and he had the wisdom to accomplish this great feat. Despite David's many abilities it was not in God's will for him to build the temple, but God was going to use David's son Solomon to build a house for his presence to dwell in (2 Samuel 7:1-29). Just as God had rejected King Saul from being king over the Israelites because of his disobedience, he rejected David's request to build him a house in order to shift his focus back to his true purpose, which was to rule over Israel.

David could have remained blind by the splendor of having a huge temple for God. Just think of all the potential revenue this temple would have brought David's kingdom as people from all over the world would no doubt desire to see this great wonder. David knew, however, that no wealth could ever be sufficient enough to buy his freedom if he fell into the hands of an angry God because of his disobedience. From this day forward don't just look at your rejection as punishment for wrong doing. Check your life to make sure that it's lining up with the word of God. However, after you have examined your life parallel to the word of God, and it seems as though the doors of progress are still closing in your face, just stay faithful to God.

You have to know and believe in your heart that through this rejection God is going to reveal purpose in your life. Whether you are rejected by a job, a school, a church, family members, or as Christians even by society, remember that you are accepted by God through the blood of Jesus Christ. It may not look like it right now. It might not feel like it right now. However, the following scriptures should give you the reassurance to know that God has indeed accepted you as his own prized possession:

Then Peter began to speak: "I now realize how true it is that god does not show favoritism but accepts men from every nation who fear him and do what is right (Acts 10:34-35 NIV)

We are confident, I say, and willing rather to be absent from the body and to be present with the Lord. Therefore we labor, that, whether present or absent, we may be accepted by Him (2 Corinthians 5:8-9 NIV).

He hath chosen us in Him before the foundation of the world, that we should be holy and without blame before Him in love, having predestined us to be His own adopted children by Jesus Christ, according to the good pleasure of His will, to the praise of the glory of His grace, wherein He hath made us accepted in His Beloved (Ephesians 1:4-6 NIV)

The Inward Voice of the Holy Spirit

By now we should know at least two ways that the Spirit of God speaks to his people: through trouble and through rejection. Now I want to focus on the inward witness of the Holy Spirit. In the Old Testament the Spirit of God came upon certain people in order to carry out specific assignments. Let's take a look at some scripture references to support this.

And the Spirit of God came upon Azariah the son of Oded: And he went out to meet Asa, and said unto him, Hear ye me, Asa, and all Judah and Benjamin; The LORD is with you, while ye be with him; and if ye seek him, he will be found of you; but if ye forsake him, he will forsake you. 2 Chronicles 15:1-2 KJV

The Spirit of the Lord GOD is upon me; because the LORD hath anointed me to preach good tidings unto the meek; he hath sent me to bind up the brokenhearted, to proclaim liberty to the captives, and the opening of the prison to them that are bound; Isaiah 61:1 KJV

And the Spirit of God came upon Zechariah the son of Jehoiada the priest, which stood above the people, and said unto them, Thus saith God, Why transgress ye the commandments of the LORD, that ye cannot prosper? Because ye have forsaken the LORD, he hath also forsaken you. 2 Chronicles 24:20 KJV

As we can see from the above reference scriptures the Spirit of God moved on ordinary men in order to speak extraordinary truths. Notice that these men were not just ordinary men. All three of these men Azariah, Isaiah, and Zechariah were all prophets of the Lord. These men were all messengers hand selected by, and spoke as formal representatives, of the God of Israel. The intention of their message was to convince the people to reconfirm to the Godly standards that had been instituted in the Torah which had been written by the prophet Moses, or they would have to face impending judgment in which God had already revealed to the prophets.

In other words, they were holders of God's divine will for his people on this earth. Prophets would usually act as advisors to the king of Israel, providing them with Godly instructions in order to insure that the kingdom was being governed accordingly. Unfortunately, even then you had false prophets who operated in the wrong spirit and would provide the king with the erroneous counsel, which would bring damnation on the king and the kingdom. While the Spirit of God had the right to come upon whoever he wanted to, everyone wasn't given this great privilege.

At this point in time the Spirit of God hadn't been given because Christ had yet to be born, he had yet to be crucified, and he had yet to be glorified. Therefore their were only a select few who ever experienced the Spirit of God in this way, usually to carry out a specific task, and more often than not these men were prophets. However, a major shift in the Spirit realm would soon take place.

A Shift in the Spirit Realm

The prophet Joel foretold of a day when the Spirit of God would certainly indwell ALL believers. Joel 2:28 states, "And afterward, I will pour out my Spirit on all people. Your sons and daughters will prophesy, your old men will dream dreams, your young men will see visions (KJV)." Jesus reminds his disciples of this in John 16:13 when he states, "But when he, the Spirit of truth, comes, he will guide you into all truth. He will not speak on his own; he will speak only what he hears, and he will tell you what is yet to come (NIV)."

These prophecies were both fulfilled in the book of Acts when on the day of Pentecost the Spirit of God filled the Apostles and also three thousand other people who accepted Christ on that day. They all begin to speak in other tongues as the Spirit gave them utterance.

The Spirit of God would no longer just come upon certain people to accomplish certain tasks. Now everyone who accepted Christ as their Savior would receive this wonderful gift of the Holy Spirit dwelling on the inside of them. The indwelling of the Holy Spirit brought power to the believer. He also brought about a new way of thinking and new direction as he realigned our thinking to be in accordance with the word of God. One other thing that He brought, that we so often overlook, was the ability to know our future.

So many people still feel as though they have to run to a prophet in order to receive a word from God. Many are even paying prophets and even fortune tellers to tell them their future. You should never have to pay anyone to tell you your future. Instead, just listen to the Spirit within for he knows your end even from your beginning. 1 Corinthians 2:12 states, "Now we have received, not the spirit of the world, but the spirit which is of God; that we might know the things that are freely given to us of God

(KJV)." This is a great paradigm shift from the Old Testament in which the prophet was the primary means of discovering one's future. Notice that Jesus told his disciples that the Spirit of truth will tell them what's to come.

The Holy Spirit wants to tell you what lies ahead for your life. He wants you to know that the situation that you are going through right now is just temporary. Where you are from and what you have been through doesn't determine where you are going. God has a great future for you and he wants you to know that. It's only when you begin to listen to the inward witness of the Holy Spirit that you will discover God's true plan for your life.

What the Holy Spirit Doesn't Sound Like

In order to know what the Holy Spirit sounds like you have to know what he does not sound like. Often times in the Old Testament the voice of God would speak in a very dramatic and fear provoking way. In Exodus chapter 19:16, God came and rested on Mount Sinai to speak with Moses and the rest of Israel. His presence was accompanied by thunders and lightning's, and a very thick cloud covered the mount. When he spoke it was with a voice of a trumpet which was so loud that all the people in the camp trembled. Naturally this voice invoked a feeling of extreme fear within the people who heard it. On this occasion however, God's intention for speaking to the people was to invoke fear within their hearts.

God had previously informed Moses earlier in chapter 19 that he would speak to the people directly so that they would trust Moses' leadership completely. The great wonders that they saw and heard would also cement the people's faith in God's awesome power just as God had demonstrated to them when he brought them out of Egypt. The people would know for a surety that it wasn't just Moses speaking, but it was God speaking to him in order to give them divine instruction.

Contrary to the Mount Sinai experience when God spoke to Israel in a loud, thunderous voice, He is never recorded speaking this way in the New Testament. Actually, if you were to do a detailed study of the Scriptures, you would discover that for the most part God didn't speak this way in the Old Testament either. However, since the voice on Sinai lingered so heavily on the hearts and minds of so many Israelites, they often made the mistake of thinking this was the only way God spoke. Therefore if God didn't speak in a very dramatic fashion, they would miss his voice.

Even in today's world we expect God's voice to be accompanied by the horn section of the world's largest marching band and numerous other theatrics. I don't know if it's because we have grown accustomed to listening to high definition surround sound or if it's because our faith is so weak that we feel we need something outlandish to get our attention. Even in today's churches people have grown so accustomed to hearing extremely loud music accompanied by the sometimes overly charismatic preacher, that they tend to equate this as the voice of God. Therefore when God speaks in a different way we miss out on what God is trying to tell us.

We should never put God in a box. The fact is that God can speak however he chooses to speak. After all, he is God. However, through the majority of the Bible we see God speaking in a very different way. There is an Old Testament passage of scripture that speaks volumes as it relates to hearing from God, and as it relates to recognizing the voice of the Holy Spirit. 1 Kings 19:11-12 (NIV) reads as follows:

The LORD said, "Go out and stand on the mountain in the presence of the LORD, for the LORD is about to pass by." Then a great and powerful wind tore the mountains apart and shattered the rocks before the LORD, but the LORD was not in the wind. After the wind there was an earthquake, but the LORD was not in the earthquake. After the earthquake came a fire, but the LORD was not in the fire. And after the fire came a gentle whisper.

What the Holy Spirit Does Sound Like

In the previous verses of scripture, Elijah was looking for God to speak in some extraordinary manner. Elijah felt that because the wind was so powerful that surely this had to be God speaking through the wind, but God wasn't in the wind. If not in the wind, then this was surely God speaking through the earthquake seeing as though it exhibited such great force, but God wasn't in the earthquake. After the earthquake came a great fire. Elijah probably assumed that since God hadn't spoken through the wind or the earthquake, without a doubt this had to be God speaking through the fire, but God wasn't in the fire.

Instead God spoke to Elijah through a gentle whisper. How often we look for God to speak to us in some spectacular way, only to be misguided by what we thought was God, but it was really the enemy making us a slave again to fear. Paul states, "For you did not receive a spirit that makes you a slave again to fear, but you received the Spirit of sonship. And by him we cry, 'Abba, Father' (Romans 8:15 NIV). Contrary to the voice that spoke on Mount Sinai, the voice of the Holy Spirit no longer invokes fear. Many of today's church leaders attempt to speak in a way that brings fear. They do this to manipulate the people to give more money and to garner a certain level of respect for themselves to make people afraid to speak up against their practices. They also use this fear as a means of manipulation to trick people into following their will, instead of God's will for their life.

If you are being motivated to do anything because of fear then you can be sure that this is not the Holy Spirit speaking to you. Just as God spoke to Elijah in the passage in 1 Kings, the Holy Spirit also speaks to believers in the quietest whisper. Although this voice may not seem as powerful as compared to the voice that spoke on Mount Sinai, the effectiveness of the voice is still the same. To the believer, God's voice is always discernable. Jesus makes this clear in the following verses of scripture: "To him the doorkeeper opens, and the sheep hear his voice; and he calls his own sheep by name and leads them out. And when he brings out his own sheep, he goes before then; and the sheep follow him, for they know his voice (St. John 10:3-4 NKJV)."

Two things stand out from the above reference scriptures. Number one, it's not until the sheep come out of the sheepfold that Jesus can begin to lead them. This paints a very vivid picture of spiritual separation. Those who belong to Christ have separated themselves for special service for him. They no longer belong to the crowd, and thus are not able to do everything that the crowd does. They belong to God and have to begin following his voice above all others. Number 2, we see that if a person always knows where they are going then they are not allowing God to direct their steps. How do we know this?

The scripture says that when he brings his sheep out, he goes before them and then they follow him. You can't go ahead of God and then tell him to catch up with you. Instead you have to trust God enough to follow him even when you might not know exactly where he's taking you. We see this in the story of Abraham. Abraham didn't know where he was going, but when God told him to leave, he trusted God enough to step out in faith. The reason why he stepped out with no ideal of where he was going was because he knew the voice of God. Therefore, no matter where he went, as long as he could consistently hear God's voice he would never be lost.

My Sheep Hear My Voice

This is the same way the Holy Spirit speaks to us today. He has already gone ahead of us and surveyed the path. He knows what our next move should be before we even take it. We have to check our spiritual ear to make sure that we are hearing, and following his voice and not another's. As we can see in St. John 10:5, God's sheep will not follow a stranger's voice. This is just like a child and a parent relationship. As we grow with our parents we develop a special ear for recognizing our parent's voice. Therefore if a stranger attempts to lure us in to following them, we want follow them because their voice is foreign to us.

As with anything authentic, there are always imitators. Just like a kidnapper attempts to fool a kid by disguising their voice to sound like the parent, so does Satan attempt to fool believers by attempting to sound like God. If we listen closely, we will notice obvious differences in Satan's voice than in God's voice. God calls his sheep by name, however, it requires a certain level of sensitivity to hear and recognize his voice. Although we haven't received a spirit that makes us a slave again to fear, that doesn't mean that we are above correction.

This is important to know because one way the Spirit leads is by an inner conviction of the heart. John 16:8-11 states, "When he comes, he will convict the world of guilt in regard to sin and righteousness and judgment: in regard to sin, because men do not believe in me; in regard to righteousness, because I am going to the Father, where you can see me no longer; and in regard to judgment, because the prince of this world now stands condemned (NIV)."

The initial impact that the Holy Spirit would have on the world was the fact that he would bring conviction on the world. In other words he would convince mankind that they were sinners in need of a savior. The Bible says that a man's ways are always right in his own eyes. Most of us can attest to the fact that at one point we felt like that we knew it all and we really didn't need anybody to tell us anything. This was the mindset that we all possessed before we accepted Christ, this is still the mindset for all of those who have yet to accept Christ, and even some of us who have accepted Christ still feel as though we know everything.

However, the Holy Spirit came into the world to show us that he was the only source of divine truth. Only through him could we discover that it was solely because of the shed blood of Jesus Christ that we could be saved from eternal damnation. The life that we lived apart from Christ was a life full pride and ignorance. All of us who have accepted Christ however, did so because we came under the conviction of the Holy Spirit which caused us to repent from our sins and turn away from our old lifestyle. Unfortunately, most of us lose that initial conviction that we had when we accepted Christ, after he has come into our lives. Therefore we revert back to our old way of thinking and find ourselves being led more by what we believe to be true, rather than the infallible truth that the Holy Spirit communicates to us through the conviction of our hearts.

Don't Lose Your Convictions

There are a lot of Saints who are walking around in confusion because they have lost their convictions. If you are confused about your purpose in life and find yourself being tossed to and fro between careers, companions, churches, or even what ministry you should be operating in, then you are not being led by the convictions of the Holy Spirit. The Bible declares that God is not the author of confusion (1 Corinthians 14:33). God will not tell you to do one thing today, and then turn around and tell you to do something different the next day. If you are constantly feeling as though God is changing his mind about his purpose in your life, then obviously it's you who are unstable.

James lets us know that a doubled minded person is unstable in all his ways (James 1:8). As a believer you have to know that God doesn't change (Malachi 3:6). Since God doesn't change it's our job to learn all we can about him. Ephesians 1:17-18 says, "I keep asking that the God of our Lord Jesus Christ, the glorious Father, may give you the Spirit of wisdom and revelation, so that you may know him better. I pray also that the eyes of your heart may be enlightened in order that you may know the hope to which he has called you, the riches of his glorious inheritance in the saints (NIV) …"

Knowing your calling gives you such a hope and confidence because you know that you are fulfilling the will of God for your life. The only way to know God's calling for your life is to have the eyes of your understanding enlightened, which only comes by receiving revelation knowledge of who God is. The more you learn about God, the more you learn about yourself. This knowledge is only gained when you receive the spirit of wisdom. How do we receive this? Proverbs 1:7 tells us how: The fear of the LORD is the beginning of knowledge, but fools despise wisdom and discipline (NIV). The only way to gain this knowledge is to walk in the fear, or reverent respect of the Lord, and this lifestyle is lived out by walking in total obedience to the inner convictions that are brought about by the Spirit. Then and only then can you know for a surety the purpose that God has for you.

A New Direction

One way that conviction serves in leading us, is by giving us new direction. One definition for conviction as defined by Webster's dictionary is the state of being convinced of error or compelled to admit the truth. Their may be some idea that you have held to be true for a very long time, yet the closer you get to God, the clearer it becomes that you were in error in your belief. As Christians, our hearts and spiritual ears should always be open to receive new direction and instruction from the Lord as it pertains to how we should live our lives. This goes far beyond the initial step of salvation. Your own rationale is limited in determining what the will of God is for your life, therefore we have to empty ourselves of our own ideologies and take on more of the Spirit of God if we are to walk into divine destiny.

Take Peter for example. In Acts 10, the Holy Spirit speaks to Peter to let him know that, contrary to his previous belief that the Gentiles couldn't receive the gift of the Holy Spirit because they were unclean, God didn't have any respect of persons. This meat that nothing, God had made was to be considered unclean. Because of this revelation that Peter received from the Spirit of God and his obedience to the conviction to go to the house of Cornelius, salvation and the free gift of the Holy Spirit were provided not only to the Jews, but to everyone who would accept Christ as savior.

We see a similar situation with Paul in Acts 16. The Bible says that Paul and his companions had been forbidden by the Spirit from preaching the gospel in Asia. They then attempted to go to Bithynia, but once again the conviction of the Spirit kept them from going there as well. That night Paul had a vision of a man in Macedonia who needed his help. It was clear now that God was leading him to Macedonia to offer assistance to someone who was in need. Do you see how important it is for us to be sensitive to the convictions of the Holy Spirit?

If Peter had of ignored the conviction to take the gospel to the Gentiles, Cornelius and his entire household would not have received Jesus Christ. If Paul would have ignored the convictions and went his own way, then the person that God had predestined him to help in Macedonia would have never received that help. The Spirit is saying the day you hear his voice, harden not your heart (Hebrews 3:7). If God is speaking to your heart concerning something you need to be doing, or something you need to stop doing, then make sure that you listen to his promptings. We can't do our own thing; instead we have to only do what the Spirit is commanding us to do.

Remember he knows the path that you need to take in order to discover your divine purpose in life. It's important that we keep a humble heart before God, and listen closely to the convictions that he lays on our hearts. Remember the Holy Spirit never brings condemnation, in attempt to victimize you by what you use to be in your past, but he brings conviction in order to lead you into the truth of what he has predestined you to be and accomplish in your future.

Unshakable Faith

I ended the last section by talking about the importance of following the conviction of the Holy Spirit. The conviction that I referenced there was being convinced of error, in order to revert to the truth. Another way of defining conviction is an unshakable belief in something without need for proof or evidence. When you have this kind of conviction then you are sure of what you are hoping for in the spiritual, even though you may not currently see in the physical how it's going to work out. What does this type of conviction sound like? It sounds like faith. Hebrews 11:1 (NIV) defines faith as being sure of what we hope for and certain of what we do not see.

Faith gives us the confidence to look at what appears to be a bad situation, and see the potential for greatest. It gives us the assurance to be able to stand in the midst of the fire, just like the three Hebrew boys, and know that we will not be consumed. Most of all it gives us a hope that what we are seeing now is just temporary, and in due time the promises of God will begin to manifest in our lives. Faith however is only proven to be authentic when it is put to the test. Just like Job, the three Hebrew boys, and countless other saints were put in situations that challenged the validity of their faith, so will all of God's children have to endure situations that will challenge the legitimacy of their faith. I heard Bishop Neil Ellis, the senior pastor of Mount Tabor Full Gospel Baptist Church, say that a faith that has not been tested, is a faith that cannot be trusted.

Can your faith be trusted? Are your convictions strong enough to sustain you through life's most complex situations? Or will you wave the white flag the moment your opponent delivers a shocking blow? True convictions are only certified when a person faces a difficult situation that should have made them lose trust in God, yet they are able to weather the storm with their faith in God growing stronger than ever before. This is the conviction that the Holy Spirit brings to the believer. He assures us that no matter what we may be going through on today, that God is still faithful and everything that he has promised us shall come to pass. This faith preserves us in tough times because we know that no matter what the enemy attempts to do in our lives, he can't take our promised inheritance.

The enemy would love to make you doubt God and keep you in a state of constant confusion and anxiety about your tomorrow. As I stated before, the Bible says that hope deferred makes the heart sick (Proverbs 13:12). A lot of people have driven themselves to physical sickness and mental deterioration because they don't possess a heavenly hope, which is an unwavering faith in the eternality of God. Instead they only hope in the temporal things which they can see, which is really not faith at all. Therefore if the enemy attacks their possessions they quickly give up hope. They lose their joy, their peace, their confidence, and some even lose their will to live. The writer of Hebrews urges the believer to preserve their confidence: "Therefore, do not throw away your confidence, which has a great reward. For you have need of endurance, so that when you have done the will of God, you may receive what was promised (Hebrews 10:35-36 NASB)."

Our confidence in God and our patience during tough times assures us that we will receive everything that he has promised. Just like he told the woman with the issue of blood, let it be according to your faith. The believer's faith postures them to receive the blessings of God. I like the word that is used in the KJV translation of Hebrews 10:35 when it says that our confidence has great "recompense" of reward. A recompense is something given as a reparation, or compensation for a loss. When someone gets hurt on the job and it's the job's fault then they receive compensation. While the compensation doesn't take the pain away, it's usually more than enough to make up for a lot of the pain and emotional distress that they have had to endure.

What God is saying is that the promises that he has for you are so great that they will make up for everything negative that you have ever experienced in your life. Because you have this assurance of these great things that are to come, you can peacefully endure your temporary light afflictions because you know that the blessings of God will far exceed the pain. Staying humble before God and resting in his promises will provide you with the fortitude needed to make it through any struggle.

Following the Peace of God

With all that being said, true faith gives the believer peace in whatever situation they may find themselves in. This God-given peace robs fear of its authority. This peace also clears up any confusion in the believer's life. 1 Corinthians 14:33 says, "For God is not a God of disorder but of peace (NIV)." Keep in mind that this peace is not the same peace that the world contains which is contingent solely on conditions. The world views peace as having a bank account full of money, being in perfect health, having the perfect family, and living in a mansion on the hills. This is the counterfeit peace that Satan encourages. The problem with this peace is that it's only short-term. Sooner or later the conditions of all of our lives will change.

Our health will begin to deteriorate. Our finances could take a hit. As life progresses our love ones will begin to die. When all of these things happen, if we have the counterfeit peace that the world offers, then we will not be able to maintain. Jesus offers a different peace. Jesus states in John 14:27, "Peace I leave with you; my peace I give you. I do not give to you as the world gives. Do not let your hearts be troubled and do not be afraid (NIV)." The peace that Jesus was leaving was the inner peace that only the indwelling of the Holy Spirit could offer. This peace is not conditional, but it is positional. This peace is routed in our relationship with God as our Father.

Knowing this gives the believer the assurance that no matter what situation they may go through, their "Abba" will never leave them nor forsake them. Because the world didn't give this peace, the world will never be able to take it away. This peace is one of the spiritual fruits that are discussed in Galatians chapter five. Because this peace is a spiritual fruit, then everyone who possesses the Spirit of God should possess this peace. Christians should never walk around complaining about how bad they are having it. We should never allow what's going on in the world to rob us of our joy.

We have a promise that God will supply all of our needs (Philippians 4:13). Therefore we have no need to worry about the basic necessities of life. Even when we face difficult situations that would make the normal person complain and even lose hope such as the recession that the world is currently in, the peace of God which surpasses all understanding will guard our hearts and our minds in Christ Jesus (Phil. 4:7 NIV) and will help us remain confident in the promises of God no matter the current economical climate.

This is the Way, Walk in It

What am I saying? The Spirit of God doesn't want us to walk around in a constant state of worry. Instead he wants us to rest in the peace that the Spirit makes available to all those who will accept it, knowing that God has everything under control. Once the believer has found rest in the peace of God, then this same peace will begin to guide them into their destiny. You no longer have to be torn between multiple opinions struggling to find peace in which road to take. If you seek God with all your heart, then he will give you peace on which decision you need to make.

Whether it's deciding on a career, a companion, a school, a church, or even a permanent place of residence, God has the answer for you. Stop guessing about your future. Stop being led by your feelings and emotions. Stop allowing the enemy to distort the clear direction that God has given you in an attempt to lead you down the wrong path. Trust the Spirit of God. Give him complete control of your life. Draw closer to him everyday through a daily diet of reading his word, prayer and meditation on that word. As you meditate on the word, then you should learn how to apply it to your everyday life. If you consistently do all these things, then you will begin to discover what God's purpose is for your life.

Isaiah 30:20-21 states, "Although the Lord gives you the bread of adversity and the water of affliction, your teachers will be hidden no more; with your own eyes you will see them. Whether you turn to the right or to the left, your ears will hear a voice behind you, saying, 'This is the way; walk in it.' " God is saying to his people, no longer will he hold back direction from you. No longer will you have to walk around aimlessly trying to decipher which road to take. Once you humble yourselves before God, and incline your ears to his wisdom, you will hear his voice clearly saying, "This is the way, walk in it."

CHAPTER 7

Ready For Purpose

So far we have discussed what the prerequisites for living a Spirit led life are. We've talked about how to develop a deeper relationship with God in order to consistently receive clearer direction. We've also talked about the voices that we shouldn't listen to and the voices that we should listen to as it relates to discovering God's purpose for our life. The only thing left to talk about now is how to discover what our purpose really is. This next section should go by rather quickly.

I want to be clear I'm not writing this book to tell you what your purpose is. That's for God to know, and for you to find out. My aim is simply this:

1. To position you to be able to receive Godly direction
2. To make you observant so that you will recognize purpose when it reveals itself
3. To help impart spiritual truths unto you that will empower you with the spiritual tenacity needed to hold on to that purpose once you have discovered it.

With that being said I want to begin this next section with a question. Do you know what your purpose is?

What is My Purpose?

Purpose is defined as the reason for which something exists or is done, made, or used. While everyone has a purpose, our purposes are never the same. Also our purpose in life is rarely ever what we think it should be. When I was about 9 years old I saw my first Bruce Lee movie. Bruce Lee was invigorating. He was innovative. He was a revolutionary. Before Bruce Lee, most action movies seemed to be the same. They did all the same moves, had all the same plots, and featured all the same people. However, when Bruce came along, he forever changed the way the world would view martial arts. He would especially have a great impact on how I viewed my life at the time. Everything that he did stood out to me. His talk was calm, yet confident. His walk was smooth, but deliberate as though he would think every step out before taking it.

In battle he was graceful, delivering each blow with precision in order to properly dismantle any opponents who dared to challenge him. While small in statue, he packed a punch that looked as if it had the power of ten men. Perhaps the greatest trait of Bruce was the fact that his roles were always reminiscent of the underdog. Bruce would always play the smallest, most insignificant character that would take on the most powerful villain, and win. In case you haven't figured out by now, I was a huge Bruce Lee fan.

When I saw Bruce fight for the first time I immediately felt like I had discovered my purpose in life. From that time forward I worked extremely hard to be just like Bruce Lee. I practiced his kicks. I mimicked his punching style. I bought a set of nun chucks in an attempt to learn how to use them just like Bruce Lee. I also purchased every book that I could find about Jeet Kune Do which was the fighting style that Bruce had pioneered. I truly believed that my purpose in life was to be the next big martial arts star. I had yet to understand however that my purpose in life wasn't mine to define.

But I Thought...

How many of you when you were young had already mapped your life out? You knew what you wanted to do in life. You knew what career you wanted to pursue. You knew who you wanted to marry. You knew where you wanted to live. Well, at least you thought you knew all of these things. Once you become a Christian however and begin spending time with God, then he begins to change your purposes to align with his will for your life. Maybe I shouldn't say change your purposes. After all, he already knew what he predestined you to do even from the foundation of the earth. Perhaps a better word would be he changes your perspectives in life, and causes you to see what he sees for your life.

I thought that I was destined to be a great martial artist just like my then idol Bruce Lee. However, God knew that he had destined me to do something different. If we were to think back over our life and meditate on what we wanted to do, we will begin to thank God for giving us a clearer perspective. For instance, if some of you would have married that person that you thought you were destined to marry, then your marriage would have probably already ended in divorce. If you had of chosen that career that you thought was best for you, then you would probably not have a job because the market for that job is pretty much nonexistent and you would have had to go back to school for another four years to learn a new trade, or settle working at a job that was beneath your qualifications.

What if you had of been hired at that job that would have only paid ten dollars an hour, then you would have never applied for the job you have now that makes triple that amount. I'm sure many of you, including myself, are saying thank God that he didn't let me do what I wanted to do. Although many of you are probably breathing a sigh of relief seeing as though you dodged a big bullet; there is still one very important question that demands an answer. Are you doing what God has purposed you to do?

A Lack of Defined Purpose

The answer to this question is imperative to anyone who desires to stay in the will of God. It's also a very important question because lack of defined purpose, breeds a lack of contentment. In turn, a lack of contentment leads to a lack of commitment. When a person doesn't have a defined purpose in life then they will never feel completely satisfied in anything that they do. Is that the story of your life? Do you constantly search for new companions, new jobs, or maybe even new ministries trying to fill a void in your life that hadn't been completely filled by your previous void-filler?

No matter what you accomplish, or what moves you make in life, do you constantly find something negative that causes you to seek something different? Because of your lack of contentment you can never fully commit to anyone, or anything. This type of person will also be easily manipulated into believing that their life doesn't have a purpose. If this is you, then you are a prime candidate for being misled by the enemy into believing that God doesn't have a purpose for your life. This however couldn't be further from the truth.

As I stated earlier, Ephesians 2:10 states, "For we are God's workmanship, created in Christ Jesus to do good works, which God prepared in advance for us to do." This verse of scripture reassures us all that there is a reason for our existence and therefore no one can ever say their life doesn't have purpose. This is especially true for the believer. While God has an individual purpose and plan for everyone's life, all believers share some common purposes.

CHAPTER 8

The Common Purposes

As a believer, we all share in the death, burial, and resurrection of Jesus Christ (Colossians 2:12, Romans 6:5). We also all possess certain inalienable rights that have been bestowed upon us because of our heavenly citizenship (Philippians 3:17-21, 1 Peter 2:9). Along with these great heavenly benefits, comes great responsibility. This is not a one person responsibility such as when Moses was given the task of leading the people of Israel out of Egypt. Although Moses had advisors and assistants to help him oversee the Israelites, the majority of people still looked to him to bear the bulk of the responsibility sometimes even doing things for them that they were more than capable of doing for themselves.

Neither is this responsibility similar to that of the Judges of Israel who had the task of ruling and guiding Israel back to God when they strayed away and worshiped other gods. The judge would have to single handingly save an entire nation out of the hands of their enemies because of their rebellion to the God of their fathers. Needless to say this would be a great responsibility for anyone to take on. This is not the responsibility that I'm talking about in this situation however. The responsibility that I'm referring to is a shared purpose that all believers have to share.

Share in Christ's suffering

I want to know Christ and the power of his resurrection and the fellowship of sharing in his sufferings, become like him in his death… Philippians 3:10 NIV

In this you greatly rejoice, though now for a little while you may have had to suffer grief in all kinds of trials. These have come so that your faith—of greater worth than gold, which perishes even though refined by fire—may be proved genuine and may result in praise, glory and honor when Jesus Christ is revealed. 1 Peter 1:6-7 NIV

Dear friends, do not be surprised at the painful trial you are suffering, as though something strange were happening to you. But rejoice that you participate in the sufferings of Christ, so that you may be overjoyed when his glory is revealed. 1 Peter 4:12-13 NIV

To this you were called, because Christ suffered for you, leaving you an example, that you should follow in his steps. 1 Peter 2:21 NIV

At the core of basic Christianity is the need to learn how to endure suffering. This is the reason I chose to begin this section of study with suffering because how you deal with suffering will determine the level of power and discipline that you exercise in every other area of your Christian life. The Bible clearly talks a lot about suffering; however I want to concentrate on the above reference scriptures to illustrate this great truth. Paul states in Philippians 3:10 suffering, in well doing, helps the believer walk in fellowship with Christ. Most Christians only want to walk in fellowship with Christ as it relates to receiving material blessings. We usually don't want any part of having to endure being mistreated, being false accused, being lied on, and the likes thereof.

Peter was willing to fight for Jesus in the garden of Gethsemane, but he wasn't willing to be identified with him when he was taken captive, when he was beaten, and when he was crucified unjustly. In fact Peter denied even knowing Jesus. Isn't that just like most people today? They love you as long as everything is going well, yet when you face difficult times they are no where to be found. However, if you are going to have fellowship with someone, then that fellowship shouldn't break because of difficult times in life. If anything the fellowship should become stronger when the pressures of life are mounting because that's the time the person needs you the most.

As believers, we should never allow anything to break our fellowship with each other, nor with the triune God. This includes suffering. 1 Peter 2:20 let's us know that suffering, in doing good, yet still finding the fortitude to endure in your faith, is a gracious thing in the eye sight of God. In fact, verse 21 of the same chapter lets us know that we have been called to suffer. Why? Christ wants to make sure that your faith in him is unconditional. During Jesus' earthly ministry, many of the disciples who started with him eventually turned and walked away. 1 John 2:19 states, "they went out from us, but they did not really belong to us. For if they had belonged to us, they would have remained with us; but their going showed that none of them belonged to us (NIV)."

What Jesus was saying was that these people had a familiarity with him, and they were fascinated with what he was able to do for them, but they lacked true fellowship. They wasn't in it for the long term, they were only concerned about what Jesus could do for them then. That's why you shouldn't worry about people who leave you. If they left you then they were probably never with you from the start. Be glad that they left you before the storm clouds begin to brew in your life. Because it's when you go through tough times in life that you really need the people you are connected with to have your back. This is the same type of dedication that Christ expects from his people. He wants to know that no matter what happens in life, your dedication to him will not be compromised.

Philippians 1:29 says, "For it has been granted to you on behalf of Christ not only to believe on him, but also to suffer for him (NIV)." It's not enough just to believe in Christ, but you have to be willing to experience many of the things he went through in order to have true fellowship with him. He has to know that your heart is forever chasing after him, and even if others walk away, he can count on you. In case you haven't gotten the picture yet from all of the above referenced scriptures, one of the purposes of the believer is to suffer. This suffering is not the same as suffering for doing wrong.

Biblical Suffering vs. Lack of Stewardship

Some of you think your poor economic status is the result of you suffering for Christ, when in all actuality it's just a result of your lack of knowledge concerning how to manage your money. Some of you believe your job laying you off was just a form of suffering that Christ used to test your faith, when you really got laid off because you were thirty minutes late for work everyday. In both of these situations the suffering was well deserved. Suffering for Christ's sake however is being able to still show your neighbor love even though you know that they have been telling lies on you. Suffering for Christ's sake is being able to rejoice when the job lays you off, but you know that you are an excellent worker.

Suffering for Christ's sake is when people do all kind of evil against you, but you never attempt to render evil for evil. Instead you pray for your enemies that God will bless them in spite of all the wrong doing they are practicing. If you can suffer with Christ, then you can reign with him as well (Romans 8:17). Suffering gives the believer fellowship with Christ Jesus. Fellowship is the tie that binds all believers. Patient suffering yields great perseverance (Romans 5:3). Perseverance equals completeness in the believer's life and where you have completeness, there will be no lack (James 1:2).

Bear One Another's Burdens

Brothers, if someone is caught in a sin, you who are spiritual should restore him gently. But watch yourself, or you also may be tempted. Carry each other's burdens, and in this way you will fulfill the law of Christ. If anyone thinks he is something when he is nothing, he deceives himself. Galatians 6:1-3 NIV

> We who are strong ought to bear with the failings of
> the weak and not to please ourselves. Each of us should
> please his neighbor for his good, to build him up. For
> even Christ did not please himself but, as it is written:
> "The insults of those who insult you have fallen on me."
> Romans 15:1-3 NIV

We found out in the last section that one of the purposes for ministry
was to suffer with Christ. We learned that suffering should be a shared
trait that all believers will have to endure. Where there is suffering, there
you will also find burdens. Whether it's the physical burden of having to
deal with a sickness, or the emotional burden that we bear in the death
of a loved one, our burdens do become difficult for us to attempt to bear
alone. This is why one of the purposes that should be common among all
Saints, is to bear one another's burdens. Romans 12:15 says, "Rejoice with
those who rejoice; mourn with those who mourn (NIV)."

Not only are we to rejoice with those who have experienced a victory,
but we are to be compassionate to those who have experienced defeat.
Many Christians today do the exact opposite of this. When it is that
someone gains a victory that overshadows our on, we immediately begin
planning for their downfall. We hate it when someone get's a new car, a
new job, or a new house if it wasn't us gaining these things. We hate it
when someone else's marriage is working out, and our marriage seems to
be on the rocks. We hate it when someone else get's a promotion on their
job. Today's world and church are so self-centered that we don't want to see
our fellowman succeed. In fact we wait patiently for the day to see them
fall, and we secretly rejoice on the inside when they do.

Paul informs the church at Galatia that when they saw a brother
overtaken in a fault, those who were spiritual should go and restore that
person. Paul had to add the term spiritual because he knew that everyone
who was in the church was not spiritual. It's the same way today. Many
of the people, who worship with you on Sunday, are the very same people
that would attempt to condemn you if you were overtaken in a sin. That's
why it's good for all believers to have a spiritual accountability partner.
You need someone who you can trust to reveal the most intimate details
of your life and someone who you can rest assured that they will be a safe
keep for these details and not tell anyone else.

You need someone who you can tell your biggest struggles and temptations and know that they are not going to condemn you, but they will gently help restore you to the truth. They want allow you to bear the burden yourself, but they will help lighten your load. Truthfully speaking all of us should be this trusting and caring with the burdens of our brothers and sisters in Christ. Even if someone is not a Christian and choose to confide in you, don't condemn them because of their shortcomings, help ease their loading by offering them a solution in Jesus Christ.

A Shoulder to Lean On

Hurricane Katrina, the earthquake in Haiti, the tsunami in Indonesia, and countless other natural events have led to the lost of many lives and the lost of countless homes and jobs for millions of people. Thank God for the financial support that was given and the large number of food supplies that were shipped to the people who lost so much because of these devastating events. Many churches had fundraisers collecting clothes, shoes, food, sending up prayers, and basically doing anything they could to offer the victims support during these troubling times.

Also, many who were not Christians, however they saw a need, jumped in to show their love and support in whatever way they could. The question still remains however, what did you do? Maybe you weren't in the position to offer financial assistance, but did you send up prayers for them. Let me ask you another question. What are you doing to help lift the burdens for the people in your community who have lost jobs? What are you doing for the ones in the neighborhood that are homeless? If you have the means, are you offering your financial support, or are you just telling them you will pray for them? If you have unused rooms in your home, are you offering them to someone that you know is homeless? Are you offering people a shoulder to lean on?

To bring this into perspective, when is the last time you offered assistance to someone in your church who you knew was caring a load that was becoming too heavy for them to bear? As Christians, we are commanded to let our light so shine in this world that men may see our good works and glorify our father (Matt. 5:16). With the recession that we are facing, the rising cancer epidemic, and the growing disrespect for the truth of the word of God, our world is in a dark place. We as Christians have to allow our lives to shine in hopes that someone might see the good that we are doing, and glorify God.

Many people in the world are heavy burdened with a lot of hurt and a lot of pain that they have been trying to bear on their own. Often times the burdens of life become so heavy that many people resort to drugs, alcohol abuse, and sex just to cope with the pain. For some, the hurt becomes so great that they choose suicide as a means to escape their tumultuous life. We as Christians have a duty to let the world know that there is a better way. Christ invited all those who were burdened and heavy laden to come to him and he would give them rest (Matt. 11:28). As ambassadors for Christ and as co-heirs with him because we share in his sufferings, believers have the ability to offer this same rest.

It's not that we can change what's going on in people's lives, but we can help lead them to Christ who can give them rest even in the midst of what they are going through. We can also help bear their burdens by offering them a shoulder to cry on, an ear to listen, and financial support when they are facing a financial difficulty. Most importantly we need to offer prayers for them that God would sustain them in what they are going through and if they haven't, they would realize their need for a savior and give their hearts to God. This is what sharing in another's burdens is all about.

It's the Christian's duty to help share the load with their fellowman. We should constantly look for something that we can do for our brother instead of always just focusing on ourselves. It's satisfying to know that you are being a help to your fellow brother and it's even more invigorating knowing that helping one another is pleasing unto God. The writer of Hebrews sums this up quite well in the following verse of scripture:

> Remember those in prison as if you were their fellow prisoners, and those who are mistreated as if you yourselves were suffering... And do not forget to do good and to share with others, for with such sacrifices God is pleased. Hebrews 13:3 NIV

Grow In Your Faith

As a believer we should be striving daily to develop a deeper relationship with Christ. The more you read his word, and soak in its truths, the more you should become impregnated with power to actively live a holy life. Also as you begin to feast on the word of God daily, your faith should continually grow. Romans 10:17 says, "…faith comes from hearing the message, and the message is heard through the word of Christ (Romans 10:17 NIV)." With modern day technology, taking in the word of God has become more feasible than ever before.

Those who can't read can listen to tapes and CDs that contain either sermons preached at their local churches, sermons from other notable preachers and teachers whose foundation is routed in the unadulterated word of God, or they can even listen to the Bible on CD which is being offered by such companies as Zondervan who were the developers of the series the Bible experience.

For those who can read, but have a hard time understanding the normal 1611 King James Bible there are a number of good alternatives. There are Bible commentaries that will help you study properly. There are also great study Bibles with footnotes which will give you a clearer understanding of harder to understand passages of scripture. I would like to caution you however not to get so wrapped up in reading footnotes about what the text says that you don't give the Holy Spirit an opportunity to minister to you personally concerning the text. With that being said however, there are a number of great Bible translations that I find quite sound.

Some of my preferences include the New King James Version (NKJV), the English Standard Version (ESV), the New Living Translation (NLT), and my personal favorite is the New International Version (NIV). I can't tell you which one is right for you. Try reading a text from each one before you make your choice. Be sure to choose one that doesn't jeopardize the integrity of the message that is intended to be conveyed by the original writer of the text. Choosing the best text can be stressful, but if you take out time and study the background on each text, along with staying forever prayerful, you will make a good choice.

We Are Without Excuse

The whole point I'm trying to make is that no one can make an excuse for not studying the word of God, and thus increasing their faith. In fact it's not just a suggestion, it's a command. The Bible commands believers to study to show themselves approved unto God (2 Tim. 2:15). Keep in mind that the word of God is no value unless it is received and lived out in faith (Hebrews 4:2). You know that the word has been received in faith when you see your life style begin to change. We should be dying to our old way of thinking, and developing a more Christ-like mindset everyday. This means that the word of God should be moving beyond your ears and making it to our hearts. For it's with the heart that one believes.

The devil will do everything he can to keep this from happening because he knows that if we have the word of God in our hearts, then we have the only weapon we would ever need, with unlimited ammo, to defeat him every time he attacks. He doesn't want to do battle with a person who is full of God's word and faith because he knows he can't win that battle. Having God's word and faith in that word is a deadly combination.

Faith in God's word makes the word come to life. There would be no limit to what you would be able to do if you begin to proclaim the word of God in faith. Jesus states in Mark 11:23, "I tell you the truth, if anyone says to this mountain, 'Go, throw yourself into the sea,' and does not doubt in his heart but believes that what he says will happen, it will be done for him (NIV)." Nothing would be impossible for you.

This is why Satan doesn't want your faith to grow. Instead he wants to steal the word from you before it has a chance to manifest in your heart which produces faithful, powerful living (Mark 4:1-20, John 10:10). Faithful living is fruitful living. John 15:16 let's us know that God's children have been appointed to bear fruit. But not just any fruit, fruit that will last. When your faith is strong, even when everything around you is barren, you can still bare fruit. Even when the rain has ceased and the world appears to be in a drought, God will supernaturally make a way for his people to produce. This is the same thing he did for the Israelites in Egypt. No matter what plague was taking place in Egypt; the Israelites who were living in Goshen were unaffected.

I'm not saying that you want have seasons of struggle. I'm not saying that your faith will not be tested through various trials in life. What I am saying is that the problems of this life will not be strong enough to make you lose your faith. Why? Because the closer you get to God, the more you learn of God's faithfulness. So even though you may be experiencing tough times, you know you have a promise from God which has now manifested in your heart. And that promise is that God will supply all your needs according to his riches in Glory. His riches are limitless; therefore none of your needs will ever go unsatisfied.

Increasing Your Faith

In order to increase your faith in an individual, you have to know that the person is faithful. As applied to the faithfulness of God, Charles F. Pfeiffer makes the following proclamation: "the term faithful as suggesting that God is worthy of love and confidence from man, and that He will keep His promises with respect to both rewards and punishments." We have to know that everything that God has promised in his word, he is faithful to fulfill them. In fact even when we waiver in our faith, God's character requires him to remain faithful (2 Tim. 2:13). God proclaimed to Moses concerning himself that he was compassionate and gracious, slow to anger, and that he abounded in love and faithfulness (Exodus 34:6).

God rewards those who diligently seek him (Hebrews 11:6). The more of God's word you take in, the more your spiritual appetite will increase (Matt. 5:6). As a result of your constant word intake, your faith will also increase. John 15:7 says, "If you remain in me and my words remain in you, ask whatever you wish, and it will be given you (John 15:7 NIV)." When you begin to petition God according to His word, and not because of your own selfish gain, your words accompanied by faith will move God's hand to action in your life. Make God's word come to reality in your life.

Share Your Faith with Others

Faith is the foundation of Christianity. You believe in Jesus Christ by faith, and are saved. The journey of faith doesn't stop their, however. The process of sanctification requires the believer to continue developing in their faith. Hebrews 11:6 tells us that without faith it is impossible to please God. If you take a deeper look at faith, you will see that faith determines the beginning of the Christian's life, and faith will also determine the end of the Christian's life. Hebrews 12:2 let's us know that we have to look to Jesus who is the author and finisher of our faith. Only Christ can continue to develop our faith unto perfection. Growing in your faith in Christ is essential to the spiritual development of every believer.

Growing in your faith in Christ and increasing your knowledge of his word is also essential to the believer's witness. If you don't grow in your faith then you will never be able to confidently teach others how to follow Christ. Hebrews 5:12 states, "...though by this time you ought to be teachers, you need someone to teach you the elementary truths of God's word all over again (NIV)." It's time that we check our foundation and make sure that it's built soundly on Jesus Christ. Having a strong foundation in Christ gives the believer access to unlimited favor from God. In fact Jesus said that anyone who has faith in him will do even greater works than he did during his earthly ministry (John 14:12). That's a bold statement, but I believe that Jesus made this statement because he knew that the future generation would have excess to such a vast array of technology.

With so many advancements in technology we will have an opportunity to reach an enormous amount of people with the gospel. The disciples would have been limited in who they would be able to reach due to transportation and technology restraints. Although their impact on the world would be life changing, the number of people that they would be able to reach wouldn't come close to the number of people that we would be able to reach. If we couple our faith, with the vast amount of ministry outlets that are available to us from radio to television, the impact would be astounding. Thank God that television networks such as TBN, DAYSTAR, TWN, and countless others are acting as a vehicle and voice to spread the message of the faith all over the world. Many churches are also sending missionaries to foreign countries and to unprivileged third world nations to share the good news.

Are You Sharing Your Faith?

While all this is great, there is still a lot of work that needs to be done. Jesus told his disciples that the harvest is plentiful, but the laborers are few (Matt. 9:37). Jesus didn't just stop there however. He then told his disciples to ask the Lord of the harvest to send out workers into the harvest field (Matt 9:38). The harvest field is the world. The harvest is those who have yet to be reached with the saving message of Jesus Christ both foreign and domestic. There are millions all over the world who have yet to hear the message of Jesus Christ.

To bring this closer to home, there are also millions domestically who haven't had the message of faith presented to them. To be honest half of the people in your neighborhood have probably never heard the message of the gospel. That's where we come in at. As disciples we are commanded to go out and make other disciples. In fact, this was the last thing that Jesus told his disciples to do:

> Then Jesus came to them and said, "All authority in heaven and on earth has been given to me. Therefore go and make disciples of all nations, baptizing them in the name of the Father and of the Son and of the Holy Spirit, and teaching them to obey everything I have commanded you. And surely I am with you always, to the very end of the age."
> Matthew 28:18-20 NIV

When people think of purpose, they usually think of what will garner them the most money, honor, or respect. Most people are so selfish and narrow minded that they only focus on discovering a purpose that will allow them and their family to live the rest of their life comfortably, and not how they can use their purpose to be a benefit unto others. 1 Peter 4:10 states, "Each one should use whatever gift he has received to serve others, faithfully administering God's grace in its various forms (NIV)." Your purpose in life is never designed to be used for your own personal satisfaction. In fact it's just the opposite. Your purpose in life is to use whatever gifts God has blessed you with to serve others. The greatest service that you could ever render to anyone is to lead them to Christ Jesus.

As Christians we have a divine mandate to let the world know about the salvation that has been bought for them through the shed blood of Jesus Christ. Some may say well I'm not a minister how can I ever lead people to Christ. On the contrary, all of us are ministers. All of us have been given ministry gifts from God to be used for the edification of the body of Christ. We have a promise from God that he would surely be with us always. We also have the indwelling Spirit of Christ which gives us the power needed to boldly proclaim the word of God and exercise our gifts for the glory of God. With all of these factors at play within us, we have no excuse for not telling someone about the goodness of God.

We should be witnesses on our jobs. We should be witness in our local communities. We should be witnesses in our schools. You should use every opportunity possible, and exhaust every resource possible to let someone know about the goodness of God. This requires a lot of hard work; however the reward of seeing souls saved will be well worth it. Those who have been given many gifts, and those who have been blessed financially, should use these assets to further the message of the faith in every way possible.

You could support local missionaries in their travels to foreign lands to spread the gospel. You could support local and/or national television ministries in their endeavors to reach as many people as possible with the word. If you are a minister and have the means to do so, you could start a radio or television ministry, or do like I did and write a book in hopes of furthering the gospel of truth. We should make use of every resource that we have and explore every avenue that has been provided to us in order to insure that no one goes unreached with this great saving message of Jesus Christ.

Declare his glory among the nations, his marvelous deeds among all peoples. Psalms 96:3 NIV

Be Good Stewards of Your
Gifts and Talents

Each one should use whatever gift he has received to serve others, faithfully administering God's grace in its various forms. 1 Peter 4:10 NIV

Now it is required that those who have been given a trust must prove faithful. 1 Corinthians 4:2 NIV

So it is with you. Since you are eager to have spiritual gifts, try to excel in gifts that build up the church. 1 Corinthians 14:12 NIV

But to each one of us grace has been given as Christ apportioned it. This is why it says: "When he ascended on high, he led captives in his train and gave gifts to men." Ephesians 4:7-8 NIV

Oh how people so often take for granted the gifts and talents that God has so graciously bestowed upon them. A lot of people use their gifts and talents to bring glory and honor to their selves. Some use their gifts to bring glory to the devil. Some are highly aware of their gifts; however they choose not to even use them. Still others feel as though that they don't have any gifts or talents and as a result their gifts go unutilized. I chose to include this section here not because everyone has the same gift, but because everyone in fact does have a gift. As a Christian, one of your purposes in life is to develop and be a good steward in the gifts and talents that God has given you.

When God created you he didn't just create you to take up space in this world. He created you for a specific purpose, and he has a specific plan for your life. Your gift may not be the same as my gift, but whatever gift you have, the same Spirit that is working in me, is the same Spirit that is working through you. 1 Corinthians 12:4-6 states, "There are different kinds of gifts, but the same Spirit. There are different kinds of service, but the same Lord. There are different kinds of working, but the same God works all of them in all men (NIV)." Stop letting the enemy make you feel as though you don't have a gift. The reason he does that is because he doesn't want your gift to ever manifest. Instead he wants it to lie dormant and as a result those who would have benefited from your gift will go unreached. It's our job to discover what gifts we have, and to begin working on perfecting those gifts that God has given us in order to bring glory to him.

But I Don't Know What My Gift Is…

For some of you it may be quite easy to determine what your gifts and talents are. Still for others, identifying your gifts might not be as obvious. Some people discover they have a gift in a specific area of ministry after they have amazingly overcome a dramatic experience in that particular area of their life. For instance, many women discover that they have a gift for battered women's ministry after they have survived an abusive marriage. Many former drug abusers discover that they have a gift for dealing with addicts who otherwise would never be able to overcome their addiction.

A lot of times your greatest frustration will reveal the area of ministry that you should be functioning in. If you find yourself frustrated over and over again concerning the way the finances are being handled at your local church assembly, then maybe you should be working in the finance department. If you find yourself shrieking in response to every wrong note the keyboardist plays no matter how microscopic it may be, then you may have a gift for music ministry. If you find yourselves always feeling obligated to help people who are in need, or offer your assistance to people in need, even to people you may not even know, then you may have the gift of helps.

Often times our gifts do not reveal themselves until we are forced to assume a position that maybe we didn't want or one that we didn't think we were capable of fulfilling. Joel Osteen, who is now Pastor of Lakewood Church in Houston Texas which according to Church Growth Today is America's largest and fastest growing church, never thought that he would preach the gospel. In fact he stated that he was content with just working behind the scenes at Lakewood Church, which was founded by his father

John Osteen, as the producer of his father's televised sermons in which he did for 17 years.

According to Joel his father encouraged him to preach, however he declined. As time went by he began to feel compelled to accept his father's invitation to preach the gospel. Coincidently only two weeks after he preached his initial sermon, his father died. Joel was chosen to assume the role of the pastor, a position in which he didn't even think he would ever be able to fill. It was only because of his father's encouragement that a gift that had been lying dormant within Joel ever came into the forefront.

The Buried Talent

Unlike Joel, everyone will not have to discover their gifts in such dramatic fashion. However, similar to Joel, many people will discover their gifts when and where they least expected it. Maybe you have yet to have that light bulb moment in your life. However, if you continue to seek God through prayer and reading his word, and you are actively living out your faith, God will reveal the gifts and talents that he has placed inside of you. Only be faithful to use your gifts and talents for the glory of God. Don't be like the servant in the illustration that Jesus told his disciples in which a master gave his servant a talent and he buried it in the ground (Matt. 25:18). The talent in this context was referring to money; however the story contains the same principal as it relates to your physical talents.

If you need more money, then learn how to invest wisely the money that he has given you, and use the talents and abilities that he has given you to maximize your wealth. Deut. 8:18 says, "...for it is he who has given you the power to get wealth (NIV)." The servant, who was given five talents, went and gained five more. The servant, who was given two talents, went out and gained two more. They used the talents that they had been given to garner more talents. These servants were such smart investors that they were able to double their net worth. As Christians, our talents should have the ability to reproduce fruit in our lives. If God can trust you with a little, then he can trust you with a lot.

God has given you the ability to achieve everything that he has predestined you to accomplish. If you are seeing fruitfulness in your ministry and in your finances then that means that your gifts are not lying dormant, but your gift is growing your potential to do, and to have more. This does not only have an affect on your life, but your gifts and talents have the capability to positively affect others. When God sees you using your gifts to help others and thus growing the kingdom, he can trust you enough to bestow more gifts upon you. He knows that you are not going to be selfish with your gifts. He knows that you will not use your gifts and talents for the wrong reasons. Instead, God knows that you are going to use your gifts as vehicles to further his kingdom. Then and only then can you step into the overflow.

The Faithful Servant

Many people are asking God for more gifts and talents, but they don't use the ones they have. He gave you a gift to sing praises unto his name, but you let fear keep you from singing. He gave you a gift to preach, but because you are afraid of what people may say, you choose to just sing in the choir instead. He gave you the ability to use your talents to foster wealth, yet you continue to operate in a position that doesn't allow your true gifts and talents to make room for you. You constantly ask God to give you more, but you haven't learned how to be faithful with what he has already given you. You have to understand that to whom much is given, much is required. Before God will agree to give you more he has to know that you are going to use the gifts and talents that you currently have for the right reasons. Then God can declare that you are a faithful servant.

The servant who hid his talent showed that he lacked the responsibility needed to be a faithful steward of God's resources. Instead of investing his talent in order to gain interest, he chose to just put his talent under the mattress. Therefore, it didn't have any way of growing interest. As a result the one talent that he had was taken away from him and given to the servant who already had ten talents. The reason God did this is because the servant who had ten talents had already proven that he was faithful with what God had entrusted to him. He could now step into a season of more than enough.

Are you using the talents and gifts that God has given you, in order to gain more? Or are you concealing your gifts and talents because of fear or laziness, and continuing to operate in lack? Are you being selfish with your gifts only using them for personal gain? Or are you using your gifts as ministering tools to advance the message of the faith and to stir up gifts and talents that have been lying dormant in others?

Using Our Gifts to Edify the Church

No matter what your particular gifts or talents may be Christ commands that you be a good steward of them. If you don't know what your gifts are then seek God through prayer and through studying his word and he will reveal them to you. Once you discover what your gifts are you have to remain faithful in using them for the good of the kingdom. Use your gifts, in conjunction with your fellow brothers and sisters in Christ's gifts, in order that the end result will result in glory and honor for God and growth in your local church. Never use the gifts that God has given you for selfish gain. Freely you have received; freely shall you give (Matt. 10:8). Paul tells us to try to excel in the gifts that help build the church. Our main goal in ministry should be to make sure that our gift is benefiting our local church assembly and ultimately serving to grow the entire kingdom of God.

Don't let money and notoriety become your principal motives for pursuing one particular ministry over another. Christ called you to grow in the ministry that he had preordained you to be in, not to be ineffective in a position that satisfies your need for power and acclaim. Remember all of the gifts that were given serve important functions in the body of Christ. None of them can function in and of themselves, but they feed off each other to insure that the body of Christ operates more proficiently. The effectiveness of your fellow brothers and sisters in Christ will largely be contingent on your faithfulness in utilizing the gifts and talents that God has given you. If you don't use your gifts and talents, then God may give it to someone else who will be faithful with his investment.

Whether it's money, be good stewards of your money. Apply principal to how you manage your money, and you want have to constantly ask God for a financial miracle. Consider the ant, how they store their provisions in summer and gathers its food at harvest. Don't let the world shape your thinking and cause you to become so much in debt that when the seasons change in your life, you don't have sufficient provisions. If it is gifts, then use the gifts that God has given you as avenues for first glorifying God, for helping others, and for generating wealth in your life. If you learn how to manage your little, when God grants you with more, you will be equipped to handle the overflow.

Serve One Another

You, my brothers, were called to be free. But do not use your freedom to indulge the sinful nature; rather, serve one another in love. Gal. 5:13 NIV

Jesus called them together and said, "You know that those who are regarded as rulers of the Gentiles lord it over them, and their high officials exercise authority over them. Not so with you. Instead, whoever wants to become great among you must be your servant, and whoever wants to be first must be slave of all. For even the Son of Man did not come to be served, but to serve, and to give his life as a ransom for many." Mark 10:42-45 NIV

For who is greater, the one who is at the table or the one who serves? Is it not the one who is at the table? But I am among you as one who serves. Luke 22:27 NIV

Sitting down, Jesus called the Twelve and said, "If anyone wants to be first, he must be the very last, and the servant of all." Mark 9:35 NIV

...whoever wants to be first must be your slave—just as the Son of Man did not come to be served, but to serve, and to give his life as a ransom for many." Matt. 20:27-28 NIV

> Your attitude should be the same as that of Christ Jesus:
> Who, being in very nature God, did not consider equality
> with God something to be grasped, but made himself
> nothing, taking the very nature of a servant, being made in
> human likeness. And being found in appearance as a man,
> he humbled himself and became obedient to death—even
> death on a cross! Phil 2:5-8 NIV

Take a close look at the above reference scriptures and see if there is anything that jumps out at you concerning the nature of Christ. In case you haven't figured it out by now, the familiar characteristic in which you will see in each verse concerning the nature of Christ is the fact that he was a servant. He wasn't a selective servant, he was servant of all. In other words he didn't only serve those who had the power to elevate his social status. Christ made it his personal business to serve everybody and he proved this by dying on the cross so that all that believed in him would receive salvation. The apostle Paul let's us know that our attitude should be the same as Christ Jesus. That means that if we desire to be like Christ, we have to learn how to serve.

This is a huge problem in our world today. This is also becoming a problem, and has been for some time, in the church. Everybody wants to be served and no one wants to serve. Christ makes it clear that in order to be the leader, you must first be a servant. This is because leading and serving are synonymous with each other. A great leader is always looking how he can serve his followers. Christ illustrates this when he washes Peter's feet. Peter vehemently tried to talk him out of doing this; however Jesus was illustrating a very powerful picture of Biblical servitude. One of the problems that we are seeing in the church today is a lot of leaders who step into leadership before they learn how to serve. In fact, a major contributor in the influx of new churches, are people who refused to submit to authority in their local churches.

Please note that there are no authorities accept the authorities that God has instituted. Therefore, to disobey those who have authority over you, is a direct act of disobedience against a God ordained institution (Hebrews 13:17). Of course all of this is subject to whether or not the leadership you are under is abiding by the written word of God rather than manmade dictates that deter from the faith. However, if the leadership you're under is abiding by the truth of the word of God, then you have no excuse not to serve well in that ministry. This has to be a two way thing though. As we can see from the above referenced scriptures, leadership has an even greater responsibility to serve the people. This is the difference between choosing to serve, and choosing to be a servant.

Choosing to Be a Servant

I happened to be doing a study one day about servant hood and I came across a lesson from a group call Acts 17:11 Bible Studies ministries. During the article the following statement really stood out to me:

> "When we choose to serve, we are still in charge. We decide whom we will serve and when we will serve. And if we are in charge, we will worry a great deal about anyone stepping on us or taking charge over us. But when we choose to be a servant, we give up the right to be in charge. There is great freedom in this. If we voluntarily choose to be taken advantage of, then we cannot be manipulated. When we choose to be a servant, we surrender the right to decide when we will serve. We become available and vulnerable. In the discipline of service, there is also great liberty. Service allows us to say "no" to the world's games of promotion and authority. It abolishes our need and desire for a 'pecking order.' Service banishes us to the mundane, the ordinary, and the trivial."

This particular section of the study really stood out to me because it described Christ's earthly ministry perfectly. Christ didn't choose to serve. If Christ had of chosen to serve, then he wouldn't have had any obligation to stay on the cross and die for such wretched people. He could have made his dying on the cross conditional by only choosing to die for the people who had treated him well. If he would have chosen to serve, it's no way he would have ever been able to submit to the government officials of his day seeing as though he knew that the entire government rested on his shoulders. Neither would he have abided by such civil laws such as paying taxes to Caesar seeing as though he was the King of Kings. But Christ didn't choose to serve; he chose to be a servant. There is a very distinct difference in the two.

A servant unbiasedly serves everyone. A servant also always considers others more important than themselves. A servant doesn't need a title to make him feel important; instead he is happy just to be known as a servant. A servant doesn't want to sit at the table in order to be waited on; he wants to be the one who is serving the table. If you look throughout Christ's entire earthly ministry you will soon discover that Christ was the ultimate servant.

Learning to Serve

As Christians, we should look for opportunities to serve others. Whether it is sacrificing eating at Apple Bees to buy groceries for someone who is in need, or sacrificing a Saturday of college football to cut your neighbor's grass, servitude should be an everyday practice of our lives. Christ makes it very clear, he didn't come to be served, but he came to serve. Likewise, we as Christians should never look for anyone to serve us, but we should go out of our way to serve others. It doesn't matter what your title is on earth, when God sees you he only sees a servant. It's only when we humble ourselves to be a servant that God can exalt us to be a leader. With that being said we should never use serving others as a ploy to gain notoriety. Keep in mind that God knows the motives of your heart. However, as Galatians 5:13 says, the Christian's purpose in serving should always be to glorify God and we should always serve one another in love.

Love Your Neighbors

The entire law is summed up in a single command: "Love your neighbor as yourself." Galatians 5:14 NIV

A new command I give you: Love one another. As I have loved you, so you must love one another. John13:34 NIV

Be devoted to one another in brotherly love. Honor one another above yourselves. Romans 12:10 NIV

Now that you have purified yourselves by obeying the truth so that you have sincere love for your brothers, love one another deeply, from the heart. 1 Peter 1:22 NIV

This is the message you heard from the beginning: We should love one another. 1 John 3:11 NIV

And this is his command: to believe in the name of his Son, Jesus Christ, and to love one another as he commanded us. 1 John 3:23 NIV

And he has given us this command: Whoever loves God must also love his brother. 1 John 4:21 NIV

To list every scripture reference concerning the word love would require me to write a completely separate book just about the subject matter. In fact, that might not be a bad idea seeing as though love is the "heart" of the Christian faith. Tina Turner wrote a song called, "What's Love Got to Do with It." Perhaps my book would be titled, "Love Had Everything to Do with It." If you notice I used the word "had" to signify the past tense. The reason being is because everything that is living and breathing in the world today is a byproduct of the love that was demonstrated by God giving his only begotten Son as a ransom for our sins. What's so amazing is the fact that love had to be established even from the foundation of the world.

Adam and Eve sinning in the garden was not an after thought for God. Isaiah 46:10 let's us know that God knew the end, even from the beginning. Therefore a redemptive plan to save humanity, hinged on love, from its otherwise hopeless state had already been predestined even before the fall. To make this more personal, God had already predestined you to be adopted as his children through Jesus Christ, in accordance with his pleasure and will, to the praise of the glory of His grace, by which He made you accepted in the Beloved. This means that even before you accepted Christ, even before your conception, God had already accepted you in the Beloved. I know it's enough to give the toughest man the chills. To think that someone could love you, when by nature he knew your heart would be deceptively wicked and hostile towards him baffles the mind.

This type of love goes in stark contradiction to the type of love that is being exhibited in today's world. We tend to only love those who will reciprocate this love. We love those who look like us, who dress like us, and who like the same things we like. We tend to love the ones who have the same struggles we have, or who share our same successes. We love the ones who show us respect, and for the most part we love those who have our same last name. However, true love should never be based on whether or not the love is reciprocated. Christ says as he has loved us, we "must" love one another. Did Christ only love those who loved him back? Did Christ only love those who were a part of his circle? Did Christ only love those who showed him respect, or for those who were a part of his family?

The answer is obviously no. In fact the type of love Christ demonstrated surpassed anything people had ever seen before. In Matthew 9:11 Jesus' disciples are questioned by the Pharisees concerning why Jesus was eating lunch with tax collectors and sinners. In those times, tax collectors were considered some of the most immoral people alive. Because of this, they were usually frowned upon and considered as social outcast. No self respecting righteous person would be caught in the same vicinity as these men. However, because Jesus was eating with them the Pharisees assumed that he was in agreement with them, and thus he was as wicked as they perceived the tax collectors to be. Of course, this was not the reason Jesus was eating with them, but Jesus had other reasons which were centered in love.

True Love Doesn't Bring Condemnation

Jesus didn't want to make people feel alienated because of their lifestyle; he wanted to show them that he loved them even though he may not have approved of their practices. When Christians today don't agree with someone's lifestyle choices they usually disassociate themselves from that person or that group. We focus so much on the lifestyle of the person that we forget about the humanity of the person. Instead of showing love to the person as Christ commanded we do, we focus primarily on the sin, and leave the person unhealed. Trying to change one area in a person's life only solves one of what could be many problems in that person's life. However, if we begin to feed them the word of God in love, not just concerning their issue, but just about who Jesus is and the victory that was won for them on Calvary, a change will take place on the inside.

Through the word of God, and the love that we show, we give the word of God an opportunity to bring conviction on the person's heart. They begin to see things differently then they saw before. Once the Holy Spirit brings illumination of the word, then the word of God will require a response from the individual. They will not feel comfortable doing the things that they were once doing because the word has been put into their hearts and it starts to change the way they think, and thus their actions. They have come face to face with the word of God, and their hearts have been overshadowed with the sweet love, and truth of the Holy Spirit. This is not a love that brings condemnation, but a love that brings conviction, life evaluation, and ultimately it leads to life reformation.

Keep in mind that the key to all of this is whether or not the word of God has been presented in love. We as Christians can cause something as powerful as the word of God to lose its power when we present it in the wrong way. We shouldn't talk about people to death, but we should begin loving them to life. This requires us to look beyond the person's faults and see their need for help. Jesus understood this perfectly. In response to the Pharisee's question Jesus answered and said, "It's not the healthy that need a doctor, but the sick." Jesus then told them to go and learn what this means: I desire mercy not sacrifice.

The Pharisees probably talked about mercy; however they were hypocritical in their approach towards those who needed mercy. On the contrary, Jesus was actively demonstrating compassionate love towards all those in distress as a typing shadow of the love that he would show on Calvary's cross when he would die for the sins of the entire world, not just a select few. The Pharisees were good at talking love, however towards those that they considered sinners and thus inferior, they looked down on them in disgrace.

True Love is an Action

Just like the Pharisees love is a word that routinely proceeds out of our mouths, but it doesn't come from a deep affection that is genuinely routed in our hearts. As you can see however, whenever Christ used the word love he was referring to a deep routed affection from the heart that translated into actions. In other words true love should always be accompanied by actions that reflect the love of God in our hearts. How you treat others will be a direct reflection of the heart you have for God. John 14:15 states, "If you love me, you will obey what I command (NIV)." The Christians love for God will produce faithful living in every aspect of their life. This is especially true in relation to how we treat others, especially other believers.

How can you love God, in which you have never seen, but hate your neighbor who you see everyday? Of course this is a rhetorical question. The only way to truly love God is to love your neighbors. This love doesn't just apply for the neighbors that you get along with, but this extends to your enemies as well. In fact Jesus tells us to love our enemies and pray for those who persecute us (Matthew 5:44). So does that mean you have to pray for that person that lied on you? It most certainly does. Does that mean you have to pray for that person who mistreated you? Absolutely! Does that mean that you have to pray for that person who hated you without a cause? Neither is that person excluded from your prayers, or from your love.

Did Christ exclude you from his plan of redemption when you did all of the above things and more to him? No he didn't. Therefore, as a Christian we have to demonstrate love towards everyone, even the ones who don't appear to deserve it. Just remember none of us deserved the grace and mercy of God, but he gave it to us anyway. No one should be excluded from our circle of love. Unfortunately, many of today's churches only choose to show love to certain people. We show love to the liar, but we hate the fornicator. We show love to the cheater, but we hate the adulterer. As Christians we can never discriminate against anyone in regards to showing love. That doesn't mean that we love the lifestyle that they are practicing, but we have to recognize that they still have a soul that needs to be saved.

True Love Doesn't Discriminate

One of the most discriminated groups of people in the church today is homosexuals. Instead of embracing them as human beings that are "sick" and in need of a physician, we usually treat them like aliens with an incurable disease. We say we still love them, but our actions say otherwise. We discriminate against them so much that they feel alienated, and usually just quit coming to church, or worse yet they go find a church that makes them feel comfortable by condoning their actions. Usually once they get with a group of people who show them love and acceptance, even though they may be compromising the truth of the word, it's usually hard to win them back.

Christians should never love from a distance. The same way we embrace the liar, we should embrace the homosexual using our outward showing of love to stir up an inner conviction in their hearts. Everyone has an inward ability to recognize what's morally right and wrong. Sometimes, however, it takes love to break down the wall of pride that they have built up against the truth. A little love can go a long way. Our showing of love allows the Holy Spirit to break up the fallow grounds of a person's heart, and then the scales can begin falling from their eyes. This can't be a one time showing of love and affection, but this has to be an ongoing demonstration of true Christian love in hopes that our persistence in showing them the love of Christ will eventually help them discover the truth of the word of God, which will lead to a reformed lifestyle and a victorious Christian life.

Love Makes Faith Work

As I stated earlier, love is the heart of the Christian faith. This is because love makes faith work (Gal. 5:6). Without love your faith in God would be null and void because God's moral fiber is love. If you want to be sure of your faith, then examine your love. Love assures the Christian's discipleship. John 13:35 says, "By this all men will know that you are my disciples, if you love one another (NIV)." Perhaps the most well known chapter concerning love is Romans 13. When you are examining your love, you should consider the material discussed in this chapter as a guide. Ask yourself the following questions.

1. Is your love patient and kind when dealing with others regardless of their lifestyle practices?
2. Does your love envy others accomplishments or even their failures?
3. Is your showing of love only done to boast about what you do for others, or are you rude when offering your assistance to others because you're really not doing it from the heart?
4. Does your love only seek how it can benefit you? Are you irritable or resentful when you show acts of loves to others?
5. Does your love rejoice in wrongdoing, or does it rejoice in truth?

If your love doesn't rejoice in truth, then it's not really love. If your love is impatient, and lacks the tolerance to endure mistreatment or hurt, then your love is questionable. The only way to continue towards Christian discipleship, you have to grow in your love. In fact, Christ informs his disciples that the greatest commandment in the Law was to love the Lord God will all their heart and all their soul and all of their mind which is the first commandment (Matt. 22:37). Christ didn't stop there. He continues by saying that there was another commandment just like the first one, and that was to love their neighbors as themselves. This was an astonishing statement because by saying this Jesus was equating the love of our neighbors, with the love of God.

Jesus made this statement because he knew that by showing love for one's neighbor, a person was showing love to God. As I stated earlier it's no way to love God without loving your neighbor. It's also no way to love your neighbor, unless you love God. Ultimately what Jesus was saying was that if a person walked in perfect love for God and for their neighbors, then they wouldn't break any of the other commandments as they all revolved around how we treated God, and how we treated our neighbors. No matter what a person's moral or religious beliefs may be, we have a responsibility to show them love. This is not always easy to do. Love of this nature takes hard work, but be sure that the wages for all your hard work, carried out in love, will be well worth it.

God is not unjust; he will not forget your work and the love you have shown him as you have helped his people and continue to help them. We want each of you to show this same diligence to the very end, in order to make your hope sure. We do not want you to become lazy, but to imitate those who through faith and patience inherit what as been promised. Hebrews 6:10-12 NIV

Glorify God through Praise and Worship

I've discussed a small number of purposes that are common among all believers. I want to culminate this section by discussing two more common purposes for all believers, and they are praise and worship. There are two main definitions for praise. One of these definitions means to express approval, commendation or admiration for someone or something. We praise our children for doing well in school. We praise a friend's accomplishments when they gain a great victory in life. We praise someone's nice car or nice home. We praise a pastor's dedication in preaching the word of God and in shepherding the flock of God.

We as Christians also praise the dedication and great works of past champions in the faith such as the Apostles Peter and Paul, and in modern days times the Evangelist Billy Graham and the Bishop T.D. Jakes. While it's good to express approval for those who are continuing diligently in the faith, this praise should never be confused with the praise that we offer God.

This brings me to the other type of praise, this definition being the extolling or exaltation of a deity. In Christianity we praise the one true God, the supreme deity. There is no customary way to praise God. In fact, the Bible offers many ways to praise God. Some of the many ways to praise God are through singing songs (Ps. 40:3, 47:6), through playing music (Ps. 33:2, 92:1, 98:5, 147:7, Ps. 150), to exalt his name with words (Ps. 145:21), to praise him with a dance (Ps. 150:4, Jer. 31:4), through the lifting of our hands (Ps. 28:2, 63:4, 119:48), and even through prayer (Ps. 143:6, Ex. 9:29) just to name a few. Keep in mind that this is not an exhaustive list. Therefore, we shouldn't use this list to make a guideline for praising God.

Instead we should praise him in the manner in which he moves us to do. The main thing is that we continue in our praise to God and for nothing, or no one else. We should never praise anything or anyone as a deity in our life. This invokes the anger and the wrath of God as he has commanded, "You shall have no other gods before me (Exodus 20:3 NIV)." God proclaims in Isaiah 42:8, "I am the LORD; that is my name! I will not give my glory to another or my praise to idols (NIV)." God is a jealous God. We have to be careful not to give anything precedence over God in our lives. Whether it's our careers, our possessions, our spouses, our boyfriends or girlfriends, our thoughts or desires, nothing should ever cause us to praise it more than God. Not only should we not offer praise to anything or anyone as deity, but we have to be careful that we don't receive praise from others as though we were deity.

The Danger of Stealing God's Praise

The thought of receiving praise that belongs to God should be the last thing on any Christian's mind. We should constantly guard our hearts and mind from feeling deserving of praise or honor. This is an easy way to become arrogant and puffed up, which leads to God having to humble us. The Apostle Paul constantly reminded the churches that his motives for doing well was never intended to garner praise from men as he understood that God was the only one deserving of such praise (1 Thess. 2:6, Gal. 1:10, 1 Cor. 10:33).

Although Jesus was very much equal to God, he never accepted praise from men, yet always reverted praise back to his Father. John 5:41-44 states, "I do not accept praise from men, but I know you. I know that you do not have the love of God in your hearts. I have come in my Father's name, and you do not accept me; but if someone else comes in his own name, you will accept him. How can you believe if you accept praise from one another, yet make no effort to obtain the praise that comes from the only God (NIV)?"

Exalting ourselves to god-like status comes with a rather high price to pay. One that not even the richest of the rich could afford. Jesus told us in his word that whoever exalts himself will be humbled, and whoever humbles himself shall be exalted (Matt. 23:12). Don't think so highly of yourself that God has to allow something to happen to you in order to bring you back down. Willingly humble yourself before God and he will exalt you in your due season (1 Peter 5:6). Don't be like King Nebuchadnezzar who God humbled by public humiliation. God took him from standing confidently on two feet as King of Babylon, to walking on all fours and eating grass with the beast of the field. This had to be very embarrassing for King Nebuchadnezzar but at least this experience made him recognize the only true God. Others haven't been so fortunate.

Acts 12 tells the story of King Herod who had to face the ultimate punishment because he accepted praises that belonged to God: On the appointed day Herod, wearing his royal robes, sat on his throne and delivered a public address to the people. They shouted, "This is the voice of a god, not of a man." Immediately, because Herod did not give praise to God, an angel of the Lord struck him down, and he was eaten by worms and died (Acts 12:21 NIV). Notice that God brought immediate judgment on King Herod for this blasphemous act. He didn't even have an opportunity to apologize to God for his ignorance.

This goes to show you that the very moment you begin to exalt yourself in your own thinking, could be the very moment that God brings judgment on you. I warn you to please be afraid of trying to take glory that belongs to God. Maybe you are saying that this will never be you. But if all of us were to really take inventory on our lives, we would probably find areas that we accept more praise than what we deserve. Whether it's a pastor receiving too much praise from his congregation, a musician that takes all the credit for his talent, a singer who takes too much credit for her singing abilities, or a political leader who garners a little too much respect, it's time to make sure that we are reverting all praises back to God. In fact, in everything we do, in everything that we accomplish, as believers we have to be sure to shift ALL the glory back to God.

Praise is Mandatory

Let your praise for God be an outward showing of an inward gratification that you have for him. God's glory should shine so brightly through us in this world, that when people see our good deeds they should immediately offer praise unto God (Matt. 5:6 NIV). Now we know that praise is mandated for all believers (Rev. 19:5), but did you know that praise is also mandated for everything and everyone that have breath in their body? Psalms 150:6 let's us know that everything that has breath is commanded to praise God.

The beasts in the field are commanded to praise God. The birds of the air are commanded to praise God. The adulterer is commanded to praise God. The liar is commanded to praise God. The atheist is commanded to praise God. God reigns on the just as well as the unjust. That means that even the people who may not recognize him as God, still owe him praise because it's only because of him that they are living and breathing. We shouldn't just be praising God in order to receive blessings, we are praising God because he is worthy of all praise, and because he continues to give us grace and mercy even though we don't deserve it.

We praise God just because he is God. Even when we don't feel like it, even when we are exasperated in our spirit, we should continually offer God a "sacrifice" of praise (He. 13:15 NIV). After all, look at the sacrifice that he offered for you, in order that you may have an eternal resting place in his kingdom. While praise is commanded for everyone, worship is only possible for believers. While praise is more often than not done with your lips or through external means, worship is usually done from the heart. The Christian's worship is more than just a traditional form of worship that we usually associate with our "worship service" at our local churches.

I Live to Worship You

Worship is an experiential response of the believer by words, acts, and service which he exalts the living God.[4] With that being saying we can

4   Elmer L. Towns. *Theology for Today* (Ohio: Cenage, 2008), 902.

consistently see in the Bible that worship applies to how Christians honor God with their whole lives. Therefore worship is more of a lifestyle rather than a singular act. True worship can only be born through a relationship with God. It's only when you develop a personal relationship that you can actually appreciate who God is. Humbleness of heart has to precede your worship.

Time and time again we see in the Bible where men and women of God would worship him in response to his greatness. These people were usually awe stricken at God's awesome power and his righteousness in judgment on their behalf, so much so that they would usually bow their faces to the ground as a sign of their humility towards him (Ge. 24:26, Ge. 24:48, Ex. 4:31, Nehemiah 8:6, Ps. 95:6).

At the Passover, the Israelites would always bow down and worship God showing their deep appreciation for sparing them when he struck the Egyptian homes with death (Ex. 12:27 NIV). When the wise men saw baby Jesus for the first time, even though he was just a baby, they proceeded to fall down and worship him (Matt. 2:11). That's because they recognize that he would be the savior of the world. When is the last time you bowed down and worshiped the King of Kings? True thankfulness for God's holiness demands an immediate worship. When Moses was permitted to see the back parts of God, as soon as he saw them he "immediately" fell down and worshiped God (Ex. 33:23). Worship brings the believer into a constant reminder of all that God is and all that he has done for us.

It takes us beyond the veil of our own self-righteousness, and allows us to behold Christ's blood that is forever sprinkled on the mercy seat for us. When we routinely worship God, we will always possess a humble disposition because worship helps us recognize how undeserving we are of God's grace and mercy. This humbleness will translate unto how we live our lives. Romans 12:1 reads as follows: "Therefore, I urge you, brothers, in view of God's mercy, to offer your bodies as living sacrifices, holy and pleasing to God—this is your spiritual act of worship (NIV)."

Now you may say, why am I offering my body as a living sacrifice unto God? We do this because he is so merciful. What if it doesn't appear that his mercy is being shown in my life right now? That's not possible because God's mercy endures forever (Ps. 136:1 NIV). In fact, each day you wake up it's a brand new mercy (Lamentations 3:1). You may see now why you should offer your bodies a living sacrifice unto God, but now you are trying to figure out how you do that.

You present your body as a living sacrifice unto God, Holy and acceptable by not offering the parts of your body to sin, as instruments of wickedness, but rather offer yourselves to God, as though who have been brought from death to life; and offer the parts of your body to him as instruments of righteousness (Ro. 6:13 NIV). You have to put to death the sexual cravings and evil desires that would attempt to make you walk in your former way of life (Col. 3:5 NIV). Maybe your next question may be, how do I control these evil desires?

That's a good question, but God has an answer for that too. In Galatians 5:16 God let's us know that if we let the Holy Spirit guide our lives, then we won't practice what our sinful nature desires (NLT). The reason being is because the Holy Spirit will only lead you and guide you in the truth of the word of God. It's up to you, however, to follow the promptings of the Holy Spirit. When our lives align with the word of God then this pleases God, and our lives become a spiritual act of worship unto him.

Relationship Birth's Worship

There are a few important details that are associated with worship that I want to touch on before I close this section. First, in order to worship God you have to "know" him. In other words you must experience Christ on a personal level and be convinced within yourself that he is the one true God. When Paul visited Athens he read an inscription on their walls which read, "TO AN UNKNOWN GOD (Acts 17:22-31)." They were worshiping something that they didn't even know. Paul was going to use this as opportunity to introduce Jesus to them in hopes that they would develop a personal relationship with him. Jesus states the following in John 4:23-24 (NIV): Yet a time is coming and has now come when the true worshipers will worship the Father in spirit and truth, for they are the kind of worshipers the Father seeks. God is spirit, and his worshipers must worship in spirit and in truth."

What stands out the most with this scripture is the fact that when Jesus made this statement he was talking to a Samaritan woman. If you know anything about Jewish history, Samaritans and Jews were like oil and water, they just didn't mix. Yet what Jesus was telling her was so profound. What Jesus was saying was that the time would come, and had already come, that no matter what your ethnicity, social class, or gender; the true worshipers would worship him in spirit and in truth. How do we worship God in spirit and in truth? We worship God in spirit and in truth by keeping all his commandments that he has commanded in his word.

Mark 7:7 reads, "They worship me in vain; their teachings are but rules taught by men (NIV)." Jesus was quoting from the book of Isaiah concerning the spiritual hypocrisy of the Pharisees. He stated that these men honored him with their lips, but their hearts were far from him. They were holding fast to the traditions of man, and not the word of God, thus their worship was in vain. The only way to affectively worship God in spirit and in truth is to walk in complete obedience to the word of God as the Spirit teaches you its truths, not traditions that have been passed down in your local churches. This brings me to my next point.

God Doesn't Share His Worship

Secondly, we should offer our worship to God and to him only. Exodus 20:5 states "Do not bow down before their gods or worship them or follow their practices. You must demolish and break their sacred stones to pieces (NIV)." In this scripture, God is speaking to Israel concerning serving the gods of the nations that they would be conquering. He warns them sternly not to bow down to these gods or to practice their worship practices. In the world that we live in, there are many "gods" attempting to make us bow down to them. It may be money. It may be careers. It could even be religious leaders. Any natural thing that you put in front of God has just taken his place of importance in your life.

It's imperative that we forever guard our hearts and minds against anything that will attempt to distract us from worshiping God. Even though God had given the Israelites strict warning, they still ended up bowing down and worshiping these other gods (Deuteronomy 29:26).

This probably happened because instead of them being obedient and demolishing those created gods made by man, they allowed them to stay around and eventually succumbed to the desire to worship them. They exchanged the truth of God for a lie, and worshipped and served created things rather than the Creator (Ro. 1:25). They were operating in the sin of idolatry. They had forgotten that God was a jealous God and wouldn't share his glory with another.

Are their some things in your life that you know are becoming the object of your affection, rather than God? If so, it's time to destroy whatever that something is. If it's a person, please don't take this as an opportunity to "literally" destroy them. But their may be some relationships that you will have to allow to dissolve because you know that it's not beneficial to your relationship with Christ. Don't wait. The longer you allow that thing to stay around, the more and more you will be tempted to serve it. Jesus understood this concept when he was dealing with Satan in the desert.

The longer he allowed Satan to stay around in his weakened state, the easier it would have been for him to be manipulated. Satan came to Jesus and promised him all these great things if he would bow down and worship him; however Jesus didn't entertain these thoughts. Instead, he resisted Satan with the truths of the word of God. In response to Satan's offer Jesus makes the following statement: Luke 4:8, "…It is written: 'Worship the Lord your God and serve him only (NIV).' "

Satan couldn't stay around when Jesus begin to defend himself with the Word. Some of you however, are powerless when Satan comes to tempt you because you don't have any word on the inside of you. You have to bear in mind, Satan doesn't want your praise, he wants your worship. The reason being is because he knows that anyone can praise God, but only those who have a relationship with God can worship him. Therefore, he will do anything to steal worship for himself that he knows belongs to God. That's why it's important to have a firm foundation in the word of God so that you want be fooled.

The Importance of Orderly Worship

Getting back to Israel, many of the nations that they were conquering were practicing religious worship that hinged on sin and degradation. Many of these cultures practiced temple prostitution as a form of worship, while others would burn their sons and daughters in the fire as sacrifices to their gods. God warned them not to worship him in this way as these things were detestable in his sight (Deut. 12:31). While the above two examples may be a little bit on the extreme side of worship practices, many of today's churches still do practice worship that is not Biblical. This brings me to my next point, worship has to be orderly.

As Christians, how we conduct ourselves in this world should be an exact representation of the orders that have been laid out in the word of God. This is our spiritual act of worship. What a lot of us miss, however, is how we should conduct worship in our local church assemblies amongst other believers. While I'm not saying that every church should utilize hymn books, however I don't see anything wrong with that, nor am I saying that anything new and progressive such as using a full band with lead guitars and multiple keyboard players verses the traditional church organ is on the extreme side, however what I am saying is that however you choose to worship God it should be done in decency and in order. Paul discussed an issue with the Corinthian church concerning the manner they conducted their worship service.

As in every spiritual gift, worship is to be used as a way to edify the church (1 Cor. 14:12). Also, just like any other gift, if abused it can cause more damage than it can help. This was the problem that Paul was seeing with the Corinthian church and he addresses this issue in chapter 14 of the book of 1 Corinthians. The church of Corinth were zealous for spiritual gifts, however they hadn't fully learned how to utilize the gifts that God had given them, in particular the gifts of tongues. Apparently people were speaking in tongues without providing the revelation of what they spoke. Although this would have been a benefit to the person's spirit who spoke in tongues, their speaking wasn't fruitful to the ones who heard them speak without the proper interpretation (1 Cor. 14:6-12).

In fact, this would have caused confusion among those who heard these inexpressible tongues, without the proper interpretation. As Paul states, God is not the author of confusion (1 Cor. 14:33). We should never allow our spiritual gifts, no matter how zealous we are to use them, cause confusion in the church. When we do this, no matter how spiritually gifted we may be, we are not helping to edify the church, but we are contributing to its downfall. As Jesus said, a kingdom divided against itself cannot stand (Mark 3:24).

Therefore even in our worship, it has to be done in unity with the other believers in the church. Even Paul, although having many spiritual gifts, knew that he had to exercise order when it came to using his spiritual gifts. Paul states in 1 Cor. 14:18-19, "I thank God I speak in tongues more than all of you. But in the church I would rather speak five intelligible words to instruct others than ten thousand words in a tongue (NIV)."

Often times when it appears that we are doing less, we are really doing more. Keep in mind that Paul never told us not to use our spiritual gifts. Instead he says that whether we are singing a hymn, giving a word of instruction, or whatever spiritual gift we are utilizing, to use it for the strengthening of the church (1 Cor. 14:26 NIV). Paul again focuses on the use of tongues when he says that if anyone speaks in a tongue, two or three at the most should speak, one at a time, and someone must interpret (1 Cor. 14:27 NIV). If there is no interpreter then the person should keep quiet (1 Cor. 14:28).

In regards to prophesying, Paul states that two or three prophets should speak, and the others should weigh carefully what is said (1 Cor. 14:29). If a revelation comes to someone who is sitting down, the first speaker should stop, for they should all prophesy in turn so that everyone may be instructed and encouraged (1 Cor. 14:30-31).

Again I pose the question: was Paul trying to hinder people from utilizing their gifts? Absolutely not! Paul's aim in giving them instruction was merely to ensure the proper growth of the church. While Paul mainly focused on the gifts of prophecy and tongues, this same concept of order applies to all the spiritual gifts that are used in the worship service. The singers can't sing over one another. The preachers can't preach over one another. The teachers can't teach over one another. But as Paul states, everything should be done in a fitting and orderly way (1 Cor. 14:40 NIV).

This is the only way to keep peace in the house of God during our worship services. You have to be in control of your spiritual gifts. If someone is operating in a particular gift and you feel as though you want to worship God in that same area, then wait until they finish so that whoever needed to hear what they were saying or doing, has an opportunity to do so.

There is a time for corporate worship, such as during the singing of hymns, corporate prayers, and during certain times of the service dedicated for that. Other times, we have to make sure that we stay in the order of the service and don't allow our act of worship, to be a source of divisiveness in the church. When we come to worship services we are not coming to see who can worship God the best. After all, true worship comes from the heart. We are coming to participate with other like-minded believers in expressing our gratitude for who God is and to exalt his Holy name together. We are not seeking to edify ourselves, but are looking to use our worship to edify one another: Let us therefore make every effort to do what leads to peace and to mutual edification (Romans 14:9 NIV).

Worship Reveals God's Purposes

The last important point that I want to point out about worship, is that worship helps guide us to divine purpose. Worship puts the believer in tune with the Holy Spirit, and allows them to hear God's voice more clearly concerning his will for their lives. Acts 13:2 states, "While they were worshiping the Lord and fasting, the Holy Spirit said, "Set apart for me Barnabas and Saul for the work to which I have called them (NIV)." As Barnabas, Paul, and some of the other prophets were worshiping the Lord and fasting, God spoke new direction into the lives of Barnabas and Paul. I like the word that KJV uses when it states that as they "ministered" to the Lord. The verb tense of the word "minster" means to attend to the wants and needs of others.

Now it would be absolutely absurd to think that God needs something from us. Nowhere in scripture does God ever say that he needs anything from us. In fact, God let's us know that if we chose not to worship him, the rocks would cry out (Luke 19:40). God is not codependent on us, we are codependent on him. It's in him we live, move, and have our being, we are his "offspring (Acts 17:28 NIV)." Acts 17:25 states, "And he is not served by human hands, as if he needed anything, because he himself gives all men life and breath and everything else (NIV)." Seeing as though God has existed eternally even before the creation of the world, then we know that he doesn't need anything to sustain him as he has everything he needs within himself.

A Sacrificial Worship

We now know that God doesn't need our worship, so why does he want our worship? Contrary to what many believe, God is not a narcissistic tyrant who needs worship to stroke his ego. In the Bible, the words worship and sacrifice are used in the same sentence several times (Is. 19:21, 2 Kings 17:36, 1 Sam. 1:3). This let's us know that our worship is a sacrifice unto God. How is that? Joshua 22:27 states, "We will worship the Lord at his sanctuary with our burnt offerings, sacrifices, and fellowship offerings (NIV)." The Israelites used sacrifices and offerings as a way of worshiping God. The problem was that no matter how much they offered God, it would never be enough of a "sacrifice" to restore their relationship with God which had been compromised because of Adam and Eve's sin.

Hebrews 10:1 states, "The law is only a shadow of the good things that are coming-not the realities themselves. For this reason it can never, by the same sacrifices repeated endlessly year after year, make perfect those who draw near to worship (NIV)." When Christ came into the world he informed us that these "type" of sacrifices and offerings were not desired by God, nor did they please him (Hebrews 10:4-6 NIV). The truth was that the blood of bulls and goats didn't have the power to take away sins. However, the sacrifice that Christ made by willingly laying down his life was sufficient enough to make perfect all those who are being made holy. In other words, Christ made the first sacrifice.

He promised that for all those who would believe in him, he would put his Spirit on the inside of them and their sins and lawless acts would be remembered no more (He. 10:17). Without the shedding of blood there is no remission of sin. Whenever you think about shedding blood, it always brings the word "sacrifice" to mind. When people donate blood to the local hospitals and blood banks they are doing it voluntarily and not out of obligation. So what does this have to do with worship?

Let's say for instance you were riding down the road speeding during heavy rain. You lose control of the car and slam into a tree throwing you out of the front windshield into a large field. A person who was riding in the car behind you quickly calls 911 on your behalf. When the emergency personnel get to the scene of the accident they find you severely injured and on the verge of death, however you are not quite dead yet. They think that they may be able to save you, however they have to act fast. You have lost a ton of blood and are in desperate need of a blood transfusion. There is one problem however. You have a very rare blood type and they can't seem to find anyone who shares your blood type.

You lay in the hospital bed clinging for dear life, however the more the time goes by, the more you begin to doubt whether or not they will ever find a donor. Your death sentence appears more and more inevitable. Just when you have all but given up hope, the nurse runs in to inform the doctor they have found a match. The person's identity of course has to remain anonymous. What is certain, however, is the fact that you are going to live. If you had a chance to meet this person, how would you repay them?

This is what Christ did for us. Before we accepted Christ into our lives, we were all wretches whose fate was sure to be everlasting damnation. No matter what we did to get into right standing with God, it would never be good enough to rectify our wrongs. For the most part, many of us didn't even attempt to correct our wrongs. We lived life worshipping the created things, rather then the creator; something that God strictly forbad us to do in his word (Ro. 1:25, 2 Kings 17:35, Deut. 5:9, Exodus 34:14). We worshipped everything, but the one who deserved the worship.

In spite of the world's constant rejection of him, God still sent his son Jesus to die for all those who would accept him. He paid the ultimate sacrifice for the world. This sacrifice would deliver us from our certain "death sentence," and would secure our seat in Heavenly places. Did we deserve this unbelievable act of benevolence? No, we didn't. Yet, God still did it for us. So how do you plan to repay him?

Of course, we know that we are no longer required to offer God blood sacrifices and offerings to appease for our sins. However, now we are commanded to offer God a living sacrifice by keeping our bodies holy and by living holy lives. This requires us to walk in total obedience to the word of God as it relates to how we should treat ourselves, and how we should treat others. We have been brought near unto God through the shed blood of Jesus Christ; however it's how we live our lives that will determine how deep our relationship is to God. Living a holy life will be a sacrifice, yet we know that this is a reasonable sacrifice considering all that he did for us.

Some days you might not feel like treating your neighbors right, however you have to do it because this is your spiritual act of worship. Some days you might not want to study the Bible, but you have to do it because this is your spiritual act of worship. Some days you might feel tempted to defile your body by engaging in premarital sex, adultery, or through the use of drugs or alcohol. However, your desire to worship God should far exceed your desire to satisfy flesh. This is of course if we are continuing in God's word, praying and fasting, and living holy lives. It's only when we begin to present our bodies to God as instruments for righteousness that we can truly know what is pleasing unto God for all Christians, and ultimately what is pleasing to God for our individual lives. Only through true worship, can we discover our purpose.

Why Do We Worship?

Again, why do we worship God? We worship God because he didn't allow us to die in our sins and go to Hell. Instead, he died for our sins, so that we could have eternal life. He made the ultimate sacrifice for us even though we constantly rejected him. For that we owe God worship. Another reason that we should worship God is because he is holy. Psalms 99:5 states, "… worship God because he is holy (NIV)." Psalms 96:9 says that we should worship the Lord in the splendor of his holiness. If you don't think you have anything else to worship God for, then you should worship him just because he is Holy. True worshippers never worship God for what he can do for them; they worship him because of his character. They worship him because he is righteous. They worship him because he is holy. They worship him because he is just. If you are worshiping God because you are caught up in what he can do for you as it relates to material possessions, then you obviously have a misconception of what worship really is.

A true worshipper is a person who has fallen in love with the very essence of God. The essence of God incorporates everything that He is. When you fall in love with God in this way, then you can't help but feel obligated to give him your entire being, because you realize all that he gave for you. This total commitment to God will be seen through how you live your life. You will live your life in total adherence to the word of God, and this spiritual act of worship will be pleasing in the sight of God. When you have this type of reverence for God, it no longer matters what God does to please you, the only thing that matters to you is whether or not you are pleasing him. Although you may not be worshiping God in order to receive a return, our sacrifice will demand a return. The return for serving other gods is destruction (Deut. 8:19), but the return for worshiping the one true God is far greater than anything we could ever imagine:

> Hebrews 12:28—Therefore, since we are receiving a kingdom that cannot be shaken, let us be thankful, and so worship God acceptably with reverence and awe, for our "God is a consuming fire (NIV)."

CHAPTER 9

Define Your Vision

"That which you desire you can envision. That which you consistently envision you come to believe. That which you believe is manifest in physical form. That which is manifest in physical form you can experience in your life. Look at your current Life experience and you will have discovered what you envision." - *Chuck Danes*

Proverbs 29:18 "Without a vision, the people perish (KJV):"

In the last chapter we discussed many of the purposes that were common among all believers. In this chapter we are going to discuss how to define God's vision for our lives on an individual basis.

Who Am I?

Who do men say I am? I use to wonder, when Jesus asked the disciples this question, whether or not he was asking them to define him. After careful studying however, it became crystal clear why Jesus asked this question. He didn't ask this question because he needed definition, he asked the question because he already knew who he was, he just wanted to see if those who were connected to him, knew who he was as well. This is perhaps one of the most important questions ever asked as it relates to discovering purpose. However, this is a dangerous question to ask if you don't have any ideal of the answer yourself.

In fact, some of you only bought this book because you thought that by some divine revelation I would be able to define what your purpose is in life. However, that's not the reason I wrote this book. I wrote this book in hopes that through the scriptures that were given, and spiritual insight that was given to me in interrupting them, that someone would be more equipped to answer the question, Who am I? For some of you the question still lingers, where do I fit? What is God's unique purpose for me? Why was I created? If you are still asking these defining questions, then you are still in danger of being manipulated into believing a false truth about yourself. In fact, the reason why some of you are where you are at right now is because you have been letting too many people define you.

The truth of the matter is no one can define you but Jesus Christ. How does he define you? Through his word! Everything that you need to know about yourself, and thus your purpose, is laid out for you in the Holy Bible. Through the word of God you can effectively answer the question, who am I? How you answer this question will determine which path you follow from this day forward. Will you continue to be a victim of your past mistakes and failures? Or will you step into the destiny that God has for your life? Will you let ethnicity or family stereotypes keep you from fulfilling your purpose? Or will you rise above the negativity and break every generational curse that has ever tried to attach itself to you?

No matter what you accomplish some people will only see you for who you use to be, or from where you came from. You have to know however that as a believer your destiny is never connected to where you came from, your gender or ethnicity, or from your family connections. Some of you are actually looking at where you are at right now saying that there is no way that God has a specific purpose for my life. You have to engrave the following truth in your mind: your current location doesn't determine the future destination that God has for you.

Envision Your Destiny

At the start of this section I used a quote from the famous author and public speaker Chuck Danes, who is the founder of Enlightened Journey Enterprises located in Oklahoma City. I want to be very clear here, just because I used this particular quote, does not mean that I support everything that Chuck Danes says. Chuck focuses on empowering people to discover and to begin utilizing their unique individual abilities to achieve their purpose in life. I, on the other hand, believe that an individual's true potential is only realized when they accept Christ into their life. What I do agree with Chuck on is the fact that if you desire something long enough, you will start to envision it.

That which you consistently envision you come to believe and that which you believe is manifest in physical form. I do want to point out the fact that just because you desire something, and envision it, and then it manifests itself in your life, that doesn't mean that you have discovered your true purpose. Since what you envision begins with your desires, it's important to make sure that you desire the right things.

I quoted Psalm 37:4 earlier which says that if you delight yourself in the Lord, then he would give you the desires of your heart. The word delight in the verb tense means to give great pleasure or joy. So what gives God pleasure? Contrary to popular belief God doesn't get pleasure in making our flesh happy. Paul writes that nothing good dwells in our flesh (Ro.7:18 KJV). Galatians 5:17 goes on to let us know that the sinful nature desires what is contrary to the Spirit. We can't trust our own desires as legitimate sources for determining our life's purpose. The reason why some of us are where we are right now in life is because we listened to our fleshly desires, instead of the Spirit of God. The flesh only desires what feels good. However, anything that would inconvenience the flesh or that will make it work a little bit harder than what it was use to is usually rejected.

We can't bring pleasure to God by seeking what pleasures our flesh. At one time all of us sought pleasure rather than God. Titus 3:3 states, "At one time we too were foolish, disobedient, deceived and enslaved by all kinds of passions and pleasures. We lived in malice and envy, being hated and hating one another (NIV)." Before I accepted Christ, I had very different aspirations for my life. My aspirations were usually driven by self-centred desires, which usually consisted of how much money I could make.

Now I wasn't trying to be a drug dealer, or start a criminal enterprise in order to acquire instant wealth. As I stated earlier, in the early parts of my life I strove to be the next Bruce Lee. I thought that maybe I would star in multiple movies, start my own chain of martial arts studios, and then retire at about age forty with multiple houses, multiple cars, and tons of money in the bank. I wasn't looking for ways to help others; I was only looking for how I could better myself.

This way of thinking continued throughout my life as I grew older. Although I changed my mind many times concerning what I wanted to be in life, the choices that I made were always driven by how much money I could make and what would assist me to live a comfortable, carefree life. Although I'm not saying that being wealthy is wrong, the acquisition of wealth should never be your primary motivation for doing anything. The Bible says that those who desire to be rich fall into temptation and a snare (1 Tim. 6:9). The Bible informs us that even as our riches do increase, never to trust in them (Ps. 62:11) and those who trust in their riches will eventually fall (Pro. 11:28).

Riches are only temporal. That's why the Bible tells us not to store them up down here on earth (Matt. 6:19), rather he tells us to store up treasures in Heaven (Matt. 6:20). Never let money determine your purpose or you will most certainly miss out on what God has for your life. Sure, if what you decide to do brings you great wealth, then this would obviously be very pleasing to you, but how do you think it would make God feel if what you do isn't pleasing unto him?

Often times God will withhold certain things that you have been asking him for because he knows that you have the wrong motives in asking him for these things. James 4:3 states, "When you ask, you do not receive, because you ask with wrong motives, that you may spend what you get on your pleasures (NIV)." This further confirms that God is not concerned whether or not you acquire great wealth, before you discover what his will is for your life. For most of us, we wouldn't be able to handle great wealth. In fact, it would probably be a snare to us and would lead us into trusting our wealth more than God. This of course would not be pleasing unto God.

So the question still remains, what gives God pleasure? David gives us the answer to this question. David states in Psalm 147:10-11, "His pleasure is not in the strength of the horse, nor his delight in the legs of a man; the Lord delights in those who fear him, who put their hope in his unfailing love (NIV)." God takes great delight in those who fear him and for those who put their hope in him. How do we show God we fear and love him? We talked about this earlier, but just as a refresher, we do this by keeping his commandments (St. Jo. 14:15, 21, 23 and 1 Jo. 1:6, 2:3, 5:3). Ephesians 1:4-6 says, "For he chose us in him before the creation of the world to be holy and blameless in his sight. In love he predestined us to be adopted as his sons through Jesus Christ, in accordance with his pleasure and will—to the praise of his glorious grace, which he has freely given us in the One he loves (NIV)."

God chose you before the creation of the world to be holy and blameless in his sight. Living a holy and righteous life brings pleasure to God. When you are trying to discover your purpose in life the first question that you have to ask yourself is whether or not you are pleasing God with how you live your life. Are you walking in obedience to the word of God? When your motivation for living is to make sure that you live a life that is pleasing unto God, then God can make your way prosperous. Ecclesiastes 2:26 says, "To the man who pleases him, God gives wisdom, knowledge and happiness, but to the sinner he gives the task of gathering and storing up wealth to hand it over to the one who pleases God (NIV)." When a person truly pleases God with their lives then God will give them wealth that they didn't even have to work for. He will do this because he knows that you didn't seek wealth before you sought his kingdom. This is what he did for King Solomon.

The Lord came to Solomon and told him that he could ask whatever he wanted from him and it would be given to him (1 Kings 3:5). Solomon could have asked God for anything that he wanted including great wealth, long life, great power, and for a kingdom that would last for eternity. Instead, Solomon asked God for wisdom and knowledge to carry out the purpose that he had for his life, which was to be king of Israel (1 Kings 3:9). Solomon's response pleased God. It showed God that Solomon had a heart to please him first before he accomplished anything else in life. Because of this, not only did God give him great wisdom, but he gave him wisdom that would be unmatched by anyone during his lifetime, and for eternity (1 kings 3:12). Because Solomon had a heart to please him, God also gave him both riches and honor, more so than any king in his lifetime (1 Kings 3:13).

The Rewards of Pleasing God

Solomon's story should illustrate an important truth to all believers: there is great reward in pleasing God. With that being saying, there is only one way to truly pleasure God and that is to walk in obedience to his word. Let me restate this to make sure that you understand how important this is. The only way to truly discover your purpose and to begin utilizing the gifts and talents that God has given you to be everything that he has ordained for you to accomplish in this earth, is to hide God's word in your heart, and to begin walking in total obedience to his word. The word of God has all the instructions you would ever need to please him. Therefore, the more of God's word you take in, the more your desires will begin to shift towards what pleases him.

The word of God also allows you to effectively define God's vision for your life. Studying the word of God should be the most exciting time of every believer's day. When you read it, you are actually reading your past, present, and your future. David said that he rejoiced in following God's statutes as one rejoices in great riches. Why? His word contains the blueprint for obtaining riches in every area of our lives. Christ wants to give us abundant joy, abundant love, abundant happiness, and abundant peace. If you walk in obedience to God's word, God will give you favour in his sight and in the sight of man (Pro. 3:4). Psalm 84:11 states, "For the Lord God is a sun and shield; the Lord bestows favour and honour; no good thing does he withhold form those whose walk is blameless (NIV)." When your ways are pleasing to God he want withhold anything that you need to carry out his plan and purpose for your life.

Without a Vision, the People Perish

Proverbs 29:18 states, "Where there is no vision, the people perish (KJV):" A vision that can't be defined is a vision that can't be achieved. If you are unable to define the vision that God has for your life, then you will continue to walk around aimlessly with no direction, no stability, and no purpose. On top of that you will not be able to answer the important question: Who am I? Everything you do will be marked by confusion and unbelief and according to the Bible anything done in unbelief is sin. Christ does not want you to live this way. He wants you to know that he truly has a unique purpose for your life. The very first purpose that you should have is to become more and more like Christ.

As you become more and more like Christ, and draw closer and closer to him, the more you will begin to discover the person that God has created you to accomplish. David said in Psalms 25:3 that no one whose hope is in God will ever be put to shame. Some of you have dreams and hopes that you have been holding in for a long time. However, you are afraid that if you attempt to do them that it will end in failure, which will bring you shame. No one whose hope is in God will ever be put to shame. As we stated earlier, as you delight in the Lord, or find out what pleases him, then he will begin to change your desires. Therefore the things that you ask God will start aligning with his will and plan for your life. You want ask God for anything that you know will not pleasure him, and if you do he will quickly let you know that he has something different for your life.

We have to do like David and ask God to show us his ways for our life, and to teach us his paths (Ps. 25:3-5). Psalm 119:105 picks it up and says, "Your word is a lamp to my feet and a light for my path (NIV)." I can't stress this enough, when you begin to walk in the word of God, and use it as a guide for every decision you make, you will save yourselves a lot of wrong turns. Proverbs 2:8-9 states, "for he guards the course of the just and protects the way of his faithful ones. Then you will understand what is right and just and fair—every good path (NIV)." Ephesians 5:10 tells the believer to find out what pleases God. Stop guessing at your purpose. Stop asking other people to tell you what your purpose is. God rewards those who diligently seek him (He. 11:6). Jeremiah 29:13 lets us know that if we seek God with our whole heart, then we will most certainly find him.

Seek God through reading his word, through prayer, and by applying his word to your daily life and he will reveal to you what his purpose is for your life. Once God reveals it to you, you will know it. He will cause a strong conviction to set on your heart and to dwell in your mind. You want be able to eat from thinking about it. You will stay up at night with it running through your mind. You want be able to effectively stay in the position that you are currently in because it will eat away at your spirit man so much. You will feel out of place because you know that you are not where God wants you to be, or you are not fulfilling what God has called you to fulfill. The Bible says that whatever your hand finds to do, do it with all your might, for in the grave, where you are going, there is neither working nor planning nor knowledge nor wisdom (Ecclesiastes. 9:10).

Don't perish with your vision. When God places something on your heart to do then don't wait, do it quickly. There are other people who are depending on you fulfilling your purpose. If Christ hadn't of fulfilled his purpose to die on the cross, then none of us would of ever had a chance at eternal life. If Esther hadn't of become the queen of Persia then she wouldn't have been in the position to prevent a mass genocide of the Jewish population in Persia. If Moses would have never fled to the desert to escape the wrath of Pharaoh, then he wouldn't have had his encounter with God and the Jews may still have very well been slaves, or even worst completely eradicated. If Martin Luther King Jr. wouldn't have ever had a dream for equality among blacks and whites, and those of every other ethnicities, then the United States may still be segregated.

Maintaining Your Vision in the Midst of Chaos

My point is this, no matter what your current situation looks like, no matter how bad it may seem, if you stay in the will of God, then it will all eventually turn out for your good (Ro. 8:28). Don't look for God to take you out of the circumstance you may be in now. God might have you there for a specific purpose. Learn how to look for purpose in whatever situation you may be in. Once God has revealed to you your purpose, then write it down and make it plain (Hab. 2:2). As you begin to walk in your purpose, don't become beside yourself because of people who don't support your vision.

Keep in mind that when God gives you a vision, a lot of times people want understand it. Just know that when God gives you a vision, he will provide provision in order for it to come to fulfillment (Is. 55:11). Even when it appears as though the vision is taking a long time to manifest, wait for it. Stand on what God has promised you and know that in God's appointed time, he will bring it to past (Hab. 2:3). Don't wait anxiously; wait in expectation of what you know God is going to do. Don't doubt why you wait, rejoice why you wait. Don't let anything cause you to lose sight of the vision that God has shown you.

It's not what it looks like

As we stated in the previous section, once God gives you the vision that he has for your life, and you have written it down and are working towards it, don't allow situations and circumstances to cause you to lose sight of your vision. Eyes are the gateway to the soul. Your sight shapes your thinking, and thus your actions. If you go outside and see storm clouds, you're likely to grab an umbrella. If you walk outside and see dead snake skin, then you're more than likely to assume theirs a snake close by. This will cause one to pay careful attention to every step they take so that they will be sure not to be caught off guard by the snake. I think you get what I'm trying to say.

What we see has a direct correlation to what we do. In a world full of so much bad, sometimes it's hard to see anything good. Many times what we are seeing in our present makes us forget what God has already shown us in the past. Your vision can't be steered by what you are currently seeing. Your vision has to align with what God sees. Also your vision can't be defined by what other people see. Many of us have had to deal, or are dealing with this same dilemma in our lives right now. God has given you a glimpse of where he was carrying you or what the finished outcome of your journey would be.

God gave you a sneak peak of that new job that will be double the salary compared to what you make right now. God has given you a snippet of your new ministry which was going to go far beyond all of your expectations. God has given you a vision of the missionary work that he is going to use you to do in foreign countries. However, what do you do when what you are currently seeing isn't corresponding with what God has shown you?

I think the best way to answer this question is to ask someone who has been in that same situation and overcame it. Although there are countless others who have been in this situation, the "Hall of Faith" is practically running over with them, I want to take a moment to focus on Joseph. Joseph was the next to youngest son of Jacob (Israel) who had a total of 12 sons in all. His father adored him dearly. In fact the love that he had for Joseph seemed exceedingly greater than the love he had for any of Joseph's brothers and he showed it by given Joseph a beautiful coat of many colors.

To further compound the jealousy of his brothers, Joseph had a dream that all of his brothers were going to be under him. This was very disturbing not only to his siblings, but also his father seemed to take offense to what Joseph had "seen." Have you ever had a dream, a vision, or great idea that you truly believed was heaven sent and you shared it with a friend or family member, only to have them attempt to discourage your dream by distorting what you thought you saw. For example, if you say that God showed you that you were going to own your own business, they say," Where are you going to get the money from to start the business?" You say that you want to go back to school and they say you're too old. You say that you want to buy a new home and they say you will never qualify for the loan. We call these people "dream killers."

Beware of the Dream Killers

It's important to let you know that your vision or dream and the fulfillment of the vision never occur at the same time. Between your dream and the fulfillment of this dream their will be some struggles, some sufferings, and even doubt may attempt to rear her ugly head. These all play a huge part in trying to "kill" your dream. Therefore we call these the dream killers. Dream killers come in all shapes and sizes. They come in all creeds and nationalities. They come in all forms and they come from many different directions. Dream killers can be obstacles that arise in your life that seem impossible to hurdle. Dream killers can be a sickness that all of a sudden attacks your otherwise perfectly healthy body. Dream killers tend to bring about "little foxes" of disbelief that invade your mind to make you doubt the promises of God.

In Joseph's situation, his dream killers were the people in which he trusted the most, his brothers. They were afraid that Joseph would achieve greatness that would far exceed anything that they would ever accomplish, and they were determined to keep this from happening. While dream killers are frequently internal or external problems that arise in an individual's life, more often than not they tend to be people who are the closest to you just as in the case with Joseph. These are usually the people who you trust the most. These are the people whose opinions you hold near and dear to your heart. While many of us have a certain level of confidence in our own gifts and abilities; theirs always someone whose counsel we place even above our own.

The people whose opinions you value the most are also the people who can have the greatest impact, whether good or bad, on how you view yourself. Usually either they don't believe that you are capable of accomplishing what you have envisioned, or they really don't want to see you accomplish what they know that you are capable of accomplishing. Either way it's extremely important that you don't allow yourself to become connected to those who would attempt to abort the promises that God has for your life. You have to disconnect from anyone who would attempt to kill your dream. You have to walk away from anyone who because they don't see what you see, will attempt to make you think you saw something different. Simply put, you can't listen to everyone's opinion.

We All Need Someone

None of us, no matter how gifted, will be able to carry out our vision on our own. Although we frequently desire to be able to take credit for the largest majority of what we accomplish, that's hardly ever the case. Proverbs 15:22 states, "Plans fail for lack of counsel, but with many advisers they succeed (NIV)." Proverbs 20:18 states, "Every purpose is established by counsel (KJV)…" No mater who you are, or how big of an imagination you have, you are going to need someone to help you work your plan. It's extremely important however that you connect with likeminded people. Just like wise counsel can make plans succeed, foolish counsel can cause plans to fail.

Amos 3:3 asks the rhetorical question, "Do two walk together unless they have agreed to do so? The answer is obviously no. In 2 Corinthians 6:14 Paul warns the believer not to be unequally yoked with unbelievers. The obvious difference in viewpoints will cause divisions amongst the two in how they carry out the plan, and a kingdom divided against itself will be impossible to stand. Don't connect with people who are driven by ambition; you need to connect with people who are driven by purpose; a purpose that has been revealed to them by the Spirit.

Further Paul tells the believers in Philippians 2:2 "to make his joy complete by being like-minded, having the same love, being one in spirit and purpose (NIV)." While the unbeliever's aim is to please their flesh, the believer's purpose is always to please God. Stop taking advice from visionless people. This is probably what David meant when he said not to dwell in the council of the ungodly. In case you didn't already know, just because a person confesses to know the word of God does not mean they know the God of the word. You have to make sure that the instruction you follow is in accordance with the word of God. As I stated earlier, the instruction you choose to follow will determine the future you create. Listening to the wrong counsel will cause you to stray away from your inheritance. That's why you have to break ties with anyone or anything that would try to kill your dreams, and thus destroy your inheritance.

Beware of the Dream Snatchers

Dream killers are people or things that would attempt to keep your destiny from ever coming forth, while "dream snatchers" are the people who would attempt to steal your dream that God has destined for you. We are going to get back to Joseph shortly, but in Judges Chapter 11 we are introduced to a man named Jephthah who dealt with a similar situation as Joseph. The Bible says that Jephthah was a mighty warrior, however he had one problem; his family. His father's name was Gilead, but his mother was a prostitute in which the Bible never mentions her name. Gilead eventually had kids by his wife. Because Jephthah was the son of a prostitute his siblings drove him away in an attempt to "snatch" away his portion of the family's inheritance.

They ran him out of town and labeled him an outcast. Can you imagine being driven away from your family because of something you had no control over? Can you imagine the trauma that Jephthah must have felt knowing that the people he loved the most didn't feel the same way about him? For a brief moment Jephthah probably felt worthless. For a short period of time Jephthah probably felt tempted to doubt whether or not God even had a plan for his life. The enemy would love to make you doubt whether or not God has a purpose for your life even after the Spirit has already given you a glimpse of what that purpose was. More than that, the enemy would love to "steal" your inheritance leaving you with nothing. In fact, since the beginning of time this mindset has been the foundation for Satan's very existence.

Don't Let Satan Steal Your Inheritance

John 10:10 states, "The thief cometh not, but for to steal, and to kill, and to destroy:" The reason why some people will call your idea a bad idea, is because they want to snatch it for themselves. The reason why some people will get offended by your success is because they don't understand how you came from the same school as them, the same church as them, maybe even the same family as them, yet it seems as though that you have gained a victory that threatens to eclipse theirs. Isn't it funny how people will love you as long as you are on the same level as them, however when the doors of progress are opened in your life, they quickly begin bringing all types of accusations against you. As a believer however, this shouldn't be a shock to you.

The Bible says that the devil is the accuser of the brethren. The devil constantly makes false accusations against God and God's people. He is the father of all lies. He will tell you that God doesn't love you. He will tell you that you are not a child of God. The devil will try to bring condemnation in your life in order to make you focus more on your past, rather than the future that God has for your life. It's extremely important that we be not ignorant of Satan's vices. You have to make sure you know what God has already said about you, rather than what Satan is currently saying about you. If you are not sure of your identity in Christ, then the devil can easily tell you that you are something or somebody that you are not. He can easily prevent you from walking into the destiny that God has for your life.

That's why theirs so many people who feel as though that God has no purpose for their life because they have been listening to the devil for too long. The devil has set attack against the mind of God's people. He has set up workshops in the passageways of our minds and him and his imps are tugging at the very core of our thought process trying to intercept every good thought, and replace it with a seed of negativity. He attempts to replace faith with doubt. He tries to replace joy with sorrow. He loves to feed your mind with negativity. He understands that nothing he could ever do will hinder God, however if he can make you doubt God, then he can delay your destiny from coming forth.

Perhaps more alarming is the fact that the devil will use whatever means necessary to abort the plan and the purpose that God has for your life and family is no exception. In fact, family tends to be who the devil will use more times than not. He loves to use the people who are the closest to you because their opinions tend to have the greatest impact on the choices you make. That's why it's imperative as believers to take on the mind of Christ. Philippians 2:5 says, "Let this mind be in you, which was also in Christ Jesus (KJV)." When you take on the mind of Christ, you understand that everything that is happening to you, no matter how bad, is all working together for your good.

When you take on the mind of Christ, suffering becomes an intricate part of your lifestyle. Because you realize that in order to reign with Christ, sometimes you will have to suffer. The mind of Christ is a mind of humility, selflessness, and of unity. In other words if suffering keeps me humble, makes me look at the bigger picture which is always bigger than me, and causes me to become united with Christ, then I can rest assured that it will all be worth it in the end.

Go Get Your Inheritance

Just like Jephthah, you have to know that God is in the midst of your chaotic situation. Jephthah is a perfect example that even when people count you out, God can still use you for His glory. When you are a child of God, family may walk away, friends may walk away, but once you are declared a child of God you are endowed with an inheritance that no one can ever take away. Don't believe me? Let me give you a few scriptures that confirm this truth:

> Ephesians 1:13-14: And you also were included in Christ when you heard the word of truth, the gospel of your salvation. Having believed, you were marked in him with a seal, the promised Holy Spirit, who is a deposit guaranteeing our inheritance until the redemption of those who are God's possession—to the praise of his glory (NIV).

> 1 Peter 1:3-5: Praise be to the God and Father of our Lord Jesus Christ! In his great mercy he has given us new birth into a living hope through the resurrection of Jesus Christ from the dead, and into an inheritance that can never perish, spoil or fade—kept in heaven for you, who through faith are shielded by God's power until the coming of the salvation that is ready to be revealed in the last time (NIV).

Now do you believe me? What God has in store for you, no one or nothing can ever take it away. Jephthah would eventually become one of Israel's greatest judges and warriors. The one that was ostracized by his family, deported from his land, and originally denied access to the inheritance is now the one who has been chosen by God to lead the entire nation of Israel. This story should serve notice to you that the situation that you thought was going to destroy you, God is going to turn it around and cause it to exalt you. The very same people that counted you out, God is going to cause them to become stepping stones for your next elevation. So don't become weary while doing well, for in your due season God is going to take you from where you are right now to where he has destined you to be.

CHAPTER 10

The Pathway to your Destiny

Sometimes the road to destiny will be a bumpy one. Often times you may have to take detours in order to avoid potholes and other obstacles in the road. In Spite of all this, if you continually listen to the voice of the Spirit, then you will eventually arrive at your destination. Sometimes on the road you will run over rocks and debris that will damage your exterior. Fragments of your past will attempt to lead you back down a road that God had already led you off. People that you love most will cast stones at you in an attempt to stop your progress. Just as in the case with Job and so many others, it's nothing like suffering to bring about humility in our lives. And he who humbles himself shall be exalted.

In the last chapter we talked about Jephthah and how his family attempted to steal his inheritance. Just like Jephthah, Joseph's siblings were determined to steal his inheritance. Joseph's brothers thought the only way that they could prevent Joseph from being over them, the only way to keep Joseph from gaining an inheritance, was for them to kill Joseph. They figured that if they killed the dreamer, they could ultimately destroy the dream. God was with Joseph though and caused Joseph's older brother Reuben to speak up on his behalf preventing him from being killed, instead requesting that he be sold into slavery. This one act would begin a sequence of turbulent events in Joseph's life. As the old saying goes, "when it rains it pours." Joseph was finding out the reality of this statement from first hand experience.

First of all he is sold into slavery by his brothers and dragged away to a foreign country. After that Joseph would be falsely accused of sexual assault by Potipher's wife and imprisoned for a crime he didn't commit. He then would go on to be forgotten by friends who he helped, who had promised in turn to help him. While the Bible doesn't record it, I'm sure Joseph may have had a moment where he cried out to God and said, "Lord, what's next?" Is that you? Do you feel like that every time you try to do well, nothing good comes out of it? Do you feel like that every time you look around you all you see is problems? Have you ever felt so desolate, that you were tempted to waive the white flag and call it quits?

If so, then I would like to take a moment and welcome you to the club. Because at some point in all of our lives, all of us have felt the pressure of life's burdens weighing down on us. All of us have had that moment of self-pity where we felt like not only had family and friends forsaken us, but God had forgotten about us as well. All that Joseph had to go through, and even all that you are facing right now, should reveal to you the reality that God's presence in our lives doesn't exempt us from suffering. However, as we stated earlier in the case with Job, suffering for righteousness sake identifies us as a child of God.

Christ made the following statement in John 16:33, "I have told you these things, so that in me you may have peace. In this world you will have trouble. But take heart! I have overcome the world (NIV)." So in other words, it's not a matter of if you have troubles, but when you have troubles. I like how Paul puts it in 2 Corinthians 4:8. Paul says, "We are hard pressed on every side, but not crushed; perplexed, but not in despair (NIV);" Theirs one thing that is a surety for all believers; suffering is inevitable.

The great thing about suffering is the fact that it lacks the power to destroy life's purpose. In fact, suffering can have some great redeeming benefits. That's why the Bible says blessed is the man who endures temptation, for when he is tried he shall receive a crown of righteousness (Ja. 1:12). Suffering puts the believer in the necessary posture to be able to handle the blessing that God has prepared for them. If God blesses us without struggle, then many times we may be tempted to become conceited. If the blessing comes without opposition, than you may be tempted to feel as though you are where you are because of something you did.

Developing Christ-like Character

Unfortunately, this is the downfall of so many people. God will grant them a promotion, only to have to script them of it because the sense of entitlement that they developed because of it. With that being said, suffering is necessary. Suffering produces the type of character that God can use. Psalm 34:18 states, "The Lord is close to the brokenhearted and saves those who are crushed in spirit (NIV)." Psalm 147:3 states, "He heals the brokenhearted and binds up their wounds (NIV)." When you have been broken and call out to God from a sincere and humble heart then he will hear you and come to your rescue. Psalms 147:3 let's us know that he will bind up our wounds. In other words, not only will he save you out of the battle, but he will cover the battle scars.

Everything that Joseph went through helped him to develop the right attitude. Although no one wants to endure suffering, sometimes suffering is the best thing that could have happened to us. Because Joseph had suffered so much, when God did bring his dreams to past he was able to appreciate them more. Also, in spite of how his brothers had treated him, Joseph was able to forgive them because he knew that what they had meant for bad, God meant it for his good.

The pathway was rocky for Joseph, but through it all he became a better person, and not a bitter person. He understood that everything that God had allowed to happen in his life, had all contributed in making him the man that he was, and for helping him fulfill the destiny that God had for him. This is what God is saying to each and every one of you that's reading this book. Although your path may appear to be full of trouble, God is going to use this trouble to make and mold you into the man or woman of God that he has called you to be. Through your struggles, God is going to make you better. If you will only remain faithful through the pain of the process, then God will bring every dream that you thought was dead, back to life.

CHAPTER 11

Change your mind, and be Set Free

Romans 12:2 says, "Do not conform any longer to the pattern of this world, but be transformed by the renewing of your mind (NIV)." As a believer we have to take on a different mindset than the world. On the surface, life does seem hard. Through the natural eye sometimes it does appear as though God has forgotten about us. And though promises for success are great, many times it does seem like theirs no hope in sight. On the contrary, with a transformed mind one can look at disaster and see greatness. With a transformed mind we can look at where were at right now, and though it may not be where we want to be, we can still give thanks because we know that God hasn't forgotten about us.

It's only when you take on this mindset that you can successfully walk into your purpose. So how can my mind be transformed? I already quoted from chapter 12:2 of Paul's letter to the Roman church when he talks about the transformed mind. That was just for inspiration purposes. I wanted to inspire you that theirs hope, however I don't want to inspire you, but leave you uninformed. Lack of information has been the catalyst for so many untransformed lives for too long. So many ministries, preachers, teachers, etc. love to inspire people by telling them what they can do, or where they can go which usually makes a person feel good only for a moment. However, God wants us to be free to walk into our destiny. God isn't looking to give a temporary fix; rather He wants to see people's lives changed permanently. Change of this magnitude, however, has to start in the mind.

Free Your Mind and the Rest Will Follow

Theirs an old song that says free your mind and the rest will follow. I said earlier that Satan wants to set up shop in our minds. The reason why is because our actions are ultimately governed by our minds. The mind gives direction to all of our bodily organs in order for them to function properly. That is why when a person becomes brain dead, his body takes on a vegetative state. So even though the heart is beating, and even though blood is flowing, the body is in a suspended state because theirs no "direction" to tell each part what to do. If the devil can cut off your direction, then he can stop you dead in your path.

There are many Christians right now at a stand still, because it appears they have lost direction. They have a promise, they have a vision, but they have lost the map in order to get them to where they need to go. When direction is lost, hope goes along with it. And when one loses hope, if you're not careful, eventually you will also lose heart. The Bible says that hope deferred makes the heart sick. Anything that's sick and left untreated will eventually die. That's what the enemy is doing. He corrupts the mind, snatches your hope, and then he takes your desire (heart) basically leaving you spiritually dead. I think this is why so many people take on a wrong view of God, because they have allowed the enemy to poison their mind with his lies and deceit, and now when they should have a transformed mind, they have allowed their mindset to be conformed by what's going on around them.

So now we know how a mind can be conformed, however that still leaves the question, "How can my mind be transformed?" To answer this question we have to dig a little deeper into the text. If we go back to Romans 12:1 Paul says, "Therefore, I urge you, brothers, in view of God's mercy, to offer your bodies as living sacrifices, holy and pleasing to God—this is your spiritual act of worship (NIV)." The first thing that one has to do to have a transformed mind, is to "offer their bodies as a living sacrifice" unto God. Anytime I think of the word sacrifice, I immediately think of the word pain.

A Living Sacrifice

Sacrifice requires you to do something that you might not be accustomed to doing. Sacrifice asks you to step out of your comfort zone into a place of unfamiliarity. It was a sacrifice for Peter to launch out into the deep at Jesus' request, seeing as though he had been fishing all night and was probably mentally and physically exhausted. Yet, in order to be obedient to the voice of God, he launched out into the deep and caught more fish than his net could handle. It was a great sacrifice for Abraham to offer his only son to God. Nevertheless, Abraham was more than willing to do this just as long as it meant that he was pleasing God.

Although God didn't let Abraham harm his son, the fact that he was willing to offer such a great sacrifice for him, showed God that Abraham was completely sold out to him. It showed that he had developed a mind to please God with his entire being, rather than a mind to please himself. Jeremiah 17:10 says, "I the Lord search the heart and examine the mind, to reward a man according to his conduct, according to what his deeds deserve (NIV)." If God searches your heart and examines your mind, what do you think he will find? Will he find wrong and impure motives? Will he find jealousy, hatred, or envy? Would he find a mind that thinks on good things, or a mind that is depraved and only thinks corrupt thoughts?

Whenever a person has the wrong mind, then his deeds will reflect his thought process. Based on your own estimation of the deeds that you have been doing, what rewards do you think you deserve from God? Have you been spending all your time and energy seeking temporal material things on this earth, or is your mind fixed on those things that are eternal which are above? As we alluded to before, Romans 8:5 states that those who live according to the sinful nature have their minds set on what that nature desires. On the contrary, those who live in accordance with the Spirit have their minds set on what the Spirit desires.

The only way that you can truly discover your purpose and fulfill the vision that God has bestowed on the inside of you, is to develop the mind of Christ. You develop this mind by presenting your entire being: mind, body, and soul, to God to utilize it how he chooses. Presenting yourself entirely to God will be a huge adjustment compared to what you are use to and can only be accomplished when we change our old selfish way of thinking. Any change, no matter how great or small, is never an easy thing to do.

The Pain of Change

If there is one thing that will remain constant throughout all of our lives, then it's the fact that we will be forever changing. Change can be good, such as the change from renting an apartment, to owning your own home, or from working a job making minimum wage, to working a job that pays salary. When a person is single and lonely, then finding that special person is a welcomed change in their life. All of these are good changes that most of us look forward too. These changes don't cause any pain at all, but they usually bring about great joy. Then there is the opposite side of change which is very painful.

For instance, what happens when you lose your job and you can no longer afford that home you had purchased, and consequently have to move back into the apartment? Or what happens when the corporation that you were working for shuts their doors and you have to revert back to making an hourly wage, rather than the annual salary that you had became accustomed to making? What happens when that person's feelings that you had fallen in love with suddenly changes, and they don't love you anymore? Now when you had grown accustomed to having someone in your life, you have to go back to being single and lonely once again.

This type of change usually comes with great pain, emotionally and sometimes physically. Change of this nature is never really embraced, and people who experience this type of change usually feel as though they have failed in life. However, that's usually not the case. You are not a failure; change is just an inevitable part of all of our lives. Saying that, instead of resisting change, we have to learn how to embrace change with open arms.

Embracing Change

Everything must change, nothing stays the same. There are so many facets of change that will play a part in our lives. People's emotions change and so does their physicality. Technology changes and so does the seasons. In fact technology seems to changes just as fast, if not faster than the seasons change. No matter how much we love our family, eventually something will happen that will change our family makeup whether it's marriage, relocation, or death. No matter how much you love your newborn, as life goes on, they will eventually change into adults. As it is in the natural, so it is in the spiritual.

Your spirit man will be constantly changing for the rest of your Christian life. 2 Corinthians 3:18 states, "And we, who with unveiled faces all reflect the Lord's glory, are being transformed into his likeness with ever-increasing glory, which comes from the Lord, who is the Spirit (NIV)." As the Spirit comes into our lives then he immediately begins the process of making us more like Christ. He begins to change the way we think, the way we talk, and ultimately the way we live in order to make us more like Christ. Although the Spirit is willing to make you more and more like Christ, he can't change you against your own free will. You have to be willing to embrace the changes that he instructs you to make.

This requires you to spend intimate time with the Spirit by reading God's word, praying, fasting, and fellowshipping with believers, anything that you can do to change your thinking from how you use to think. Remember your sinful mind is hostile to God. It does not submit to God's law, nor can it do so (Ro. 8:7). The reason why you have a hard time obeying the word of God is because your sinful nature hates everything that God loves. God loves a cheerful giver; the sinful nature hates to give. God loves those who walk in integrity; the sinful nature loves dishonesty. God loves those who walk in obedience to his word and everything in it, the sinful nature detests the commandments of God and considers them unfair and burdensome. We who are Christians, however, are no longer walking according to our sinful nature, but we are walking according to the Spirit's guidance. To fully embrace the Spirit's guidance and to walk in total obedience to his will, we have to humble ourselves.

Change...But Why?

> And he said: "I tell you the truth, unless you change and become like little children, you will never enter the kingdom of heaven. Matthew 18:3 NIV

How many times have we said "why" as it related to some sort of change in our lives? Why did my spouse have to leave me? Why did I lose my job? Why didn't I get accepted unto this school? Why did my loved one have to die? These are many of the questions that we ask God when we encounter a difficult change in our lives. Often times, people who experience a difficult change in their lives take on a very bad disposition towards life and especially God. When we have the wrong attitude towards God we will completely close our eyes and ears and not receive anything from God. Many people steer away from the faith because something happened in their life that they didn't understand, and thus they blamed God for their misfortunes. Often times we fail to realize that God influenced the change in our lives for a reason.

As I have alluded to many times in the book thus far, it was God who influenced Abraham to leave his kindred and go to unfamiliar territory because God had purpose for him that far exceeded his current location. Just like God did for Abraham, a lot of times God will influence change in our lives in order to position us for purpose. Getting back to Joseph, when God showed him the vision he didn't show him what he was going to have to go through before it would be fulfilled. Therefore, when he was taken away from his family and sold into slavery, Joseph could have gave up on his vision and became hostile towards God, but even in the midst of chaos, Joseph remained faithful to God and held strong to the vision that God had gave him. I'm not saying that Joseph understood what was going on, but he knew that even in the midst of it, God had a plan.

Change Positions You for Purpose

Just as Joseph maintained his faith in God, in spite of very painful change, I encourage you to do the same. We can't become angry at God because our lives are not going how we planned. Remember God will cause everything that you are going through to work out for the good (Ro. 8:28). When you lost your job that wasn't God picking on you that was God positioning you for a new purpose. When that relationship went south that wasn't God trying to steal your happiness that was God preparing you for what the future held. God looked through your future and saw that if you had of stayed in that relationship then you would have missed the person that he had purposed you to have.

Stop getting angry at God; learn how to accept what God allows in your life. Remember he knows best. You might not understand it now, but sooner or later it will all make sense. We have to ask God to make us new in the attitude of our minds (Eph. 4:23). Refuse to walk around bitter and defeated. Refuse to give up on your hopes and dreams because of how your situation appears. Embrace the change that God has brought in your life, because it's through the change, and your attitude towards the change, that God will fulfill the purpose that he has for your life. You have to develop a mind that is at peace with whatever direction God chooses to take you in life.

Winston Churchill, the British politician, statesman and two-time prime minister was quoted as saying the following about change: "There is nothing wrong with change, if it is in the right direction." Charles R. Swindoll, founder of the syndicated radio broadcast insight for living, and the senior pastor of Stonebriar Community Church, in Frisco, Texas, made the following quote concerning change: "We cannot change our past. We can not change the fact that people act in a certain way. We can not change the inevitable. The only thing we can do is play on the one string we have, and that is our attitude."

New Location, Same Attitude, Same Results

The list of things that we can't change would probably be so long that it could stretch around the world twice. The only thing, however, that we can change, is our attitude towards the changing world around us and in our own personal lives. Our attitude will determine the final outcome of our lives. As Jesus states in Matthew 18:3 unless we change and become like little children we will never enter the kingdom of heaven. For the most part little children tend to be happy pretty much all the time. No matter what may be going on in their homes, or in the world around them, they can always find a reason to smile.

They have an optimism that scares some people because they are rarely ever affected by life's issues. Even when some have parents who are abusive and who try to destroy their hopes and dreams, little children keep a spirit of expectancy. Despite of what may be happening, they believe that everything will be alright. This is the same attitude that us Christians must possess. We have to find a way to smile even when the world seems to be crashing in around us. We have to possess an optimism that confuses the world and the devil.

It's not that we are not facing tough times; it's not that everything in our life is always copasetic, but it's an optimism that we possess in our God to know that he has promised never to leave us nor forsake us; he promised to be with us even until the end. That means that even in what I'm experiencing right now, God is still with me. And even though life seems to change with the blink of eye, God is still the same God and his promises endure from everlasting to everlasting. If we change locations, but possess the same attitude, then we will continually see the same results in our lives.

Peter wrote both of his letters to stimulate the believers to wholesome thinking (1 Peter 2:1). The word wholesome means promoting health or well-being of mind or spirit. God wants us to have a healthy thought process about life and the many changes that will inevitably occur in it. To do this we have to separate ourselves from negativity. People who have the propensity to only speak negativity should be disconnected from our lives. These people will not be beneficial in helping us fulfill our destiny, instead hanging with them will make us take on their bad habits such as complaining, gossiping, and living ungrateful lives.

Instead we have to connect ourselves with people who have the same mind we have, which is the mind of Christ (Phil. 2:2). We need people who think like we think in order to encourage us that we can make it through what we are going through with the help of Christ. We need people who will encourage us not to break down, before we break through. We need people who will pray with us that we will maintain our focus on God even in tough situations. We need people who will not allow us to complain around them, but will always lead us back to Godly thinking.

What is Godly thinking? Philippians 4:8 answers this question: Finally, brothers, whatever is true, whatever is noble, whatever is right, whatever is pure, whatever is lovely, whatever is admirable—if anything is excellent or praiseworthy—think about such things (NIV). When you change your thinking and learn how to embrace change as the Spirit guides you then you will walk into your destiny, and fulfill every purpose that God has ordained for your life.

CHAPTER 12

Access Granted

Congratulations your access has now been granted. Your journey towards purpose has now been set into motion and there is no looking back. The Holy Spirit has taken control of the wheel in your life, and he is guiding you towards an expected destination. Again I have to warn you that this journey will not be an easy one. Along this journey you will encounter setbacks, disappointments, and you may even encounter difficult situations in your life that will make you want to turn and go back towards a more familiar and easier path. I encourage you however to remain faithful on the path that the Spirit is leading you, and steadfast in walking in the truth of God's word. Psalms 43:3 says, "Send forth your light and your truth, let them guide me; let them bring me to your holy mountain, to the place where you dwell (NIV)."

When Christ died the veil was ripped, and now everyone has "access" to God through Jesus Christ (2 Cor. 3:16, Eph. 2:14, Eph. 3:12).We can now approach God's thrown with boldness in order to receive instruction, direction, and help in our time of need (Heb. 4:4). The ball is in your court. The Spirit is saying, "Follow me to destiny," however, it's up to you to take the initiative and follow him. If you continue in the faith like Abraham, Isaac, Jacob, Joseph, and so many other great men and women of the God did; then God will fulfill every promise that he has promised you. Let sound and godly Wisdom and discretion be your safeguard. If you allow the Spirit of truth to guide you into godly wisdom and discretion then the

Bible says that, "then you will walk in your way securely and in confident trust, and you shall not dash your foot or stumble (Proverbs 3:23 NIV)."

What a great promise. To know that no matter how many obstacles may be in our path, if we follow the direction of God then he will keep us from stumbling. He will establish our goings and will make our footsteps firm. Sometimes however we can be our on stumbling block because of doubt and lack of obedience. What is keeping you form walking into destiny?

What's Your Excuse?

In John chapter 5 we are introduced to a man who had been lame for 38 years. The man, along with many other disabled people would lie at a pool called Bethesda waiting for the Angel to trouble the water in hopes that they would be able to step into the water and receive healing for their various infirmities. The Bible never mentions anyone ever being healed at this particular pool. Howsoever, these people, who were down on their luck and plagued with infirmities, were holding on to whatever bit of hope they were able to grasp. Although Jesus was cognizant of all of these people's situations, there was one that stood out from the rest.

Jesus knew that this man had been waiting at this pool for a very long time hoping for something that would never manifest in the position that he was in. He wanted to be healed. I will even go as far to say that he wanted purpose for his life; however he didn't know how he would ever obtain this purpose in his current position. Jesus asked him did he want to get well, however instead of answering yes, the man made an excuse. We often miss what God is trying to do in our lives because we are too busy worried about what we can do, rather than what God can do. We allow our conditions to keep us in a box as to what we can have or accomplish in life. Jesus had the man's healing right in his hand; however he missed it because he couldn't see beyond his physical limitations.

Whether it be a physical limitation, a mental limitation, or a financial limitation, don't ever let your circumstance keep your from walking into the destiny that God has for your life. Stop looking at what you are able to do, and focus on what God is able to do through you. The lame man was looking to have his purpose fulfilled by other means, rather than by God. He was convinced that his destiny would be determined by someone else as he informed God that he didn't have anyone to put him into the pool. As long as his destiny was linked to other means and other people then it would go unfulfilled. For 38 long years he had looked for someone else to put him into the pool, and because of that he blamed others because he didn't step out. What's your excuse?

Stop Blaming Others for Your Misfortunes

Countless people blame their lack of effort and their lack of unfulfilled promises on others. Many blame a physical or mental condition. Some blame their past, their culture, or a generational curse. However, the only person you can legitimately blame for refusing to step into your destiny is you. Stop blaming others for your failures. Stop blaming others for the position you're in right now. Instead, take responsibility and, from this day forward, determine to step out as the Spirit guides you.

Jesus didn't entertain the lame man's excuses. Instead, Jesus told him to get up, pick up his mat, and walk (John 5:8)—to do the very thing he thought he couldn't do. Just as Jesus told the lame man to walk, I tell each and every one of you to get up and begin walking away from your excuses and toward God's purpose for your life.

Working Against The clock

Have you ever felt like time was passing you by and you had yet to accomplish anything worthwhile in life? Have you ever felt like you had missed out on your purpose in life and that you were now just living to die? If you have felt like that then you are not alone. In fact, most people have felt this way before. Some even feel this way at this very moment in there life. Not only in these times that we live do people feel as though their life has no meaning, but also many of the great patriarchs from times past felt this way at some point in time in their life.

Job writes, "My days are past, my purposes are broken off, even the thoughts of my heart (Job 17:11 NIV)." Job felt as though that life was passing him by and the thoughts and plans that he had for his life would ultimately go unfilled. Not only did Job feel this way but I'm sure Abraham must have felt this way as he waited for the promised seed, Joseph as he waited for the fulfillment of his dream, Israel as they waited for deliverance from slavery, David as he waited to become the rightful king of Israel, the woman who had been dealing with an issue of blood for 12 long years, and the lame man who had been lame for 38 years just to name a few.

Had God's purpose eluded them? Absolutely not! Everything God promised to these men and women of the faith all came to past. Let's get a little more personal. Has God's purpose eluded you? The answer again will have to be absolutely not. God has a predetermined season in order to fulfill the promises that he has purposed for your life. No matter what your age is, if God has promised you something then it will come to past. Maybe it didn't happen when you thought it was going to happen, or how you thought it would happen, but you have to know that he who has promised is faithful, and everything that he promises shall come to pass.

If God promised you something then there is no doubt that it shall come to pass. We have to discipline ourselves however to learn how to stay on the timeline of God. Isaiah 55:8 teaches us that God's ways are not our ways, neither are his thoughts our thoughts. Simply put, everything that has happened in your life all happened under the auspices of the all seeing, and all knowing God. Nothing that has happened in your life caught him off guard. That job that fired you, God knew all about it. That college that didn't accept you, God saw it happen before the foundation of the world.

You having a baby out of wed-lock wasn't strong enough to destroy the plan and purpose that God has for your life. Neither were the addictions that plagued you most of your life capable of keeping God's purpose from being fulfilled in your life. Instead God is going to cause everything that has happened in your life, the good and the bad, to work together for your good and for his glory. Stop thinking your dreams are dead. Stop thinking that your life is over. Don't just sit their and wait to die and don't die before you live.

Sure life to this point hasn't turned out as you planned. But Jeremiah 10:23 let's us know that a man's ways are not of himself, neither can man direct his own steps. Let God direct your steps and make sure that you are faithful to his every command. Always remember that God is working behind the scenes clearing a path for you to walk into your destiny even when you don't see it.

> As the rain and the snow come down from heaven, and do not return to it without watering the earth and making it bud and flourish, so that it yields seed for the sower and bread for the eater, so is my word that goes out from my mouth: It will not return to me empty. Isaiah 55:10-11 (NIV)

Work Your Plan

Once God has revealed your purpose unto you, and showed you the guidelines to follow to accomplish it, then you have to start working the plan. You can't take shortcuts as you work towards your purpose; you have to carry out the plan exactly as God instructs you. Remember it's not your plan, its God's. Proverbs 16:9 says, "In his heart a man plans his course, but the Lord determines his steps (NIV)." Only when we commit to doing things God's way will our plans succeed (Pro. 16:3). Just because your plan may seem good to you, doesn't mean the plan is acceptable to God.

When God instructed Moses to set up the tabernacle he told him to set it up according to the plan in which he had shown Moses (Ex.26:20). When God gives plans they are not negotiable. They have to be performed exactly as he has instructed. Failure to do so may lead to destruction or painful correction due to disobedience (Ps. 33:10, Pr. 14:22, Is. 19:3, Is. 23:9, Is. 30:1). No plans can prevail against the plans of the Lord (Pro. 21:30). Therefore the only way to achieve godly success is to stay true to the plans that God has placed in your heart.

If you are not clear of what those plans are then do like David did and consistently seek God in order to determine his plans for your life: Make me know your ways, O Lord; teach me your paths. Lead me in your truth (Psalm 25:4-5 NIV). Consistency in following the plans of God will produce great results. As we continue to walk according to word of God, and allow our every step to be influenced by the Spirit, then we will achieve great success and guaranteed purpose (Jer. 29:11).

Make Your Petition Known to God

The first step to receiving anything from people, or from God alike, is to first ask as Matthew 7:7 states, "Ask and it will be given to you (NIV)…" Don't take this is a license lust to ask God for whatever you want and believe that he has an obligation to give it to you. God is not Burger King, so you can't have it your way. St. John 15:7 says, "If you remain in me and my words remain in you, ask whatever you wish, and it will be given to you (NIV)." 1 John 5:14 says, "This is the confidence we have in approaching God: that if we ask anything according to his will, he hears us (NIV)."

When we make request that are in the will of God, then we can have confidence that he hears us. The only way to make sure that your requests are in the will of God is to abide in the Spirit. Let the Spirit be your guide in every decision you make and in everything that you request from God. As you seek God about that next big move in your life whether it be what your next career move should be, the person that you should marry, where you should live, or what ministry you should operate in, make sure that your request is influenced by the Holy Spirit.

Wait for God's Response

After you make your request known to God then comes the hard part, and that's waiting on his response. Even when God says yes, that doesn't mean that he is going to do what you were requesting right then. Therefore, we have to learn how to wait on God even after he has said yes to our request. This can be a very trying and tiresome process. It's like having a big check, however you can't cash it right now. The anticipation is enough to drive the most patient person wild. However, if we want to receive everything that God has promised us then we have to learn how to wait.

The Israelites had to wait for the promise to be fulfilled of their release from slavery. David had to wait for the fulfillment of the promise of him being King. The disciples had to wait on the "promise" of the Holy Spirit (Acts 1:4). Take note that how you wait is extremely important. 1 Philippians 4:6 gives us the perfect diagram of how we should wait: Do not be anxious about anything, but in everything, by prayer and petition, with thanksgiving, present your requests to God (NIV). The first thing we have to do as we wait for the promises of God to be fulfilled in our lives is to rejoice in the Lord.

David said that I will bless the Lord at all times (Ps. 34:1). That means that not only should we rejoice in the Lord when times are good, but also in the bad. We should rejoice in suffering and pain (Ro. 5:3). We should rejoice in all things, no matter what the circumstance may be (Eph. 5:20, 1 Thes. 5:18). Why is this so important? It's important because rejoicing in the Lord robs the devil of any glory he might have attempted to garner in our life. Many times when life doesn't go the way we had planned, the easiest thing to do is to complain and when we complain this robs God of his glory.

Rejoicing in the Lord, no matter what the circumstances that may be surrounding us, gives us the ability to look past our current situation and to find hope and assurance in God (Ro. 5:5). This hope and assurance allows us to focus solely on God and his promises and takes our minds off of the negativity, and thus helps us to have peace in the midst of any circumstance. The peace of God will guard our hearts and our minds and we want be weighed down by the anxieties of life. This peace will help us look at what we are going through as just a temporary problem that God is using to prepare a permanent solution in our lives.

The next thing we have to do while we wait is remain prayerful. As we petition God concerning life's most important decisions we have to remain in a prayerful state. This is not just a constant prayer for the things we want, but this should more often than not be prayers for others (1 Tim. 2:1-4). Often times as we begin to pray for the needs of others such as those in authority, those who have yet to accept Christ, those who are without jobs and without shelter, those who have been victimized by fraud and deception, etc., then it will make us reevaluate the things that we are asking for.

We may even see that what we were asking God for was arrogant and self-absorbent. Anything asked for selfish gain will not be granted (James 4:3). However, by staying prayerful under God we keep the door open for redirection from the Holy Spirit and he may even lead us to change our request in order to stay in his will. The last thing we have to do in waiting is to remain thankful. Not only should we be thankful for the big things in life such as new cars, new houses, new jobs, etc., but we should learn how to be thankful with the small things in life. Be thankful for life and everything and everyone in it. Be thankful for your health and strength even if it's not 100%. Be thankful for family and for friends. Be thankful when you have a lot of money in the bank, and be thankful when your account may not be what you want it to be.

Paul states in Philippians 4:12, "I know what it is to be in need, and I know what it is to have plenty. I have learned the secret of being content in any and every situation, whether well fed or hungry, whether living in plenty or in want (NIV)." Being thankful in every situation you encounter in life is not something that will come naturally. You have to learn how to be content. Paul said that he had learned the "secret" to being content. What was the secret? The secret was the fact that Paul had learned how to be satisfied with Jesus. When you are satisfied with God, you know that He will supply all your needs (1 Phil. 4:13).

So no matter if you have a lot, or if you have a little, if you learn how to be satisfied with Jesus you will never have to worry. Devotion to prayer and thankfulness should be a routine part of every believer's life (Col. 4:2). As we grow in our relationship with God and knowledge of God, then we should grow in patience (Col. 1:10-12). Patience is a fruit of the spirit that every believer should eagerly seek to possess. Though it may seem like it's taking a long time for God to answer you, just keep waiting.

Those who wait on the Lord, God shall renew their strength. Don't make a rushed decision because of a lack of patience and end up with a counterfeit purpose when God wanted to give you something authentic. Don't forfeit your purpose in life because you haven't learned how to wait. Instead wait patiently on the Lord, and you will receive everything that God has promised you (He. 6:15).

You've Asked, You've Waited, Now Respond

After you have asked God concerning what your next move should be, waited for his response, and heard his voice, then make sure you respond well. Do whatever God asks you to do, how he asks you to do it, and when he asks you to do it. Don't be indecisive and hesitant in completing the task that God has asked you to complete. A confident, timely response is imperative not only for you, but for those who will benefit from your obedience. Hebrews 3:15 says, "Today, if you hear his voice, do not harden your hearts (NIV)..." When God had given the Israelites instructions through the prophet Moses they responded and said, "We will do everything the Lord has said (Ex. 19:8)."

Although this answer sounded good, it wasn't followed through in their actions. The Israelites were serving God with their lips; however their heart was far from him. Actions always originate from the heart. Our actions have to correspond with what we say, and what we say has to be in accordance with the word of God. Don't say Lord I will do your will, and then don't back your words up with the right actions. Respond to God by living a holy and righteous life. Respond to God by walking in obedience to his word. Respond to God's rebuke and to his correction by making appropriate changes in your life (Pro. 29:29, Jeremiah 2:30, 7:28).

Respond to the discipline of God by separating yourself from anything, or anybody who is hindering you from walking in total obedience to God's word (Jer. 17:23). God will make known to us his will for our lives (Eph. 1:18), however we have a responsibility to respond by staying obedient to everything that God has commanded us to do. If God places something in your heart to do, do it, and do it quickly. When you respond to God in faith, then your faith will pave the way for divine guidance and provision for the task that God has assigned for you. Your faith, demonstrated by your obedience, will give you extraordinary favor in everything that you go to do and God will make your way prosperous.

If you fully obey the LORD your God and carefully follow all his commands I give you today, the Lord your God will set you high above al the nations on earth. Deut. 28:1 NIV

CHAPTER 13

It's Your Season

So what is your purpose? Why did God put you here on this earth? When God created you what did he have in mind? In case you haven't figured out by now from all that you have read thus far, the main reason God created you and me was for us to become more and more like Jesus Christ by keeping stride with His Spirit, and by living a life that brings honor to his name.

Ephesians 1:4-6, 13-14 says, "For he chose us in him before the creation of the world to be holy and blameless in his sight. In love he predestined us to be adopted as his sons through Jesus Christ, in accordance with his pleasure and will—to the praise of his glorious grace, which he has freely given us in the One he loves…having believed you were marked in him with a seal, the promised Holy Spirit, who is a deposit guaranteeing our inheritance until the redemption of those who are God's possession—to the praise of his glory (NIV)."

When we first believed in his son Christ, God gave us everything that we would ever need to live a holy and blameless life, and to fulfill every purpose that he had preordained us to accomplish. Power to live a godly life and eternal security were given to us when God deposited the Holy Spirit on the inside of us. We, although once dead in sins, have now been made alive because of the Spirit of Christ that dwells richly within us. So why are we still living the same life that you were living without the Spirit? Why are you still sitting down on gifts and talents that God has given you to utilize for the edification of the body of Christ? Why we you still living life as though you have no purpose?

Ecclesiastes 3:1 says, "There is a time for everything, and a season for every activity under the heaven (NIV):" This book that I have been given the privilege and honor to write, was written to stir each and every one of you to action, and to let you know that it's YOUR season. It's a call for all those who have been operating in the Spirit of laziness, to go to work. It's a call for all those who have been trying to do their own thing, rather than following the leading of the Holy Spirit, to allow the Spirit of God to take control in their lives.

For the one's who have felt as though they didn't have purpose, this book was written to show you that you do have purpose. For those who have been working diligently for the kingdom, this book was written to encourage you not to grow weary while doing well, for in due "season" you shall reap a harvest of blessings if you don't give up (Gal. 6:9 NIV). This book is a call for all of God's children, young and old, to begin to study their Bibles more, pray more, fast more, love more, and ultimately become more and more like Christ.

Remember each and every one of us are Christ's workmanship created in Christ Jesus to do good works, which God prepared in advance for us to do (Eph. 2:10 NIV). While it's apparent that all believers share common purposes in the body the Christ, it's also clear that God has created and designed each one of us uniquely, with a specific purpose to fulfill on this earth. Your specific purpose is not mine to define, however there are ways of determining what your purpose, or purposes are.

Ways to Know God's Purpose for Your Life

What are you passionate about? As believers we do have common interests, but there are usually things that each of us care about more than others. As we grow in Christ so will the passions that God has placed on the inside of us. Sometimes we are able to identify these passions on our own, however many times it takes a fellow brother in Christ to stir up the passions that have been lying dormant within us. Paul stirred into flame the gift of God that had been lying dormant within his protégé Timothy (2 Tim. 1:6).

What frustrates you the most? I stated earlier that many times our greatest frustrations tend to reveal God's purposes for our lives. Does how the choir is being directed frustrate you so much that you just want to scream? Then maybe it's time for you to go have a talk with the pastor to see if you could maybe help out in that area of ministry. Does the lackadaisical approach of the women's outreach ministry annoy you? Then that may be an area that you can be a help with in your local church. It's time to turn our frustrations into great ministry opportunities.

Has God given you a vision that constantly weighs on your heart day in day out? Do you stay up all night trying to fall asleep; however you can't because this vision is weighing so heavily on your mind? Do you try to do other things to take your mind off this vision, only to have the vision come back stronger than ever before? If this is you, then it's time for you to be obedient to what God is telling you to do. God is trying to communicate purpose into your life, however you have to develop enough courage to step out and do what God is telling you to do.

Time to Work

For everyone who has chosen to read this book, I truly believe that God has a great purpose for your life. While I'm not able to physically lay my hands on you, in the spiritual I pray that God would stir up every gift and talent that has gone unexploited in your life. I pray that you will begin to recognize ministry opportunities through your passions and even your frustrations. I pray that God will give you the grace and the courage to fulfill every vision that he has shown you.

For those of you who still feel as though your life doesn't have purpose, I pray that God will impregnate you with Godly desires and heavenly visions that will far exceed your greatest imaginations. I also pray that he will diminish doubt and negativity in your life, and he will begin to connect you with like-minded people who will help lead you towards your destiny. Most of all I pray that God will give you uncommon favor in everything you go to do for the kingdom.

Are you ready to begin operating in the purpose that God has for your life? Are you tired of feeling as though your life has no meaning? If so, then it's your season to walk into your destiny. There is someone depending on you to fulfill the purpose that God has for your life. Just as John prepared the way for Jesus' earthly ministry, so too, are you preparing the way for someone to begin walking into their destiny.

Most of all, it's time for all of God's people to begin working diligently to help grow the kingdom, by making sure that we are operating in the gifts and callings that God has created us to operate in. It's time out for excuses. It's time out for laziness. The harvest is truly plentiful, but the laborers are so few. That's why it's so important that we all discover what God's purpose is for our lives individually, as well as corporately. There is someone who is depending on you. So what are you waiting for? Let's go to work!

ACKNOWLEDGEMENTS

First of all I would like to give all glory and honor to my Lord and savior Jesus Christ, the one through whom all blessings flow. I thank you for giving me the vision to write the book, the spiritual tenacity to study for the book, and the stick-to-itiveness to finish the book. Most of all I just think you for choosing me to be used as a vessel to spread your gospel throughout the world by any means possible. All praises belong to you!

I would also like to thank my wife Dominique for her support throughout the tedious process of writing this book, and also just for being such a support to me in every aspect of my ministry. Without you, there would be no me. Special thanks also to my son Malachi, and my daughter Cintia. Thanks for always putting a smile on daddy's face. You want understand this now, but sometimes it was only through those smiles that I was able to get up and face another day.

Special thanks are due unto my mother and father, Joyce and Thomas Tucker. I thank you guys for always supporting me in everything that I have ever done. Your support has carried me from being a little hard headed boy who never wanted to listen to anyone, to the man that I am becoming today. I truly love you guys with all of my heart. Also thanks to all of the Tucker family for your love and support throughout the years. I know I "never would have made it" without you guys having my back.

Also I would like to extend a special thanks to my grandparents, Louise and Willie Stone. Thanks for all of you guys financial support in helping me fulfill the vision that God has bestowed upon my heart. Also thanks for all of the buffet dinners that we have eaten together over the years. Special thanks to all of the Stone family for your love and support throughout the years. I love each and everyone of you.

Thanks to my mother-in-law, Nita Harrington for everything that you do for my family and I. Without your support on many occasions I don't know how we would have made it through. God truly gave you a spirit of giving and I thank you for using it to help others every chance you get whether it's financially, or just an encouraging word. For that I thank you.

Thanks to my uncle Darryl and his wife Michelle for all of the encouragement that you guys have given me throughout the years. Your encouragement has been the fuel that kept my engine going throughout some really difficult times in my life.

I also want to give a special thanks to my cousin Jason Carter for being such a positive influence to me in word, and in the life that you live. Thank you for teaching me how to think outside of the box, and for helping me understand that if I kept God first in my life, and worked hard towards my goals, there was nothing that I wouldn't be able to accomplish.

Last but not least thanks to Pastor Kell Stone and the Gospel Tabernacle Outreach Center. Thanks for all of the support you guys have given me throughout the years. Also, thanks for putting up with my "long-windedness" without falling to sleep on me. Well, at least some of you didn't go to sleep (Ken). I love you guys so much.

I wouldn't have time to thank everyone by name with such a limited amount of time, however if you have ever given me an encouraging word, sent up a prayer on my behalf, or if you are just a fellow believer who supported my ministry, and thus the kingdom by buying a copy of this book, then I truly appreciate you and I just want to say thank you for your support. God Bless.